RE-EDUCATING TROUBLED YOUTH

Environments for Teaching and Treatment

Contributors to This Volume

KRISTEN D. JUUL, *Professor of Special Education, Southern Illinois University, Carbondale*

CHARLES L. MAND, *Chairman and Professor, Department of Health, Physical Education and Recreation, The Ohio State University*

JOANNE F. MILBURN, *Director, Hannah Neil Center for Children, Columbus, Ohio*

MARTIN L. MITCHELL, *Vice President, The Starr Commonwealth Schools*

ABRAHAM W. NICOLAOU, *Associate Professor of Special Education, Western Michigan University*

NOBEL L. SCHULER, *Museum and Fine Arts Director, The Starr Commonwealth Schools*

RE-EDUCATING TROUBLED YOUTH

Environments for Teaching and Treatment

Larry K. Brendtro

Arlin E. Ness

and Colleagues

ALDINE PUBLISHING COMPANY
New York

About the Authors

LARRY K. BRENDTRO is currently the Chairman and Associate Professor of Special Education, Augustana College, Sioux Falls, South Dakota. Formerly president of the Starr Commonwealth Schools, Dr. Brendtro has worked for over twenty years with troubled children and adolescents and has served on the faculties of the University of Illinois and Ohio State University. His numerous publications include: *The Other 23 Hours* (with A. Trieschman and J. Whittaker) and *Positive Peer Culture* (with H. Vorrath).

ARLIN E. NESS is the President of The Starr Commonwealth Schools. An Adjunct Professor on the Faculty for Exceptional Children, The Ohio State University, Mr. Ness has served as consultant to the Child Welfare League of America, the National Association of Homes for Children, and The United States Department of Health and Human Services. He is also technical advisor to the International Association of Workers for Maladjusted Children.

Aldine Publishing Company
200 Saw Mill River Road
Hawthorne, New York 10532

Library of Congress Cataloging in Publication Data

Brendtro, Larry K.
   Re-educating troubled youth.

   (Modern applications of social work)
   Includes bibliographies and index.
   1. Social work with youth—Addresses, essays, lectures. 2. Social work with children—Addresses, essays, lectures. 3. Problem children—Education.
I. Ness, Arlin E. II. Title. III. Series.
HV713.B727 1983   362.7'4   83-11787
ISBN 0-202-36033-4
ISBN 0-202-36034-2 (paperback)

CONTENTS

PREFACE

This book is based in our experiences in training professionals and developing programs to serve emotionally disturbed and behaviorally disordered children and adolescents. During thirteen years of our careers we shared the responsibility for providing leadership to The Starr Commonwealth Schools, which touched the lives of over 3000 troubled youngsters and their families. As a laboratory for studying the educational and treatment process, The Starr Commonwealth is unique. From three campuses in Michigan and Ohio, Starr's staff of 200 professionals operate alternative schools, residential and day-treatment centers, special education programs, and community service activities, and serve as consultants to schools and children's agencies.

This volume focuses on information relevant to child and youth service practitioners in special education, residential group care, social work, psychology, counseling, recreation, mental health, and juvenile justice; we have freely drawn from the knowledge base in these areas. Through experiences in teaching undergraduate and graduate students in these fields, we have constantly been challenged to relate practice to theory and research. Yet, we would be the first to acknowledge that much of what we have learned comes from the resourcefulness of the children whom we serve, and of our many co-workers, several of whom have participated in writing chapters on specialized areas.

The contributors to this volume bring with them perspectives from diverse backgrounds in special education, therapeutic recreation, social work, and psychology. All have served as faculty or consultants in the graduate *educateur* programs operating at The Ohio State University and Western Michigan University through affiliations with The Starr Commonwealth Schools. The *educateur* is an interdisciplinary generalist in the re-education of troubled children who is trained to work in a wide range of living–learning environments. The development of this curriculum has entailed the integration of a wealth of knowledge that heretofore has been fragmented and encapsulated in separate professional disciplines.

We are indebted to many people for helping to bring this book to fruition. The senior author is grateful for having had the opportunity to study or work with such giants in this field as Bill Morse, Herb Quay, Ralph Rabinovitch, Fritz Redl, Dave Wineman, and Karl Menninger.

Colleagues who have shaped our thinking include the contributors to this book as well as Jim Whittaker, Al Treischman, Harry Vorrath, Nick Long, Gisela Konopka, Alan Keith-Lucas, William Glasser, and the late Floyd Starr. Assistance in reading specific chapters was provided by Ken Kessinger, Les Carson, and Paul Koehler.

Particular thanks go to Dorothy Brobst for her support and patience and to Diane Loomis for her secretarial assistance. We would also like to give special recognition to those program administrators, Alec Allen, James Beard, James Clark, Kevin McCauley, Joanne Milburn, Martin Mitchell, Gregg Peters, and their staff who, on a daily basis, implement and apply the concepts of this book in their work with the students of The Starr Commonwealth Schools.

Finally, we reserve our deepest expression of gratitude to our wives, Janna Brendtro and Barbara Ness, who provided encouragement and suggestions that sustained our efforts; and to Daniel, Steven, and Nola Brendtro, as well as Carin, Timothy, and Carla Ness, who have every right to expect more of their fathers' time now that this book is complete.

Larry K. Brendtro

Arlin E. Ness

FOREWORD

Isn't it about time? Time that the reality of the field of the behaviorally disordered was addressed? Time that one found mention in the literature of aggression, violence, guns, and knives and the very hard to reach, distraught youngsters who are involved?

Special Education has disowned the children and youth who are the focus of this book. Federal and state guidelines often exclude them from the consideration and services of special education, with the intentions of leaving them to other agencies. The basic flaw in this pattern is that these youngsters constitute the largest group in the deviant spectrum. These youth are in our schools — teachers must deal with them on a day-to-day basis. Furthermore, they are the most difficult to understand and *by far* the most difficult to help. Their treatment requires both a high level of professional wisdom and a large investment of energy required by those who would provide these services. Our ignorance of these youngsters produces much of the burn-out among teachers of the disturbed. This book directly confronts this problem, although it is not the only syndrome discussed.

Essentially, the book integrates a number of disciplines around an ecological model, reflecting a design based on the *educateur* approach. The first chapter focuses on conceptual issues that must be confronted if we intend to do more than play pretend games in special education. What the holistic approach signifies for the various disciplines is described in detail. For once the ecological approach becomes the core and not just a comfortable ancillary aspect thrown in to be up-to-date. Around this ecological or milieu centrality an interesting cycle evolves. The internal systems that make up the milieu and give it psychological power are presented. First is the interpersonal dimension of helper–youngster relationship. Second is the peer group life, which is often seen as a major oppositional force to the treatment efforts of adults. Next, the way in which the institutions must operate to integrate the relationship and peer factors is discussed. Contrasts in organizational designs are analyzed and a problem-solving orientation emerges as the solution to integrating the treatment effort.

Lest the target of the entire endeavor become lost, the focus returns to the individual, now considered from a psychoeducational framework, in which behavior and affect are seen as two sides of the same coin. This approach is essential for appreciating the fundamental stance of the volume and unites such diverse techniques as crisis intervention and teaching social skills. The authors waste no time battling psychological windmills.

How are we to accomplish the lofty goals that have been described for a treatment program? The methodology is covered in the last section of the book. The authors do not forget that they are dealing with the treatment of seriously impaired youngsters. In place of the usual chapters on teaching subjects, which are readily available elsewhere, they begin with an astute analysis of life-space interviewing as a problem-solving intervention, followed by a chapter on how to use peer group processes effectively. Here the discussion indicates how to convert the power of the peer group to positive ends, making an ally of what some see as the enemy. There is an interesting section on role reversal, which illustrates the therapeutic impact when problem youngsters become helpers rather than the negative agents in society. Two other topics, often shortchanged, make up the complement of interventions. One deals with play and recreation, which is seen as a critical component of treatment rather than a time-filler or mere tension-reducer. The final section discusses creativity as a therapeutic experience.

Although several professionals have contributed their expertise to this book on re-education, the reader leaves it with a sense of unity about what one does and why. This is because the writers have worked together in training teachers and developing effective programs. It is clear too, that these youngsters are not viewed as lost causes, and why so many short-fall programs have only limited success. The authors' hope is based on experience that combines theoretical and practical components. It is made clear that we will not be able to help our disturbed youngsters if we continue in typical, ritualistic patterns. This text presents alternatives.

William C. Morse, Ph.D.
Chairman, Combined Program in Education
and Psychology
The University of Michigan

Introduction

He drew a circle that shut me out—
Heretic, rebel, a thing to flout.
But love and I had the wit to win:
We drew a circle that took him in.
—Edwin Markham in "Outwitted"

This book is about helping troubled young people who are searching desperately for security, identity, and purpose in their lives. Childhood and adolescence are pivotal stages in the quest to belong, to become somebody, and to be worth something. Children need stimulation, affection, and guidance in order to develop their potentials, but many are reared in environments that deprive them of these nutriments. Adolescents approach the threshold of independence with only the experiences gained from childhood; many lack the support of significant adults. Those who encounter difficulty in navigating through these turbulent years come to be identified by society as troubled or troublesome. They include:

- the rebellious youth whose actions strike out against a world that seems hostile or unjust

- the empty child starving for love but unable to reach out, frightened of being hurt again

- the lonely, insecure youngster whose spirit has been crippled by neglect or failure

- the conflicted young person desperately wanting something or someone to believe in, struggling for stability and identity in a world of confusing values.

These children and youth present challenges that do not yield to simple panaceas. Although no single approach holds all the answers, bridging various concepts of education and treatment offers the best opportunity for creating positive change. We shall refer to this process as "re-education" with full awareness that this term has been used in a variety of philosophical contexts including behavioral, ecological, and psychodynamic views.

Chapter 1 offers a selected overview of approaches to troubled children and introduces a holistic psychoeducational approach that seeks to blend academic theory with practice wisdom. The remainder of this book presents foundations and formats for successful re-education.

It is our thesis that constructing a truly powerful learning environment for troubled youth requires a holistic synergy that comes from harmonizing a wide variety of factors. Those readers accustomed to narrow viewpoints will be challenged, since we shall reach out to various disciplines, countries, and times in history in the conviction that the search for meaning is an open system.

Bridging Theory and Practice

LARRY K. BRENDTRO AND ARLIN E. NESS

All theory is gray, and
green the golden tree of life.
— Goethe in *Faust*

This civilization of vast intellectual, economic, and military power is at the same time weak and ineffectual at the basic human task of socializing children. One might presume that we would have created environments that guide all of our young toward responsible adulthood and nourish those with special needs. But large numbers of disturbed, delinquent, abused, and alienated youngsters populate our schools, community agencies, and children's institutions. Typically our efforts to meet their needs are shamefully inadequate, suggesting that we do not know enough or care enough about serving such children. This book seeks to address these tandem issues of knowledge and concern, which are essential to creating powerful environments for redirecting young lives.

EARLY APPROACHES: PYGMALION PIONEERS

Early leaders in youth work radiated an optimism in sharp contrast to many contemporary approaches, which concentrate on abnormality or pathology. Challenging prevailing attitudes of futility and cynicism, they approached difficult children with a powerful Pygmalion-like optimism, frequently achieving astonishing results.

In nation after nation such people have come forth in times of great

3

difficulty, committed to a positive vision of the strength and potential that lay untapped in troubled youth. Among these pioneers were:

- Johann Heinrich Pestalozzi (1746–1827), the Swiss educator, who gathered together homeless and unwanted children who were victims of the Napoleonic wars and founded a residential school at Stans based on a progressive, humane philosophy.
- Itard (1775–1838), the French physician, who challenged the diagnosis of experts and worked to reclaim Victor, a primitive wolf-child who had wandered wild and naked in the woods since being abandoned with a slit throat early in his life.
- Nineteenth-century American reformers such as Dr. Samuel Gridley Howe (1801–1876), who established services for all kinds of handicapped children in New England, and Dorthea Dix (1802–1887), a Sunday School teacher for female prisoners who awakened the nation's conscience to the atrocities experienced by the mentally ill, including children incarcerated in alms-houses, barns, and stables.
- Rudolph Steiner (1861–1925), the Austrian humanitarian–spiritualist, whose philosophy guided the creation of the world-wide Waldorf School movement which offered a rich environment to children with all manner of handicaps and problems.
- Makarenko (1888–1939), a Russian teacher and social worker, who accepted the challenge of developing colonies to serve the *besprizorniki*, masses of roving children who terrorized Soviet cities following the Russian revolution of 1917.
- Sir Rabindranath Tagore (1861–1941), the Bengali philosopher, a recipient of the Nobel Prize in literature, whose poetry of love reflected his own deep concern and work with children in his school in Santiniketan near Bolpur, India.
- Janusz Korczak (1879–1942), a Polish educator, who championed the rights of the young in 20 books with titles including *Children of the Street* (1901), *How to Love a Child* (1920), and *The Child's Right to Respect* (1929). For 30 years he directed the House of Children, a Jewish orphanage in Warsaw, until he became a martyr in a final act of love and respect as he declined a Nazi offer for personal freedom to accompany 200 of his children to the gas chamber at Treblinka (Kulawiec, 1974).

An outstanding pioneer in American youth work was Jane Addams (1909), who worked with Chicago youngsters at the beginning of the twentieth century. Unlike many of her day (or others who were to follow in the profession), Addams had an immensely positive and optimistic outlook. She interpreted the stealing, vandalism, aggression, defiance, and truancy of youth as the normal expression of boys in search of adventure. She recalled that coast-dwelling youth in early America could find this outlet in the mystery of ships and the thrill of going to sea. In an industrial society youth were compelled to invent their own excitement, and this was the cause of many behavioral problems.

One cannot help but note that many contemporary theories have an intellectual rather than an emotional quality to them when contrasted with the thinking of pioneer youth workers who wrote from immediate experience. In fact, very few theories about the treatment of troubled youth have been derived directly from experience. Instead, an attempt is usually made to apply an existing conceptual framework (such as psychoanalysis or behaviorism) to the treatment of troubled youth. Training curricula for professional youth workers typically emphasize content that an "expert" has mastered rather than material that practitioners themselves need to know. We have found that one of the simplest but most easily overlooked ways of determining what staff should be taught about managing troubled youth is to ask them. Perhaps this approach is seldom used because trainers are uncomfortable with the type of questions raised. It can be a humbling experience to test any theory against the wisdom and searching questions that one encounters among those who work on the front lines.

CURRENT STRATEGIES

During the second half of the twentieth century, there has been a growing body of literature relating specifically to the treatment of troubled youth. Many of the early approaches emanated from the field of residential treatment rather than from public schools. Whittaker (1979) has identified three prominent schools of thought that have been developing in parallel in recent decades. The *psychodynamic* approach dominated the residential literature in the 1950's beginning with the seminal contributions of Bruno Bettleheim (1950) at the University of Chicago Orthogenic School and Fritz Redl (Redl & Wineman, 1951, 1952) at Pioneer House in Detroit. In the 1960's the *behavioral* approach began to receive the greatest attention. A prominent example is the Achievement Place model, also known as the Teaching-Family model, developed by Phillips and his colleagues (1968, 1972). Simultaneously, *guided group interaction* strategies were also being widely employed with delinquents in correctional programs and were later extended to other types of youth and settings; this strategy first gained prominence with the work of McCorkle, Elias, and Bixby (1958) at Highfields in New Jersey. Whittaker (1979) provides a thorough discussion of these three approaches, which is summarized in Table 1-1.

Another residential model that has gained wide attention, particularly among special educators is the Re-ed concept of Hobbs (1967). Hobbs originated the Re-ed program as an American adaptation of the *educateur* common in Western Europe and Canada. The Re-ed Schools in Tennessee and North Carolina were developed in the early 1960's as short-term 5-day residential treatment facilities serving small groups of disturbed students. Generic professionals called teacher–counselors worked in both the school and group living settings. Another key role was the liaison teacher, who provided a link with the child's community ecology. Whittaker summarizes the core components of Hobbs' approach as "developing trust, gaining competence, nurturing feelings, controlling symptoms, learning middle-class values, attaining cognitive control, developing community ties, providing physical experience, and knowing joy" (1979, pp. 73–74). The emphasis on teaching joy stems from the earlier work of the Russian youth worker Makarenko.

Because of a bias toward learning, it was perhaps inevitable that the Re-ed schools would gravitate toward the behavioral approaches that were achieving dominance during the same period. More recently, Hobbs has expressed some reservation about overemphasizing this component of the re-education experience. In a review of the first 20 years of project Re-ed, Hobbs states:

> Our current view is that behavioral modification, powerful as it is, is not a sufficient theoretical base for helping disturbed children and adolescents. It pays insufficient attention to the evocative power of identification with an admired adult, to the rigorous demands of expectancy stated and implicit in situations, and to the fulfillment that comes from the exercise of competency (1979, p. 15).

With the development of the field of emotional disturbance as an area of special education, there has been a burgeoning of programs and theories. Rhodes and Tracy (1972) sought to organize these diverse concepts and identified six distinct models: psychodynamic, behavioral, sociological, biophysical, ecological, and counter-cultural.

Perhaps the broadest taxonomy of the various educational and residential remediation models for emotionally disturbed children is that of Kristen Juul (1980), who writes from an international perspective. Juul extends Rhodes' categories to nine different models and notes that they are not necessarily mutually exclusive. Tracing the psychoeducational management of troubled children back approximately 200 years to Pestalozzi, he presents the nine models in the approximate historical

Table 1-1. Differential Approaches to Group Treatment of Children and Adolescents

	Psychodynamic	Behavioral	Guided group interaction
Assumptions	Existence of unconscious, Freudian model of personality structure. Behavior connected to inner states. Conflicts revealed through play, social relationships. Group as corrective experience	Personality best understood as the sum of observable behavior. Behavior largely controlled by environment. Troubled behavior is the whole problem, not a symptom	Delinquent behavior elicited and maintained by negative peer culture. Helping others increases self-worth. Each youth responsible for own behavior, capable of change. Delinquent skills redirected in the group
Purpose	Personality and behavior change through free interaction in a carefully structured social environment	Behavior change in individual and in group as a whole by application of principles of social learning	Use of dynamics of peer group to constructively shape behavior of group members
Group population	Children 4 years through adolescence. Usually primary behavior problems—not psychotic, psychopathic, withdrawn	Behavior-disordered children; no particular problems ruled out	Primarily older delinquent adolescents, often in institutions. Not psychotic, schizophrenic
Group composition	Groups usually 6 to 10 in number. Careful balance of problem types important factor	Usually small group, homogeneous for presenting problem	Groups usually 7 to 11 in number. Common experiences with delinquent acting out
Knowledge/ theory base	Psychoanalytic theory/ego psychology. Neo-Freudian developmental theory	Social learning theory	Still developing. Connected to intensive interaction techniques (Lewin, Rogers, and others)
Leading theoreticians	S. R. Slavson, Haim Ginott, Mortimer Schiffer	S. Rose; the combined contributions of many applied behavior analysis	H. Vorrath, L. K. Brendtro, S. Pilnick, L. T. Empey
Role of therapist	Varies from totally permissive to strong role model. Generally nondirective, neutral, parental figure	Therapist indentifies antecedent reinforcers, determines new contingencies. Monitors, models, teaches, controls contingencies	Pivot of group process—controls contingencies, supports, confronts, summarizes

From Whittaker, 1979, p. 112.

sequence in which they emerged. He also emphasizes the contributions that two Austrians, Alfred Adler and August Aichorn, made to the field of therapeutic education. A summary of Juul's taxonomy follows.

1. *The developmental model.* In this view, the child's emotional and social growth proceeds through predictable stages and sequences and results from the interaction of these stages with the child's experiences. There are sensitive periods during which experiences and relationships are important or critical to the development of a healthy personality.

2. *The psychodynamic model.* This view stresses the importance of feelings and emotional needs in the belief that distorted interpersonal relationships lead to lasting personality disturbance. Treatment involves sensitizing significant people in the child's life and responding to the child's needs for relationships with mature and caring adults.

3. *The learning disability model.* Two major premises of this model are that (1) neurological dysfunctions directly hamper the child's emotional and social functioning and (2) a child's failure to learn in normal ways leads to feelings of inferiority and lowered self-esteem that may be related to other behavioral problems. Remediation usually takes the form of individualized education and prescriptive teaching.

4. *Behavioral modification strategies.* Proceeding from the assumption that all behavior is learned, these strategies attempt to modify deviant behavior in specific ways through the use of appropriate reinforcement procedures. The chief orientation in American behaviorism has been the operant approach linked to Skinner, which entails an analysis of behavior, its antecedent conditions, and its consequences.

5. *Medical and biophysical theories.* These theories propose that deviations and disturbances in behavior and learning are related to biological disorders. Such problems can be as diverse as brain disorders or dietary deficiencies.

6. *The ecological model.* Based on the assumption that the cause of the disturbance is a disharmony between the youth and the environment, intervention focuses on changes both in the child and in the environment to improve their reciprocal relationships.

7. *The counterculture movement.* This view is critical of societal institutions. Children are seen as having great potentials, which could be realized if they were unfettered from the debilitating effects of current educational programs or the social and economic system.

8. *The transcendental model.* This approach is seen in a diversity of therapeutic communities in which a central tenet is the belief in the spiritual or even mystical nature of the human personality. An example is the Rudolph Steiner Anthroprosophic Movement, which originated in Europe.

9. *The psychoeducational model.* This model synthesizes other strategies. It is eclectic and holistic, drawing techniques from other models as they are deemed appropriate. The quality of the child's total experience is seen as central to successful readjustment.

Juul documents examples of his various models as gathered from observations of schools and therapeutic facilities in 11 nations. These data led him to conclude that although theoretical categories may be distinct in rhetoric, it is difficult to identify pure examples of these models in practice. There are actually about as many models for intervention as there are programs. Juul concludes that most *practice* models are psychoeducational because explicitly or implicitly they tend to draw from several different educational and treatment frameworks. The specific model that purports to govern the operation of a program may be less important than the fact that intervention is organized around a distinct conceptual framework.

Juul notes strong national differences in the dominant models for intervention. Central and northern European nations are heavily influenced by the developmental principles of Pestalozzi. In the French-speaking cultures, Freudian psychodynamic concepts and ecological orientations predominate. In contrast to European approaches, behavioral strategies are the most widely developed in the United States, particularly in the research literature. Actual practice in this country is characterized by a diversity of approaches drawing on a wide range of philosophical and theoretical formulations.

The abundance of theories can be confusing to the practitioner who is seeking for "the way." Wolfgang and Glickman (1980) conclude that although all models have their critics, there is not now and possibly will never be research that documents indisputably the superiority of one model over the others. Thus, those working with troubled youth have available a wide range of strategies from which they can build an approach consonant with their personal philosophy and the needs of children and youth.

THE THEORY – PRACTICE GULF

Kurt Lewin once observed that nothing is as practical as a good theory. Much has been written about the difficulty of putting theory into practice; it is at least as difficult to put practice into theory. A theory may be either a help or a hindrance to the practitioner. Attempts to use a particular theory to explain complex phenomena can lead to oversimplification, confusion, or to a kind of intellectualization that has been termed hyperrationalization (Wise, 1979).

Many successful youth workers are atheoretical naturalists, using an approach that blends common sense, experience, and a love for children (Morse, Cutler, & Fink, 1964). Others are guided in their practice by behavioral, psychodynamic, or some other specific philosophy. In either case it is likely that practitioners depend heavily upon *implicit theories,* highly personal concepts and assumptions about teaching and learning that are seldom clearly identified or expressed (Hunt, 1976, 1980). Because youth workers are inclined to "do their own thing," it is an immense task to mold a human service organization to comply with a particular philosophical orientation. School administrators are notoriously ineffective at infusing their theories of education into classroom practice (Deal & Celotti, 1980), and directors of children's institutions find that their directives stop at the cottage door (Grossbard, 1960).

Many youth workers find that the formal theories that constitute their training provide an insufficient basis for practice. A classic study of psychotherapists (Fiedler, 1960) suggests that although novice therapists closely adhere to the theories and methods in which they were trained, experience leads them to develop much broader approaches. Unfortunately, it is not an easy task to transmit such practice wisdom to the beginning worker.

Perhaps the American system of training all educational and youth work practitioners within the confines of the college and university contributes to the lack of a sound theory for clinical practice. In contrast, many European programs for training youth professionals are organized around applied rather than academic models of education. For example, such applied models have led to widespread contributions in the area of therapeutic education within the French cultural sphere. Unfortunately, however, Americans are notoriously inadequate at mastering the foreign languages necessary to uncover the contributions in other cultures (Juul & Linton, 1978).

Another plague on practice in America has been the tendency to become enraptured with the latest treatment or educational fad. Searching for magical answers only to be disappointed, the practitioner discards yesterday's fashion as soon as a replacement arrives on the scene. In this "disposable" culture of plastic and paper, we have not yet achieved a lasting and substantive approach to the treatment of troubled youth. When some technique has a modicum of success in a particular situation, it becomes a panacea and is extended to new domains where it is much less appropriate (Morse, 1979).

Carbone (1980) has said that the individual who cannot explain the basis of his or her practice might be a competent technician but not a professional. By this standard the human services are short on professionalism, as most skillful practitioners frequently have difficulty in communicating the basis of their success. Neither are administrators of educational and treatment organizations immune from this inability to conceptualize practice. Too often such leaders have not been prepared to create new models of schooling or treatment but only to preside blindly over the existing structure.

POLARIZATION BETWEEN THEORIES

Few fields of endeavor have seen more strident rhetoric among proponents of various theories than has the area of emotionally disturbed and behaviorally disordered youth. As Rhodes and Paul (1978) conclude, there has been a tendency to polarize orientations as either scientific or humanistic and to see them as mutually exclusive. Both approaches, however, are essential to education: one relates to the *science* of education, the other to the *goals* of education and the human nature of learners. No single view represents the summative truth, and a reconciliation of views would deepen understanding of ourselves and our science of education.

A number of voices in the research community are now calling for greater use of other systems of "knowing" rather than over-reliance on experimental methodology. There is growing concern with qualitative as well as quantitative research. Eisner (1981) argues for the importance of both *scientific* and *artistic* study. The scientist seeks to discover *truth* in logical and consistent laws of nature; the artist seeks to find *meaning* by creating patterns and images. Both views are needed, for only binocular vision can provide depth of perception.

Combs, Avila, and Purkey (1978) have noted a useful distinction to be that of closed versus open systems. The *closed system* focuses on achieving a clearly defined objective (such as teaching a specific cognitive skill to a child). With an *open system,* one searches for the solution to a problem without knowing the desired outcome (such as exploring a child's perception of a problem). Many helping professionals find that they are more comfortable with one or the other of these approaches. Yet each has its advantages and disadvantages, and each can be successful depending on the particular situation and task.

The process of synthesizing diverse viewpoints confronts each generation anew.

Since the time of Plato and Aristotle, educational thinking about the role of the environment in learning has occasionally swung toward ex-

tremes. . . . Twenty-five centuries of humanistic insights may already
have accumulated a large fund of balanced educational wisdom. Even so,
each generation may have to rediscover old truths; indeed, each educator
may need to come somewhat independently to certain conclusions and
decisions by reflection of personal experience (Wahlberg, 1979, p. 10).

John Locke observed in his *Essay Concerning Human Understanding*
(1690) that no man's knowledge can go beyond his experience. For that
reason, we would do well to be more receptive to the truths and
meanings that emerge from the experiences of others.

PROFESSIONAL HYPERSPECIALIZATION

Another set of territorial lines drawn between practitioners are
those that demarcate professional specialties into separate enclaves
with their own concepts, programs, language, and literature. Traditionally, the two broad divisions have been between teaching and
treatment.

In the past there has been little connection between treatment
workers and the teaching–learning enterprise. The fledgling professions of social work, clinical psychology, and rehabilitation sought to
establish their identities by associating with the high-status field of
medicine. Early philosophies and methods were thus heavily influenced by the medical model, and the concept of treatment has
continued to be widely employed even though theoretical orientations
have broadened considerably. Even special education at its inception
was more a medical specialty than a field of education. Increasingly,
however, a shared body of knowledge is available to educators and
treatment personnel alike. Theories of learning, individual and group
dynamics, the family, and community ecology are now a part of the
training in most human-service fields.

Although the helping professions have long recognized the importance of cooperation, infighting among various specialties has been
intense. Such territorialism led Garner (1976) to call for "a truce in the
war for the child." Clearly there has been something of a tacit collaboration among the various helping professionals to chop up the child
into many pieces so each specialty might have its share (Morse, 1978).
Organizing child-caring programs around departmental lines contributes to this problem. Overspecialization tends to breed commitment to
the wrong constituents; other M.S.W.'s or psychologists or special
educators, the academic department, and the profession all become
more important than the program. As Leavitt, Dill, and Eyring (1973)

note, specialization has advantages but overly narrow perspectives can be dehumanizing and alienating.

The thesis that specialization contributes to the economic efficiency of an organization (originally advanced by Adam Smith in *The Wealth of Nations* in 1776) is an industrial model that does not apply either programmatically or economically to child-caring organizations. Currently there are some hopeful signs that many human-service professions including perhaps the most specialized of all, medicine, are making attempts to reassert the importance of the generalist. Likewise, we are taking a closer look at what has been passed off as interdisciplinary cooperation in the past. Calls are now being heard for reorganizing around the functional needs of children rather than around departments or professional loyalties (Brown, 1979).

The need for a holistic approach is leading to a shift in emphasis from specialization to an interdisciplinary outlook (Mearig, 1978). Growing disillusionment with the fruits of social research is increasing the demand for "people with the ability to conceptualize human behavior into systems of interpersonal, intergroup and interorganizational relations" (White, 1978, p. 131). The effective practitioner must be able to learn from experience, analyze controversial issues, and identify the pattern of meaning in a complex situation (C. Klemps, cited in Nash & Ducharme, 1978). As public policy compels schools to respond to the total child, there is a greater need for professionals who are skilled in multiple disciplines or who can successfully relate in interdisciplinary partnerships. The clear demarcations that once separated educators from treatment personnel are rapidly becoming outmoded.

TOWARD A HOLISTIC SYNERGY

Guindon (1971), writing in the tradition of the French *educateur*, argues that children need a whole world to be whole in. All of the child's potentials — physical, affective, cognitive, social, and religious — must be given appropriate "stimulus nutriments." Clearly, such a holistic philosophy challenges many existing treatment orientations. Monolithic approaches of any ilk, be they behaviorism, peer group treatment, psychotherapy, or any other circumscribed system, are called into question. While advocates of singular dogmas strive to keep their approaches pure, practitioners are becoming increasingly suspicious of simplistic outlooks. The editors of *Phi Delta Kappan* suggest that children need to be protected from charlatans and practitioners of single methodologies (*Special Education*, 1974). As Whittaker (1980) concludes, what we need most is not a single answer, but the wealth of resources of a "field of a thousand flowers." Those who become wed to any narrow outlook become dropouts from the exciting search for truth.

Diverse, even contradictory, approaches can succeed in specific situations. Freedom schools seek to abandon the rigidity of regular education, whereas back-to-basics schools reassert the discipline and control lost in the "permissiveness" of regular education. One cannot help but conclude that if programs espousing such contradictory philosophies can succeed (and there is evidence that they can), then perhaps their effectiveness is due to other factors, which they have in common.

It is safe to say that probably hundreds, if not thousands, of variables are correlated in some manner with program success. Amidst all of these complex relationships, how can the practitioner effectively sort out what is most important — which interventions have the most leverage in educational and treatment environments created for troubled youth? Somehow one must be able to identify a manageable number of variables on which the failure or success of a program substantially depends and concentrate on them, even if at the expense of many peripheral interests. *Only by attending to critical factors can one achieve a truly successful program.*

Although a vast array of potential variables affect program success, research suggests that a more limited number of factors merit special concern because of their particular power. These variables do not act individually but rather in harmony, creating a *synergistic* effect. According to this view, several components need to be carefully integrated if the program is to achieve the desired impact. Acting together, the separate variables are more than the sum of their parts. Each of these variables is important, perhaps even critical. They are typically described by the researcher as "necessary but not sufficient," since a given variable is essential but is inadequate in isolation.

The research of Clark, Lotto, and McCarthy (1980) suggests the need for a holistic outlook that encompasses multiple variables. In their analysis of 1200 studies on factors related to success in urban schools, they identify a number of salient dimensions including *strong leadership* that creates a climate of *positive expectations, reduced child–adult ratios, goal specificity,* and *high levels of parental involvement.* They also highlight the importance of a *structured learning environment;* youth who are lacking order in other aspects of their lives seem to need this compensatory structure for purposes of re-education. Gold (1978) emphasizes the importance of personal characteristics in staff who work with troubled youth including the *ability to establish warm relationships* of mutual respect with students alienated from traditional approaches. He further stresses the importance of developing *positive peer group cultures.* Garner (1982) identifies *teamwork* as essential in creating an environment where all of the needs of children and youth can be met. And in a note reminiscent of the pioneer workers with troubled youth, McClelland and Dailey (1974) found that what separated outstanding human service workers from the mediocre was not any particular skill, but an attitude of *faith in the ability of people to change.* It would appear that those committed to what they are doing have taken a giant step toward success.

Building a quality program is a formidable task requiring patience and persistence. Yet success is more than a matter of accumulating incremental gains, for at the point where the various variables come into balance a powerful synergy is released. Practitioners recognize this phenomenon as the dramatic change in an organization when everything begins to work. One can frequently hear practitioners using such phrases as "coming together," "gelling," "clicking," or "fitting into place."

Sadly, most programs are significantly out of balance in one or more of these key factors and are thus lacking the "critical mass" necessary for success. Sometimes such a program can limp along in mediocrity for many years. In other cases it is as if the people and the organization itself lose the "will to live." We have seen well-financed organizations with an abundance of staff and a reputation to match that were (to those who knew them well) abysmal failures. Likewise, we have encountered struggling, Spartan, and understaffed programs succeeding against impossible odds, sustained by the knowledge that great things were being achieved for young people.

The key to successful re-education cannot be found either in the extremes of an overly narrow methodology or in a disjointed eclecticism. We believe that a holistic understanding of the needs of troubled children supports the need for a holistic strategy for intervention. The approach of this book, therefore, is psychoeducational, because this viewpoint embodies the full range of behavioral, affective, interpersonal, organizational, and curricular factors that are critical to the re-educational process. In the following section we shall set the stage for the remaining chapters by highlighting what we believe to be the central assumptions of the psychoeducational approach.

THE PSYCHOEDUCATIONAL MODEL

As we have seen, the psychoeducational approach is a synthesis of other specific strategies that results in a holistic practice model. The quality of a child's total experience is seen as central to re-education.

The term psychoeducational accents the close connection between education, the teaching of human beings, and psychology, the study of human behavior (Fagen, Long, & Stevens, 1975). It is neither pathology-oriented nor exclusively behavioral, cognitive, or affective in focus.

There has been a lack of clarity about the precise meaning of the term psychoeducational. At one time, psychoeducational was equated with psychodynamic, as is seen in the early work of Berkowitz and Rothman (1960). With the continuing development of special education, psychiatric viewpoints came to be balanced with (or supplanted by) educational concepts, and the term psychoeducational acquired a much broader meaning. As early as 1964, Morse, Cutler, and Fink noted the distinctions between the psychoeducational and psychiatric–dynamic approaches as they were applied in special classes for disturbed children (see Table 1-2).

Unfortunately, subsequent writers have been slow to follow this lead, and confusion has persisted. Many textbooks about the emotionally disturbed follow the typology of theories offered by Rhodes and Tracy (1972) and assign psychoeducators such as Redl and Morse to the psychodynamic category. This placement probably does not represent the best fit, given their highly eclectic philosophies. Furthermore, the historic tension between behavioral and dynamic points of view spills over into definitions of the psychoeducational approach. Note these apparently unintentional distortions of aspects of the psychoeducational model as seen from behavioral perspectives: Glavin (1970) characterizes this approach as focusing on unconscious processes and encouraging acting out of conflict so that learning can occur in the presence of the "crisis teacher." Kauffman speculates that the psychoeducational life-space interview strategy "has great appeal to most individuals who are opposed on philosophical grounds to the use of explicit behavior modification techniques" (1981, p. 181).

Table 1-2. Comparison of Psychiatric–Dynamic and Psychoeducational Approaches

Psychiatric–Dynamic	Psychoeducational
Controls are loose	Controls are evident
Pupils described in psychoanalytic terms; educational aspects minimized	Pupils described in both educational and psychodynamic terms
Free expression emphasized	Achievement emphasized
Relationships marked by dependency gratification	Relationships marked by emphatic feelings

Adapted from Morse, Cutler, and Fink, 1964, pp. 121–122.

In light of such confusion it seems particularly important that we attempt to provide a clearer definition of the psychoeducational model. Although any eclectic approach precludes a simple definition, a review of a number of contributions to the psychoeducational literature yields six tenets:

1. Relationship is primary.
2. Assessment is ecological.
3. Behavior is holistic.
4. Teaching is humanistic.
5. Crisis is opportunity.
6. Practice is pragmatic.

We shall examine each of these further below.

Relationship Is Primary

The quality of human relationships is the most powerful determinant of successful programs for the education and treatment of troubled children; methodology is less important than relationships (Morse, 1981; Pappenfort, 1980). The crucial elements in the re-education process include the *adult–child relationships*, the *peer relationships* among children, and the *teamwork relationships* among adults.

Emotionally disturbed children have learned to associate adult intervention with adult rejection. Through a corrective relationship they learn to view adults in a new light. This requires accepting the child with his inappropriate behavior while simultaneously limiting it so as to avoid self-defeating and self-injurious behavior (Berkowitz & Rothman, 1960). The adult who is easily manipulated has not developed an effective relationship; in a relationship based on empathy and caring, the adult will use the most appropriate interpersonal techniques available to manage behavior (Rich, Beck, & Coleman, 1982).

Establishing therapeutic relationships with troubled youngsters involves enhancing *communication, social reinforcement,* and *modeling* (Trieschman, Whittaker, & Brendtro, 1969). Enhancing communication includes decoding the real meanings conveyed by verbal and nonverbal behavior and establishing trust with youth who are often guarded and aloof. To enhance social reinforcement, one must become a significant person to children who may have learned to devalue adults and then use the resulting influence in a constructive manner. Enhancing modeling entails becoming the kind of an adult with whom youth will identify and being worthy of this emulation.

Astute caring must respond to the child's sense of aloneness and alienation while avoiding unnecessary dependency. The child's alienation is accepted in an envelope of caring. An empathic understanding of another's life view enables the helper to share intelligently in problem-solving (Morse, 1981).

We must seek to extend the same qualities that mark a positive adult – student relationship into the peer group relationships. A climate must be created in which youngsters feel genuinely concerned for one another and become involved in helping one another (Vorrath & Brendtro, 1974). As children learn to reciprocate positive relationships with significant adults and peers, we should strive to generalize this caring behavior beyond their immediate circle of friends through service to others in the community at large (Brendtro & Nicolaou, 1982).

Administrators, professionals, and parents who are involved in re-education must deal with one another in a manner consistent with their expectations of children. The leadership and teamwork processes must model the desired relationships between worker and child and between worker and group. No one is entitled to enter into a relationship with another on the basis of unilateral conclusions, expecting to impose on the other his or her unshared definition of the problem. Cooperative problem-solving requires a climate of respect and mutual concern (Barnes & Kelman, 1974).

Assessment Is Ecological

Behavior must be understood as part of the child's life-space, which includes the transactions between the child and adults, peers, task, and educational system. The various components of the life-space have been discussed by Redl and Wineman (1952); Trieschman, Whittaker, and Brendtro (1969); Long, Morse, and Newman (1980); Prieto and Rutherford (1977) and Swap, Prieto, and Harth (1982). These transactions are summarized in Table 1-3.

Ecological study entails understanding significant transactions in the child's life-space. Table 1-3 outlines seven critical transactions that may be the source of conflict. Through ongoing assessment and communication with and about the child, one learns to know the person and environment in all facets. This is not a ritualized diagnostic procedure, and one must try to hold one's own inferences open until all the data can be known. No behavior is "crazy" when one comes to appreciate the idiosyncratic rationale that produced it (Morse, 1981).

A re-educational milieu must be developed with attention to modify-

Table 1-3. Critical Transactions in the Life-Space

Transaction	Facilitating conditions for re-education
Student–family	Positive relationships with parents and siblings; significant involvement of parents as full partners in the re-education process
Student–teacher/ counselor	The helping adult as emphatic, realistic, consistent, limit-setting, and conveying a positive model and expectations
Student–peer group	A climate of mutual respect, sharing, cooperation, cohesiveness, balanced grouping, and prosocial orientation
Student–school/ treatment organization	Clear and consistent policies, goals, and responsibilities; participative decision-making; cooperative work climate; size and organization facilitating primary group relationships
Student–activity	A curriculum or program that is relevant, challenging, involves self-directive activity and opportunities for feedback and success
Student–structure	Appropriate rules, expectations, routines, physical setting, control or consequence system
Student–self	Self-control, positive self-image, provision for physical, affective, cognitive, and social needs

ing various transactions to facilitate a positive adjustment. Intervention can be directed both at the person (e.g., increasing self-esteem) and at the environmental forces (Morse, 1965). Changing self-defeating behavior involves setting identifiable objectives in relation to the total person functioning within the life-space (Fagen, Long, & Stevens, 1975). The diagnostic task is to highlight areas of strength and to pinpoint areas of weakness requiring remediation. An environment is created so that each child can function successfully (Long, Morse, & Newman, 1980).

The most effective assessment of a child's functioning in his or her reality situation is not made by a remote therapist, but by an individual who is actively involved in the life-space. Likewise, the greatest influence in changing troubled children seldom comes from the 50-minute therapy hour but rather from adults and peers who are directly involved with the youngster in the other 23 hours (Morse, 1981; Trieschman, Whittaker, & Brendtro, 1969; Vorrath & Brendtro, 1974).

Behavior Is Holistic

Emotional and behavioral disturbance in children must be viewed in relation to normal processes of physical and psychological development. Behavioral change is highly individual yet predictable, and it occurs as new experience is built on the foundation of a child's prior experience and physical maturation (Wood, 1975).

In addition to basic physical needs, children must meet a range of socioemotional needs if they are to achieve self-actualization. These needs include:

Love—being valued unconditionally and being able to love another

Security—having predictably consistent relationships and expectations

New experiences—having increasingly broad opportunities for mastery

Praise and recognition—receiving positive reinforcement from valued adults and peers

Responsibility—having opportunities for successful experiences leading toward independence and self-control (Glasser, 1965; M. Pringle, cited in Morse et al., 1980).

Children who cannot meet their physical or psychological needs or who meet them in maladaptive ways come to be seen as disturbed or disturbing. Behavior is a source of concern when it results in personal unhappiness, conflict, and self-depreciation, or when it comes into conflict with social norms and thereby leads to feelings of alienation or rejection (Fagen, Long & Stevens, 1975).

Both the inner conflict of the disturbed child and the external conflict engendered by the delinquent are best treated by designing an environment that offers the appropriate stimulus nutriments so the child can actualize all of his potentials — physical, affective, cognitive, social, and moral (Guindon, 1973).

Every youth is unique in behavioral style and functional level. The same behavior can stem from any of a number of causes, and a given set of circumstances can produce any of a number of different behaviors (Long, Morse, & Newman, 1980). Understanding behavior requires an awareness of the cognitive, affective, and motivational processes in the child and in one's self (Fagen, Long, & Stevens, 1975). (See Table 1-4 for a comparison of the view of behavior held by the psychoeducational model with that held by proponents of behavior modification.)

The complex problems of children do not neatly fit the narrow professional skills of any single discipline. A cross-disciplinary approach is needed to achieve a holistic understanding of behavior. Without a broad knowledge of the major theories of human nature, one must rely on the superficial application of gimicky techniques (Morse, 1981). Two principal ways of achieving holistic synthesis are interdisciplinary collaboration and interdisciplinary training. In *interdisciplinary collaboration*, a team coordinates clinical and educational data and planning (Knoblock & Reinig, 1971). Such teams typically include special educators, social workers, psychologists, psychiatrists, language therapists, and other specialists. (A good example is the League

Table 1-4. Comparison of Behavior Modification and Psychoeducation

Behavior modification	Psychoeducational model
Behavior is the result of reaction to external stimuli	*Behavior* is generally the result of combined external and internal stimulation
Learning occurs primarily through conditioned positive or negative stimuli	*Learning* occurs through the interaction of these processes: Constitutional factors Maturation and development, which organize cognitive and affective structures Personal meaning and significance attached to events based on an individual's life history Consequences of behavior Creative problem-solving
Educational goals focus on repetition of the desired behavior and elimination of the undesired behavior	*Educational goals* may include changing specific behavior but generally emphasize decision-making according to a realistic and responsible plan of action

Adapted from Tessier, 1974.

School Model developed by Fenicel and described by Morse and Coopchick [1979]). *Interdisciplinary training*, while not negating the importance of collaboration, entails the development of a new type of professional with a broad general background in educating and treating troubled children (Mearig, 1978). For example, such a profession may be modeled on the European *educateur* and draw from the existing knowledge base of such fields as special education, social work, recreation, developmental psychology, and child care (Beker, 1977; Brendtro, 1980; Krueger, 1982).

Teaching Is Humanistic

All learning takes place within the context of an interpersonal relationship with teachers (Knoblock & Reinig, 1971). Behavior is the verbal and nonverbal expression of the total person, and thus the person, not the expression, is most important (Fagen, Long, & Stevens, 1975).

Humanistic teaching respects the individuality of each person and thereby seeks to ensure that legitimate adult authority is exercised with consideration for the rights and needs of children (Morse et al., 1980).

Humanistic teaching must be attuned to the affective dimension, i.e., the attitudes, values, and feelings. Although success in academic skills can enhance self-esteem, the psychoeducational approach does not favor a sterile, exclusively cognitive or skill-oriented educational experience for either normal or disturbed children (Cheney & Morse, 1980). Cognitive and affective processes are in continuous interaction (Fagen, Long, & Stevens, 1975).

"Learning must be invested with feeling to give it interest, meaning, and purpose" (Long, 1969, p. 370). Relationships between feelings and learning are seen in many ways:

> *Positive feelings about the subject matter* enhance learning.
>
> *Positive feelings about the teacher* enhance learning.
>
> *Subjects that enhance self-esteem* (e.g., "I am good at this") are more easily learned (Fagen, Long, & Stevens, 1975).

Students need the opportunity to exercise choice if they are to learn responsibility and self-control. Schools are often structured to restrict self-direction and thereby distort the learning process. Three major educational distortions that restrict flexibility and self-actualization include the following:

> *Externally dictated academic tasks* that fail to recognize the child's needs, interests, or abilities, and thus lead to passive conformity or resistance.
>
> *Restrictive competition for grades and recognition,* which pits children against one another and limits positive reinforcement to a small number of "superior" students; others are devalued. This situation fosters feelings of inferiority, envy, and distrust. Personal pride suffers while cheating and exploitation are rewarded.
>
> *Focus on narrow academic products,* which leads to the regurgitation of specific facts in the absence of meaningful understanding (Fagen, Long, & Stevens, 1975).

Humanistic teaching must provide opportunities for exploration and accommodate a variety of styles and channels of learning. Thus, the creative arts, recreation and physical activities are vital to a holistic education and deserve an important place in the program (Berkowitz & Rothman, 1960; Cheney & Morse, 1972; Huber, 1980).

Crisis Is Opportunity

Problems are a normal part of human existence. While human problems may not be inherently desirable, neither should they be viewed as entirely negative. As Edmund Cooke once said, "Trouble is what you make it." Problems can either be opportunities for growth or they can be devastating. The use of conflict situations for positive intervention was one of Redl's particularly fruitful contributions. Instead of seeing a crisis as a catastrophe, one can view a problem situation as a unique opportunity for mutual learning (Morse, 1981).

A negative definition of problems is a significant impediment to successful work with troubled youth. Young people learn from the reaction of adults that problems signify stupidity, craziness, evil, or inadequacy. Thus it is not surprising that children go to great lengths to deny problems rather than to cope with them directly. It is important that problem situations be redefined so they are no longer seen as trouble but rather as opportunities for personal growth. Those who become competent at problem-solving possess skills that are in great demand (Vorrath & Brendtro, 1974).

Conflict and stress can disrupt a child's equilibrium, creating a state of crisis marked by inner tension, unpleasant feelings, and disorganized behavior. The child who cannot cope effectively will require adult support and guidance. A small influence exerted by a significant person during times of crisis can have a profound impact on the child's development (Kaplan, 1961).

Troubled children behave in immature and destructive ways during periods of stress. Their behavior can elicit corresponding problem behavior in others, including the adult. Thus aggressive children can create aggressive adults, withdrawn children can get others to ignore them, and immature behavior in children can produce immature or angry responses from adults (Long, Morse, & Newman, 1980).

If the adult becomes entangled in the child's problems and acts out the child's feelings or behavior, a conflict cycle is generated. This conflict cycle serves to maintain negative feelings and behavior and reinforces defenses against change. Adults must be aware of their own feelings and potential reactions during conflict if they are to hope to work in a mature manner to produce change in the child (Long, Morse, & Newman, 1980).

Experience in dealing with frustration is necessary for personal growth (Fagen, Long, & Stevens, 1975). If properly managed, conflict can be used productively to teach children new ways of understanding and coping effectively with stress. Crises are excellent times for adults to teach and for children to learn (Long, Morse, & Newman, 1980).

Practice Is Pragmatic

The psychoeducational approach is a practice model that draws from a variety of educational and treatment frameworks in order to make available the greatest resources to serve children. However, the specific methods proposed by different theories may be contradictory — should one provide emotional support to a child in crisis or ignore disordered behavior? These conflicts cannot always be resolved at the level of theory.

There are any number of reasons why one intervention will be selected over another. Depending on the situation, these reasons might be based on:

> Theory — This is a *rational* method.
>
> Research — There is *empirical* evidence supporting the method.
>
> Ethics — This is what one's *values* prescribe or proscribe.
>
> Intuition — This is what *seems right*.

Certainly there are other, less desirable reasons such as expediency, ulterior motives, or unconscious motivations. However, in the final analysis most skillful practitioners choose the path that shows most promise. They employ what Lazarus (1972) calls a "technical eclecticism." Out of practical necessity they are *pragmatic*, using what works regardless of whether it is supposed to work at the abstract level (Savicki & Brown, 1981).

Unless pragmatism is tempered by a strong humanistic philosophy, it could easily become shallow and self-serving. We have chosen to conclude our definition of the psychoeducational model with an example of humane pragmatism. This classic story was first presented by William Morse (1964) at the conclusion of the First Annual Conference on the Education of Emotionally Disturbed Children at Syracuse University.

"Red Wig Therapy"

I have pictures a teacher in Florida gave me which verify it. A child was entered in a special class. He was mute and diagnosed as schizophrenic. He refused to talk to anybody and he sat hunched up so that his neck almost disappeared as his head settled on his shoulders somehow. He wouldn't talk or communicate with anybody. After a while, and it was about Christmas time, the youngsters were writing out paragraphs about what they wanted for Christmas. This was the first time he contributed and he wrote down he wanted hair because he was bald. And he was absolutely bald. He wrote that he wanted hair for Christmas. He wouldn't, of course, *say* what he wanted because he wouldn't talk, but she read his statement and said humorously, "I can't get you hair, but maybe I can get you a wig." You know, as you might say to a child. He had continually worn his hat in class to hide his bald head. Well, he became fixated on Christmas and this wig which he wanted so much and thought he was going to get. As the teacher told me, she had this thing going and she knew she had to get him a wig.

She began to explore wig-getting, for which her professional courses had not prepared her very well. And she found out that if she went across the state she could get a wig for him, although the wigmaker was distressed at the thought of designing a wig of false hair for a small child and also told her that it would cost $175, of which $25 had to be paid in advance and the rest when she picked up the wig. Now their therapeutic budget did not include money for wigs. There was no available petty cash. She went to a service club and I imagine that must have been quite a session when she said, "I want you to buy a wig for a kid for Christmas." As she said, "Me and my big mouth." I think it was really her big heart that got her involved, her sensitivity that got her involved, not her mouth; but anyway, she got the money. She went across the state and got the wig. It took quite a while for the boy to get his head fitted, get the wig made and get it back. Then it didn't fit at all well. This was because he no longer kept his head stuffed into his shoulders. He stood tall and straight. So the wig was too large in the back. She said you could have put a clothespin over the extra part. He would have worn it anyway, he was that happy, but she took it back and she got it fixed.

He was so proud of his new hair that his symptoms left him immediately and he began to converse. The picture of this happy youngster and that wig is some sight. It's a hideous wig, but it was beautiful to that child. He would not let it be washed or anything done to it if he could help it. He kept it on all the time. All the children were shown it.

After about three months the teacher had a phone call from the mother. The mother said, "You must come to the house," and there was a tenor about her voice that scared the teacher out of her wits. She said, "I think I know what he's done. He's leaned over and dropped that thing in the john and flushed it down and there is $175 bucks worth of therapy down the drain." She was afraid to ask the mother but she went out. When she got there, he was there with his red wig, so her fears were wrong. The mother put the child under light and lifted the wig. There was a crop of short, fuzzy hair under his wig. No one had ever been certain, according to the history, why he had lost his hair in the first place. But he had. And now nobody knows why he got hair, but he did. Even after peeking again to make certain, it was hard to believe for a long time. In the last picture she showed me, here was this boy with a fine thatch of his own red hair. No more wig.

Well, I would say I think a lot of our business boils down to knowing where the child is hurting. What is bothering him? Have we the sensitivity in our interactions to find it? Those who interact with children are sensitive to their needs and they'll go about doing the things that the child needs in ways that we've never called therapy before, I think. I would suggest we not wait until research proves that wigs on a bald-headed little boy are therapeutic, but to go ahead with the wig when you see the child needs it (Morse, 1964, pp. 113–115).

REFERENCES

Addams, J. *The spirit of youth in the city streets.* New York: The MacMillan Company, 1909.

Barnes, H., & Kelman, S. From slogans to concepts: A basis for change in child care work. *Child Care Quarterly*, 1974, *3*(1), 7–23.

Beker, J. On defining the child care profession VI. *Child Care Quarterly*, 1977, *6*(Winter), 245–247.

Berkowitz, P., & Rothman, E. *The disturbed child: Recognition and psychoeducational therapy in the classroom.* New York: New York University Press, 1960.

Bettelheim, B. *Love is not enough—The treatment of emotionally disturbed children.* Glencoe, IL: The Free Press, 1950.

Brendtro, L. Bridging teaching and treatment: The American educateur. *Journal of Teacher Education*, 1980, *31*(5), 23–26.

Brendtro, L., & Nicolaou, A. Hooked on helping. *Synergist*, 1982, *10*(Winter), 38–41.

Brown, R. Concepts and models in the field of rehabilitation. *Residential and Community Child Care Administration*, 1979, *1*(Spring), 7–19.

Carbone, P. Liberal education and teacher preparation. *Journal of Teacher Education*, 1980, *31*(3), 13–17.

Cervantes, L. *The dropout.* Ann Arbor, MI: The University of Michigan Press, 1965.

Cheney, C., & Morse, W. Psychodynamic intervention in emotional disturbance. In W. C. Rhodes and M. L. Tracy (Eds.), *A study of child variance, Vol. 2: Interventions.* Ann Arbor, MI: University of Michigan Press, 1972.

Cheney, C., & Morse, W. Psychodynamic intervention. In N. Long, W. Morse, & R. Newman (Eds.), *Conflict in the classroom.* Belmont, CA: Wadsworth, 1980.

Clark, D., Lotto, L., & McCarthy, M. Factors associated with success in urban elementary schools. *Phi Delta Kappan*, 1980, *61*(7), 467–470.

Combs, A., Avila, D., & Purkey, W. *Helping relationships.* Boston: Allyn & Bacon, 1978.

Deal, T., & Celotti, L. How much influence do (and can) educational administrators have on classrooms? *Phi Delta Kappan*, 1980, *61*(7), 471–473.

Eisner, E. On the difference between scientific and artistic approaches to qualitative research. *Educational Researcher*, 1981, *10*(4), 4–9.

Fagen, S., Long, N., & Stevens, D. *Teaching children self control.* Columbus, OH: Charles E. Merrill, 1975.

Fiedler, F. A comparison of therapeutic relationships in psychoanalytic, nondirective and Adlerian therapy. *Journal of Consulting Psychology*, 1960, *14*, 436–445.

Garner, H. A truce in the war for the child. *Exceptional Children*, 1976, *42*(March), 315–320.

Garner, H. *Teamwork in programs for children and youth: A handbook for administrators.* Springfield, IL: Charles C. Thomas, 1982.

Glasser, W. *Reality therapy.* New York: Harper & Row, 1965.

Glavin, J. New directions in research on emotionally disturbed children. Paper presented to Special Study Institute on Planning Research on Education of Disturbed Children, Peabody College, Nashville, TN, September 24–26, 1970.

Gold, M. Scholastic experiences, self-esteem and delinquent behavior: A theory for alternative schools. *Crime and Delinquency*, 1978, *24*(3), 290–308.

Grossbard, H. *Cottage parents—What they have to be, know, and do.* New York: Child Welfare League of America, 1960.

Guindon, J. *Les e'tapes de la re'education des jeunes delinquants et des autres.* Paris: Editions Fleurus, 1971.

Guindon, J. The reeducational process. *International Journal of Mental Health*, 1973, *II*(1), 15–26.

Hobbs, N. The re-education of emotionally disturbed children. In E. M. Bower and W. G. Hollister (Eds.), *Behavioral science frontiers in education.* New York: Wiley, 1967.

Hobbs, N. Helping disturbed children and their families: Project Re-ed 20 years later. Paper published by the Center for the Study of Families and Children, Institute for Public Policy Studies, Vanderbilt University, Nashville, TN, 1979.

Huber, F. A strategy for teaching cooperative games: Let's put the fun back in games for disturbed children. In N. Long, W. Morse, & R. Newman (Eds.), *Conflict in the classroom*. Belmont, CA: Wadsworth, 1980.

Hunt, D. Teachers are psychologists, too: On the application of psychology to education. *Canadian Psychological Review*, 1976, *17*, 210–218.

Hunt, D. How to be your own best theorist. *Theory into Practice*, 1980, *19*(4), 287–293.

Juul, K. Remediation models for emotionally disturbed children from an international perspective. Paper presented at the conference of the European Association for Special Education, Helsinki, Finland, August 3–8, 1980.

Juul, K., & Linton, T. European approaches to the treatment of behavior disordered children. *Behavioral Disorders*, 1978, *3*(4), 232–249.

Kaplan, G. (Ed.). *Prevention of mental disorders in children*. New York: Basic Books, 1961.

Kauffman, J. *Characteristics of children's behavior disorders*. Columbus, OH: Charles E. Merrill, 1981.

Knoblock, P., & Reinig, J. *Special project report: Preparing psychoeducators for inner city teaching*. Syracuse, NY: Syracuse University Division of Special Education & Rehabilitation, 1971.

Krueger, M. *Job satisfaction for child care workers*. Milwaukee, WI: Tall Publishing, 1982.

Kulawiec, E. Janusz Korszak: Educator–martyr. *Intellect*, 1974, *102*(May), 512–516.

Lazarus, A. *Multi-model behavior therapy*. Fort Lee, NJ: Sigma Information, Inc., 1972.

Leavitt, H., Dill, W., & Eyring, H. *The organizational world*. New York: Harcourt Brace Jovanovich, 1973.

Long, N. Helping children cope with feelings. *Childhood Education*, 1969, *45*, 367–372.

Long, N., Morse, W., & Newman, R. (Eds.). *Conflict in the classroom* (4TH ed.). Belmont, CA: Wadsworth, 1980.

McClelland, D., & Dailey, C. *Professional competencies of human service workers: A report to the College for Human Services*. Boston: M. C. Berand, 1974.

McCorkel, L., Elias, A., & Bixby, F. *The Highfields story*. New York: Henry Holt, 1958.

Mearig, J. (Ed.). *Working for children*. San Francisco: Jossey-Bass, 1978.

Morse, W. Summary discussion. In P. Knoblock (Ed.), *Educational programming for emotionally disturbed children: The decade ahead*. Syracuse, NY: Syracuse University Division of Special Education and Rehabilitation, 1964.

Morse, W. The mental hygiene viewpoint on school discipline. *The High School Journal*, 1965, *48*, 396–401.

Morse, W. Professionals in a changing society. In J. S. Mearig (Ed.), *Working for children*. San Francisco: Jossey-Bass, 1978.

Morse, W. The problem and promise of special education. In W. C. Morse (Ed.), *Humanistic teaching for exceptional children*. Syracuse, NY: Syracuse University Press, 1979.

Morse, W. LSI tomorrow. *Pointer*, 1981, *25*(2), 67–70.

Morse, W., Ardizzone, J., Macdonald, C., & Pasick, P. *Affective education for children and youth*. Reston, VA: Council for Exceptional Children, 1980.

Morse, W., & Coopchick, H. Socioemotional impairment. In W. C. Morse (Ed.), *Humanistic teaching for exceptional children*. Syracuse, NY: Syracuse University Press, 1979.

Morse, W., Cutler, R., & Fink, A. *Public school classes for the emotionally handicapped: A research analysis*. Reston, VA: Council for Exceptional Children, 1964.

Nash, R. J., & Ducharme, E. R. Preparing new educational professionals for non-public school settings. *Journal of Teacher Education*, 1978, *29*(4), 36–41.

Pappenfort, D. Progress report. The National Survey of Residential and Non-residential Services to Children and Youth with Special Problems and Needs. Chicago: University of Chicago, April–June 1980. (Unpublished.)

Phillips, E. Achievement Place: Token reinforcement procedures in a home-style rehabilitation setting for "pre-delinquent" boys. *Journal of Applied Behavior Analysis,* 1968, *1,* 213–223.

Phillips, E. L., Phillips, E. A., Fixsen, D., & Wolf, M. *The teaching-family handbook: Group living environments administered by professional teaching parents for youth in trouble.* Lawrence, KA: University Printing Service, 1972 (rev. 1974).

Prieto, A. G. and Rutherford, R. B. An ecological assessment technique for behaviorally disordered and learning disordered children. *Behavioral Disorders,* 1977, *2*(3), 169–175.

Redl, F., & Wineman, D. *Children who hate.* Glencoe, IL: The Free Press, 1951.

Redl, F., & Wineman, D. *Controls from within: Techniques for the treatment of the aggressive child.* New York: The Free Press, 1952.

Rhodes, W., & Paul, J. *Emotionally disturbed and deviant children: New views and approaches.* Englewood Cliffs, NJ: Prentice Hall, 1978.

Rhodes, W., & Tracy, M (Eds.). *A study of child variance: Conceptual models,* Vol. 1. Ann Arbor, MI: The University of Michigan Press, 1972.

Rich, H., Beck, M., & Coleman, T. Behavior management: The psychoeducational model. In R. McDowell, G. Adamson, and F. Wood (Eds.), *Teaching emotionally disturbed children.* Boston: Little, Brown, 1982.

Savicki, V., & Brown, R. *Working with troubled children.* New York: Human Science Press, 1981.

Special Education: A Major Event in 1973. *Phi Delta Kappan,* April 1974, *55*(8), pp. 513, 515.

Swap, S., Prieto, A., & Harth, R. Ecological perspective of the emotionally disturbed child. In R. McDowell, G. Adamson, and F. Wood (Eds.), *Teaching emotionally disturbed children.* Boston: Little, Brown, 1982.

Tessier, B. The psycho-educative model in action. A description of the Boscoville and St. Helene Reeducation Center. Montreal, 1974. (Unpublished.)

Trieschman, A., Whittaker, J., & Brendtro, L. *The other 23 hours.* Chicago: Aldine, 1969.

Vorrath, H., & Brendtro, L. *Positive peer culture.* Chicago: Aldine, 1974.

Wahlberg, H. (Ed.). *Educational environments and effects.* Berkley, CA: McCutchan, 1979.

White, W. Organizational behavior research — Where do we go from here? In E. E. Eddy and W. L. Partridge (Eds.), *Applied anthropology in America.* New York: Columbia University Press, 1978.

Whittaker, J. *Caring for troubled children.* San Francisco: Jossey-Bass, 1979.

Whittaker, J. Keynote Address, Michigan Association of Children's Agencies Annual Child Care Symposium, Albion, MI, April 1980.

Wise, A. *Legislative learning: The bureaucratization of the American classroom.* Berkeley: University of California, 1979.

Wolfgang, C., & Glickman, C. *Solving discipline problems: On strategies for classroom teachers.* Boston: Allyn & Bacon, 1980.

Wood, M. (Ed.). *Developmental therapy: A textbook for teachers as therapists for emotionally disturbed young children.* Baltimore: University Park Press, 1975.

PART I

Foundations for Powerful Environments

We believe that the dominant factors in teaching, treating, and caring for troubled children are the underlying human interactions. Regardless of the methodology employed, the outcome of our efforts hinges in large measure on the quality of these relationships. In the following three chapters we shall examine the crucial foundations of the powerful interpersonal environment, which include:

Individual relationships. Successful teachers and youth workers are able to build strong human bonds with children who may not readily identify with adults. Those who cannot form significant relationships will not be effective as communicators, models, or social reinforcers.

Peer group relationships. Successful programs are characterized by student participation in a positive, caring group climate. When students are indifferent or antagonistic to one another or to staff, the program becomes ineffective.

Organizational relationships. Adults must have the skills and motivation to forge effective partnerships with other professionals and with parents. Without this spirit of cooperative teamwork, participants lack a sense of shared mission and dissipate their energies in dysfunctional conflict.

In the following chapters we shall consider the impediments to effective individual, group, and organizational relationships as well as specific strategies for creating powerful environments for teaching and treatment.

The Interpersonal Relationship: Reaching the Reluctant

LARRY K. BRENDTRO AND ARLIN E. NESS

> O grant me my prayer that I
> may never lose the touch of the
> one in the play of the many.
> —Sir Rabindranath Tagore in *Gitanjali*

Most workers with troubled children believe that the quality of the interpersonal relationship is pivotal to the sucess of their efforts. Yet because the concept of "relationship" is so vague and diffuse, some might argue that it is devoid of any real significance. Others see relationship as important but have not found it necessary or even desirable to try to objectify the highly personal process of forming human bonds. It is apparent that many fledgling youth workers—and veterans as well—lack the skills to form constructive relationships with troubled youth. A better understanding about precisely what is meant by this term is needed if we are to master the skills and attitudes essential to relating effectively with troubled children and youth.

Educators and clinicians have long been aware of the awesome power of the helping relationship. Writing the first book for teachers to be published in America, Samuel Hall proclaimed:

If you succeed in gaining their love, your influence will be greater in some respects than that of parents themselves. It will be in your power to direct them into almost any path you choose. . . . You have the power . . . to make them kind, benevolent and humane, or, by your neglect they may become the reverse of everything that is lovely, amiable and generous (1829, p. 47).

Likewise, the literature on social work has emphasized for many decades the importance of the interpersonal relationship to the helping process (Biestek, 1957; Towle, 1936). Hollis (1965) noted that a corrective relationship can have a powerful impact on the self-image of individuals whose experience with others has caused them to view themselves in an unrealistically dismal light. Perlman (1979) concluded that relationship is the red thread that runs through every successful effort of one person to influence another in a benign manner.

In spite of abundant pro-relationship rhetoric, there has been a marked depersonalization of the helping process in teaching and treatment. This is amply demonstrated by the shift in the meanings of the terms "education" and "therapy." The word "education" derives from the Latin *educare*, a broad term that means *to nourish* and *to raise*. Today it is equated with schooling, and many contemporary educators who are preoccupied with transmitting subject matter reject a broader definition of their role. The term "therapy" also has roots that denote a commitment far beyond that of therapists today:

> The first recorded therapist, officially titled as such, was Petroclus, referred to by Homer as Achilles' *therapon*. Petroclus was the leader's professional friend; he lived in the same tent, listened all day to Achilles' endless complaints, even encouraged him to shout out his anxieties, defended and represented his client against the world, and finally perished in the performance of his duties (Thomas, 1981, pp. 40–42).

European systems of re-education emphasize the importance of the capability to form strong, healthy, parent–surrogate relationships among those recruited and trained to work with troubled youth. The German professional role is that of socio-pedagogue or *erzhier*, which means "upbringer." French *educateurs* are trained in the principle that close interpersonal relationships between staff and students are "the cornerstone of a serious re-education" (Guindon, 1970, p. 66). In contrast, all too few child-serving institutions in the United States ensure the primacy of sustained caring relationships (Thomas, 1975).

Philosophies of treatment vary in the emphasis given to relationship in the therapeutic process. Some of these differences are highlighted in Table 2-1. Okun (1976) observes that the client-centered therapist seeks an empathic, nondirective relationship as the centerpiece of treatment. Psychodynamic therapists provide a neutral, accepting relationship. Reality therapists are interested in the connection between *behavior* and *values* and seek to build a warm, even loving, relationship between therapists and client. Cognitive-behavioral therapists focus on the connection between *behavior* and *thoughts* and seek to exhort, frustrate, and command clients to change their thinking without trying to form empathic relationships. In the classic behaviorist view, relationship is not considered a significant variable in behavioral change;

Table 2-1. Relationships in Five Therapies

Client-centered	Psychiatric-dynamic	Responsibility-reality	Cognitive-behavioral	Behavioral
Empathic	Accepting	Warm nonpunitive	Instructional	Detached
Nonjudgmental	Neutral	Judgmental	Judgmental	Evaluative
Communicating unconditional acceptance	Providing benign therapeutic relationship	Expecting responsible behavior and values	Rejecting illogical thinking and behavior	Reinforcing desired behavior

Adapted from Okun, 1976. We would include, together with reality therapy, other approaches that concentrate on responsible, moral behavior including those of Dreikurs (1964), Glasser (1965), and Vorrath and Brendtro (1974).

instead, "the helper is more of a behavioral engineer: objective, detached and professional" (Okun, 1976, p. 102).

In the past many behaviorists have questioned the importance of relationship because this variable could not easily be measured. This situation is changing with growing recognition that relationship is a critical factor in successful intervention (Schwartz & Goldiamond, 1975). Phillips and his colleagues (1973) at Achievement Place reported the failure of their first attempt to replicate a behavior-shaping program for delinquents when positive staff–student relationships were missing. Schwartz (1977) reports a carefully controlled study by Sloane comparing the treatment provided by behaviorists and psychotherapists. Clients in both groups improved significantly and treatment outcomes were similar. Both groups of therapists were rated by their patients as empathic, genuine, and possessing equal degrees of unconditional positive regard. Sloane concluded that change was apparently due to some factor other than the espoused theoretical orientation. Successful patients in both groups rated the personal interactions with their therapists as the single most important element in their treatment. Some behaviorists have become uncomfortable with the mechanical notion of "engineering behavior," and Hewett and Taylor (1980) suggest substituting the more humanized concept "orchestration of success."

RELATIONSHIP DEFINED

Some years ago, as a member of the faculty at the University of Illinois, the senior author was challenged by colleagues to define relationship operationally. The result was the definition that became a central concept in the book *The Other 23 Hours: Child Care Work with Emotionally Disturbed Children in a Therapeutic Milieu* (Trieschman, Whittaker, & Brendtro, 1969). This definition is depicted schematically in Fig. 2-1. As can be seen from the diagram, relationship consists of three components: social reinforcement, communication, and modeling.

Social Reinforcement

If a child is involved in a significant relationship with an adult, that adult has powers of social reinforcement disproportionate to those of other adults in the life of the youngster. This makes the youth subject to

Elements of a Relationship   Processes of Learning

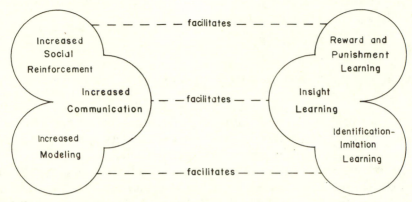

FIG. 2-1. Contributions of relationship to learning.

influence of social approval or disapproval. Thus the adult with such a relationship is not restricted solely to use of physical rewards or punishments to control the youth.

Communication

Relationship involves increased and intense communication between the parties involved. When the adult and child readily understand one another, they are able to employ a variety of verbal and nonverbal interactions to communicate their feelings. An adult in this relationship thus has available numerous potential techniques to enhance cognitive understanding and affective communication that are founded, for example, on the ability to empathize with a youngster and on a greater facility in using reasoning, explanation, suggestion, and interpretation.

Modeling

Finally, a significant relationship entails enhanced modeling. When a child chooses an adult as a model, that adult is able to influence a wide range of behaviors beyond those that are already in the young person's repertoire or that of his peers. This influence includes narrow and specific copying of behavior (imitation) as well as wholesale adoption of entire patterns of behavior or styles of personality (identification). The latter is, of course, one of the most profound means of socializing children and youth in any culture.

IMPEDIMENTS TO RELATIONSHIP

In spite of the potency of human relationship in changing behavior, those working with troubled youth encounter very special problems. Specifically, youth are reluctant to relate. In our earlier work we called these youngsters "relationship-resistant." Such youth seemingly cannot or will not allow the easy establishment of positive relationships with significant adults. Instead they display a series of behaviors that impede relationship, which are summarized below.

Barriers to Communication

Acting in ways that are secretive, guarded, aloof, suspicious, or superficial, these young people are effective at keeping adults at arms' length. They may harbor hostile feelings toward adults and may fear becoming close, as seen in the following case:

> Billy would always insist on wearing his hat, even indoors, and it usually was pulled down almost over his eyes. Furthermore, he would seldom remove his jacket even on the hottest day. If someone were to put a hand on his shoulder, he would cringe and draw away. This behavior was irritating to staff until they learned that he had witnessed his mother murder his alcoholic father; the mother had boiled a tub of water, thickened it with syrup and poured it over her husband while he was in a drunken stupor.

Unresponsiveness to Social Reinforcers

Although many troubled youth are hungry for praise, it is not uncommon to find youth who initially shun or reject such attention. Perhaps they have learned to get all of their attention through negative behavior, or for some reason human relationships have taken on a negative rather than a positive valence. The use of effusive praise can backfire when children are accustomed to adults who are punitive or abusive. Likewise, overuse of praise, especially insincere and perfunctory praise, can fail to achieve the intended results (Evertson et al., 1980).

Rejection of the Adult Model

Many troubled youth, particularly adolescents, exaggerate their difference from adults. Pledging their loyalty to the peer subculture, they go to great ends to reject adult models. In *Blackboard Jungle*, a novel about a deprived, inner-city neighborhood, Hunter (1954) tells of the experience of a teacher who brought his personal collection of records to school in hopes of influencing the students in their attitudes about good music. Rejecting his values completely, the students taunted him and went on a rampage destroying his records.

STAGES IN RELATIONSHIP-BUILDING

Clinical experience with problem youth suggests that the process of relationship-building proceeds through predictable stages (Trieschman, Whittaker and Brendtro, 1969; Whelan, 1982). These stages include:

Casing—an initial period of orientation,
Limit-testing—a period of trying out the relationship; and
Integration—adapting to a predictable style or pattern of interaction.

Each of these stages presents unique challenges and opportunities, which are discussed more fully below.

Casing: Managing Initial Impressions

The troubled youngster who encounters a strange adult enters the new relationship with many uncertainties about what might be expected. It is not surprising, then, that such a youth will need to reorient to this new reality. Humans, of course, are not alone in their need to check new and potentially threatening situations. For example, a rat placed into a strange maze may retreat to a corner from which it can carefully observe before venturing forth to explore the unfamiliar environment. Troubled youth show their casing behavior in various ways depending on their personalities.

Children with poor reality contact are particularly disoriented by new situations and frequently develop ritualistic behaviors to structure initial encounters with strangers. The senior author recalls an early experience with a 12-year-old autistic boy who began each interaction by asking the adult to change a half-dollar to two quarters or vice versa. By chance the author met this individual again some 20 years later and did not recognize this fine-appearing young man in a three-piece suit—until he asked to exchange two quarters for a half-dollar. Although all of us experience some disorientation on meeting strangers, we usually ritualize the interaction with a handshake and introduction. This autistic youth invented his own private ritual.

Most disturbed and delinquent youth case their environment in a much more flexible and adaptive manner. They will attempt to determine what power the adult has in the organization and will try to diagnose the peer power hierarchy. They will be concerned with how other youth perceive the adult, specifically, to determine what kind of person this is and what can be expected from him or her. During this period of casing, the youth will be guarded and will probably not show his or her true colors. The adult should not place too great a stock in the youth's initial presentation. For example, a frightened youth may act with great bravado, and a cool, delinquent youth may act like "goody two-shoes." Usually this is a honeymoon of relatively short duration and has little relationship to the behavior that will follow. (Years ago we learned never to take base-rate measures of behavior during this initial period.)

Many young people have learned to expect hostile behavior from all adults; it is important that one not fall into this mold. In these initial encounters, the adult must walk a middle ground between being too business-like, in which case he will be perceived as "just like the others," or too friendly, which can lead him to be perceived as a threat, a mushy pushover, a seducer, or worse. The Viennese educator and therapist August Aichorn stressed the importance of the initial encounter and described his approach upon meeting a hostile and intimidating boy:

> At first glance he seems to be the bully type. If we take a stern tone with him he rejects us immediately and we can never get a transference established. If we are cordial and friendly, he becomes distrustful and rejects us or takes this for weakness on our part and reacts with increased roughness. . . . He looks with suspicion on people who are nice to him and he is more than ever on his guard. . . . I consider the first moment of our coming together of the utmost importance. It is more than a 'feeling-out of the situation.' It must have the appearance of certainty and sureness. . . . After the sizing up of each other is over, the struggle for mastery begins" (1935, pp. 127–128).

Limit-testing: The Need for Acceptance with Control

After a youngster's initial attempt to case his environment, he will probe for more information. Because the youth can learn only so much by asking and observing, he may now need to test out reality directly through his actions. One needs to know whether adults can be trusted with secrets, how they will handle anger, and how they will respond in a wide range of situations.

Some youth cultures use a ritual called "playing the dozens" which helps serve this function of testing out the personality and power relationships of others. Basically, playing the dozens is a game in which participants take turns hurling increasingly atrocious insults about one another (or one's mother). The first person who backs off, loses his temper, or is left in humiliated speechlessness is presumably the loser. Needless to say, such a "game" can be most disquieting to the adult in charge of a group, who may become the next target of hostile rhetoric.

Whether confrontations are psychological or physical, they can be very intimidating to the inexperienced youth worker who is never quite certain of the outcome. It is important that such challenges be met in a controlled, unflappable manner, even if the adult is terrified on the inside. (This may be one situation in which it is generally not advisable to signal one's real feelings.) Being able to manage these confrontations in a matter-of-fact, nonflinching, "I've-been-through-this-before" manner will help put this stage behind.

Morse (1980) marks the importance of *differential acceptance* of negative behavior, specifically, of being able to understand and deal with aggressive youngsters without either becoming counteraggressive or condoning inappropriate behavior. Adults who reciprocate rejection will be equally as ineffective as those who fail to provide any structure. The behavior of troubled children signals a need for both acceptance and limits.

Integration: Achieving Security and Consistency

Successfully mastered, limit-testing provides a foundation for a more secure and predictable relationship between youth and an adult. Still, regardless of how stable and positive a relationship might be, limit-testing will re-emerge periodically. However, these instances will be isolated episodes and not reflect the characteristic style in which youth and adults relate to one another. Of course, if an adult is highly inconsistent, it is possible that the relationship will never progress beyond the stage of testing limits.

Table 2-2. Patterns of Consistency and Predictability By Adults

---

To a child, the adults having authority over him are the main sources of threat,
   just as they are the main sources of comfort and nurturance. If much of
   their behavior is consistent and predictable, he feels safe. When a child's
   life has no important points of consistency, his predictions are constantly
   unfulfilled.
An environment is new whenever a part of it changes. The child must immediately determine the points of predictability in the new environment. This
   usually means that he systematically breaks all the established rules — to
   find out if they are still in force.
One effective way of increasing consistency is to establish a long-term rule and
   then enforce it consistently. The rule must be chosen very carefully. A
   good rule must fulfill three requirements. It must be definable, it must be
   reasonable, and it must be enforceable.
Many of the rules that parents try to enforce are unnecessary and impractical.
   Consider whether the result of breaking the rule is likely to be as disastrous
   as alleged. Consider whether it is worthy of the effort to enforce it consistently. A rule that is not enforced is far more damaging than is no rule at all.
   If you are unwilling to enforce it, it is an unenforceable rule.

Adapted from Smith and Smith, 1966.

Adults can greatly enhance the stability of their relationships with
youth by developing a pattern of consistency and predictability in their
expectations (Smith & Smith, 1966; Table 2-2). Because troubled children have often experienced long histories of turbulent relationships,
they may require a considerable period before they abandon well-en-
trenched interpersonal behaviors. For example, the distrustful youngster has learned to be this way from significant adults who could not be
trusted; the child can be expected to generalize that style to other
relationships, a phenomenon that psychoanalytic theory calls transfer-
ence. A consistent, stable, corrective relationship offers the opportunity for breaking old patterns to form new interpersonal response
styles.

REMOVING BARRIERS TO COMMUNICATION

It is widely recognized that effective communication is essential to
successful interpersonal relationships. All of us, regardless of our
professional training, have had a lifetime of experiences in learning to
communicate with others. In most respects, communication with
troubled youth is not inherently different from communication with
others we have known, except perhaps that more hangs on the outcome. The adult must develop the ability to use verbal and nonverbal
communication with great empathy if trusting relationships are to
supplant isolation and distrust.

Verbal Communication

As in any human relationship, the parties involved must find something they have in common about which to communicate. Many skilled youth workers make a point of keeping abreast of the interests of young people so that there can be some basis for positive and meaningful communication. Describing her work with troubled minority youngsters, Beard says:

> I believe that it is important for the person interested in working with adolescents to maintain some knowledge of the current symbolism of each generation: hair styles, dress, language, music and dances, heroes, heroines, recreational activities, codes of honor and disgrace, "in" group and "out" group behaviors. . . . Detailed knowledge about the symbols is not as important as awareness and respect for their presence. Maintaining an atmosphere of comfort and openness with the young person, while expressing interest in knowing more about the meaning and function of the symbols to the group and to the client herself, moves me closer to bonding with the young person (1979, p. 98).

Sometimes youth workers have the mistaken notion that the only important conversations they have are those related to the therapeutic discussion of personal problems. One of the authors is reminded of an early experience at The University of Michigan Fresh Air Camp. It appeared as if a particularly guarded youth was beginning to relax and share important information about his background. Elated at the possibility of an important breakthrough, the author suggested, "Why don't you come and sit on the log so we can talk?" Suddenly the youth's demeanor changed and he pulled away saying, "Oh, no, don't try that psychology stuff on me!" He kept his distance for several days until he could be sure he was safe from surreptitious psychotherapy.

Probably because psychotherapeutic interactions have been glamorized in the media, it is easy for adults working in therapeutic settings to feel that only "depth" topics are important for discussion. In fact, sometimes they are irrelevant and may be used by young people to manipulate the adult by producing the supposedly desired "therapy talk." This is seen in the following experience by one of the authors.

> Ten-year-old Tony turned to me and said, "I have three vivid memories. Would you like to hear them?" Before I could respond he ticked them off. "First was the time my mother hit me on the head with a board. Second was the time she threatened my brother with a knife. Third was the time she pushed my little sister down the stairs." He looked up expectantly for my response. Convinced I was being fed material that had been used time and again on all the psychologists and social workers in his thick file, my only thought was to respond to him with "Am I supposed to get a pencil and write these down?"

It will ordinarily be most useful if communication is directed to the here and now rather than to distant issues. The Japanese have a proverb that says, "The path of duty lies in what is near at hand but men seek it in what is remote." Significant helping relationships do not dwell in the past but deal with the present and with preparation for the future. Just because communication deals with *surface* behavior does not mean that this is *superficial* behavior. What some might call "depth psychology" might better be labeled as irrelevant.

Even so, our focus on immediate, observable behavior can also be carried to the extreme. The problems of young people are frequently more than meet the eye. Some youth do harbor deep-seated problems because of conflicts that they have never revealed to another person. For example, the authors have encountered scores of troubled youngsters who have been sexually molested by adults. This abuse was traumatic and produced patterns of disordered behavior that persisted despite many attempts at direct intervention until the young person dared to trust a concerned adult enough to share the problem and to begin working through his or her feelings.

The most effective communications with troubled young people are frequently not those carried on in the sanctity of the formal therapy hour, but those that arise out of the natural course of life events in the other 23 hours. The adult who stands beside a youth at a time of personal or behavioral crisis has the advantage of dealing with material when it is direct and meaningful. Trying to reopen the issue days later in a scheduled therapy session can be next to impossible with many troubled children.

Two different models for verbal communication in real-life situations are the teaching interaction (Phillips *et al.*, 1974) and the life-space interview (Redl & Wineman, 1952). While on-the-spot, life-space communications offer great potential in the management and treatment of troubled youth, such interventions present unique challenges, which Fritz Redl often described as "therapy on the hoof." These issues will be considered in greater detail in Chapter 6.

Nonverbal Communication

Even when no direct verbal communication is occurring, powerful messages can be transmitted by nonverbal means. These messages can be conveyed by proximity, gestures, facial expressions, body position, eye contact, and tone of voice. More subtle but no less powerful nonverbal messages are conveyed in the ways we treat our time and our physical space:

—The Navahoes have a beautiful custom. If one wants to be your friend, he comes and sits with you. Navahoes believe the most valuable thing you can give is part of your time (Milburn, undated).

—Young people whose lives have been marked by ugliness can benefit from being provided an environment of beauty that communicates "this is for you because you are of value."

Just as we adults must be sensitive to the nonverbal messages conveyed by our actions and the learning environments we create, so also is it important to learn to decode the nonverbal behavior of youth in order to understand how they are feeling. Sometimes a group of children can develop elaborate systems of nonverbal communication within the peer group that are totally missed by the adult who is naive to what is really transpiring. Perhaps the adult is highly educated but is imprisoned in a "cerebral" outlook that is a by-product of rational, verbal academic traning. Intuitive ability in nonverbal communication accounts for much of the success of many volunteers, aides, and paraprofessionals who may lack formal training in verbal methods of therapy.

Troubled youth who do not trust what adults *say* can be particularly attuned to nonverbal cues that are at cross purposes with the verbal message. Savicki and Brown (1981) stress the importance of *cue congruence*, namely, that the messages sent by different channels be consistent. Examples of incongruent cues might be the following:

—The teacher directs a student to "come here right now" but telegraphs her expectation that he will not comply by walking toward the youth.

—As a youth brandishes a weapon threatening a peer, the child care worker cowers and with a trembling voice says, "You are going to put that down."

—A program with a stated mission of "changing the self-concept and behavior of disturbed children" is operated in ramshackle quarters under the direction of disheveled-appearing staff.

The most direct type of nonverbal communication between youth and adults is probably direct physical contact. Effective workers with troubled youth are usually very skillfull in the strategic use of physical contact in a warm and supportive manner. In fact, it is very hard to imagine how one could touch the lives of some troubled children without touching their person. This is particularly true with younger and more immature children. However, physical contact opens salient issues, particularly with the adolescent.

Some children seek excessive physical contact for reassurance; they may be seen by adults as either "cuddly" or "clingy" depending on how the behavior is interpreted. It can be difficult to meet one child's need for frequent contact without interfering with relationships with other children.

Some children find any physical contact initiated by adults to be aversive. These youth may recoil and demand "get your hands off or I'll give you one up the side of the face." Other youth approach adults in a playful, combative manner that may not be appropriate to the situation. Aggressive physical contact between adult and troubled youth is fraught with potential problems. What one minute seems fun can quickly become explosive as someone gets hurt and tempers flair. Children differ dramatically in their response when others enter their personal space, and adults must individualize their approach to accommodate these differences.

Like aggression, contact with sexual connotations can be inappropriate and destructive of the therapeutic relationship. Youth workers need to feel free to discuss any problems they have surrounding issues of physical contact without the fear that such problems will reflect on them personally. This is particularly crucial with respect to sexual innuendos, as seen in the following examples from child care workers in residential group care settings:

> Tony (age 10) would regularly call me over at bedtime and insist that I should give a good-night kiss. This seemed innocent enough and became a ritual. I was shocked to learn from other staff that this was part of an elaborate sexual fantasy which was related in great detail to the entertainment of other cabin-mates.

> Since Carlos joined the adolescent group he periodically sneaks up behind me when I'm not looking and plays "got-cha" with my breasts. At first I was too embarrassed to tell any other staff. I shouldn't have been since all three female staff finally discovered that he pulled this on each of us at various times.

So many factors impinge on physical contact that it is difficult to provide specific guidelines. Suffice it to say that physical contact can be a potent and effective means of communication which should be used with great sensitivity in the therapeutic relationship.

Empathy

Central to any effective relationship is the ability to feel what another person is feeling. This is a formidable task with troubled youth whose observable behavior may sometimes very effectively mask true feelings. Although some adults seem to be naturally empathic, this is probably a skill that can be learned and enhanced. Bullmer (1975) has even developed a programmed text for training in "the art of empathy" by improving the accuracy of interpersonal perceptions.

Probably no single behavior is as crucial to empathy as the skill of listening. "The importance of listening extends far beyond its value for understanding other people. The act of listening, itself, conveys important messages to others. The careful listener is paying others the highest form of compliment. He is saying in effect, 'you are a truly significant person to me and what you are saying is important.'" (Combs, Avila, & Purkey, 1978, p. 136). In spite of the adult's willingness to listen to youth, the reality may be that some young people are not particularly inclined to express themselves verbally. Such silence frequently causes youth workers a great deal of discomfort and they feel obliged to fill the vacuum with their own jabberings. At times when children are in the midst of strong emotions, they are unable to listen to anyone or to accept advice, consolation, or constructive criticism. They want only for someone to understand what is going on inside them at that particular moment (Ginott, 1965).

Regardless of whether we can create appropriate words to match the moods of the moment, we always have available our own selves to communicate our concern. Keith Leenhouts, who established the Volunteers in Probation movement in the United States, makes this point with a simple, but telling, story: "A small girl returned late after spending the afternoon with a friend. She told her parents that the reason she was late was that 'I stopped to help Sally. She fell and broke her doll.' 'Oh, did you fix her doll?' asked her father. 'No,' she responded, 'I don't know how to fix dolls. I only helped her cry.'"

As much as the adult desires to be accepting and empathic, there are always times when the behavior of youth must be confronted. Some believe it is impossible to criticize the behavior of a youth without abandoning an understanding, accepting posture. Thomas Gordon in *Parent Effectiveness Training* maintains that inevitably, in confronting the behavior, one attacks the child (Gordon, 1970). Although such a danger exists, if this were always the case, then those working with troubled youth would be in a most hopeless quandry. Successful youth workers have mastered specific techniques to challenge behavior without rejecting the young person, for example, by combining criticism with simultaneous supportive praise (Fixen et al., 1978; Vorrath & Brendtro, 1974). If one has built a positive core of interactions, specific behavior can be challenged without jeopardizing the relationship.

The Hindu poet Sir Rabindranath Tagore is best known as recipient of the 1913 Nobel Prize in Literature. He was also intensely interested in problems of children because of work with his school for such youth in Bolpur, India. In his poem "The Judge" Tagore captures the empathic spirit that must exist if the adult is to confront and correct a child's behavior effectively:

Say of him what you please but I know my child's failings.
I do not love him because he is good, but because he is
                    my little child.
How should you know how dear he can be when you try to
                    weigh his merits against his faults?
When I must punish him he becomes all the more a part of my being.
When I cause his tears to come my heart weeps with him.
I alone have a right to blame and punish, for
                    he only may chastize who loves (1916, p. 22).

Trust

Unlike other children, many troubled youngsters have not learned
to associate adults with pleasant experiences; adults have not met their
needs in predictable ways, nor could they be counted on in times of
trouble. These children can be described in Erickson's (1963) terms as
embodying "basic mistrust." They often approach adults with suspi-
cion and uncertainty, and they anticipate rejection or punishment.

> Why does the child continue to misperceive the benign adult as if he were
> dangerous and not to be trusted? Since his perceptions are based on a
> lifetime of experience, he is unable to ignore suddenly all that he has
> previously learned just because the new adult acts somewhat differently
> from others he has known. This trait of distrust has served him well on
> numerous occasions when faced with a threatening or unpredictable
> adult; it is understandable why he will now tend to act toward the new
> adult in the same manner. From his point of view, it is likely that he is
> being deceived, and that beneath the friendly "front" of the adult is a
> person who, like others he has known, is not to be trusted (Trieschman,
> Whittaker, & Brendtro, 1969, p. 66).

Those who would gain the trust of troubled youth must be committed to eliminating distrust in a patient yet persistent manner. Intrusive
attempts to get the youngster to "open up" will most likely result in
more guarded behavior. Trust is a two-way arrangement. If the adult
can find appropriate ways in which to communicate that he or she
trusts the child, then a significant step in establishing reciprocal trust
will have been taken.

Aichorn (1935) tells the story of a mother who brought her son to
him and, in the boy's presence, went on at great lengths about how
totally dishonest, deceitful, and unreliable the youngster was. After
Aichorn had had enough of this, he interrupted her and challenged her
perception of the boy by handing the youth money and asking him to
run to the corner store to make a purchase. As Aichorn predicted, the
youth returned promptly with the item and the appropriate change,
much to the embarrassment of his mother. This is not to say that we
should leave money lying around just to prove that troubled youth can

be trusted; instead, trust can be programmed in small doses in which youth are given limited responsibilities appropriate to their maturity and which are designed to convey to them our trust while avoiding the likelihood that the trust will be violated.

Theta Burke was a therapist at Michigan's Hawthorn Center. Her work brought her into daily contact with some very troubled children. She is an individual who combined a rich understanding of the behavioral sciences with the deep, humanistic insights of a poet. Her insights are all the richer because of a radiant life, which is a testimony that severe physical disability need not handicap one's service to others. The following verses were taken from one of her several books of poetry, *I've Heard Your Feelings* (Ann Arbor: Delafield Press, 1976).

— Sometimes I say I hate you
   because I'm afraid
         you don't love me.

— The rejection I imagine from you
   is but a reflection
   of the unhappiness and uncertainty
   I feel within.

— I open to you
   only those doors to me
   which I can trust your entering
   with acceptance
   But at times that trust
         may be so tenuous
   as to allow only the unlatching
   and there needs to be a gentle push
   as you knock.

— Sometimes the reaching for *something*
   feels safer and more predictable
   than allowing oneself
   to risk the reaching for *someone*
   but the risking
         is the key
   to the far greater treasure

— Reach out
   for only by your reaching
   does the other know
   he matters to you.

— I saw you being the way you are
   heard you saying ways you felt
   and I learned to be me.

If the young are to learn to be trusting in their relationships, then adults will need to model honesty and openness in theirs. This profound truth has been simply stated by Carl Rogers:

In my relationships with persons I have found that it does not help, in the long run, to act as though I were something that I am not. It does not help to act calm and pleasant when actually I am angry and critical. It does not help to act as though I know the answers when I do not. It does not help to act as though I were a loving person if actually, at the moment, I am hostile. It does not help for me to act as though I were full of assurance, if actually I am frightened and unsure. . . . I have not found it to be helpful or effective in my relationships with other people to try to maintain a facade (1961, p. 741).

ENHANCING THE ADULT AS A SOCIAL REINFORCER

In the course of our careers, the authors have interviewed thousands of people seeking to enter professional work with troubled youth. One of the questions that we have asked ourselves frequently in talking with these people is: What is there about this individual that would be attractive to a troubled youth? The answer to that question is not always readily apparent. We have frequently had grave reservations about whether certain people were in the right kind of work. No individual will have the right chemistry to meet the needs of every kind of troubled youth, and there is room for much diversity in the personalities of those who deal with young people. Although it is often presumed that effective workers should display warmth, sensitivity, flexibility, and toughmindedness, this assumption is not documented by research. A wealth of studies on what makes for effective teachers fails to point to a particular personality type as being more effective in working with youth. Shalock (1979) reviewed hundreds of such studies and concluded that about all that can be said is that people who are friendly, cheerful, sympathetic, and morally virtuous are more inclined toward success than those who are cruel, depressed, unsympathetic, or morally depraved. The practitioner did not need the researcher to reach such a conclusion.

Although some workers are naturals — virtual pied pipers with troubled youth — most of us have to make do with the personality that we have. Nevertheless, most workers can develop skills that serve to cultivate their attractiveness and minimize potential aversiveness.

Enhancing Adult Attractiveness

In studying the evaluation of adults by adolescents in a treatment center, Spotts and Spivack (ND) concluded that youth did not admire staff who were anxious or irresponsible. In fact, these qualities were not valued in either peers or adults. Responsibility, poise, dominance, and independence were viewed positively by the youth in both staff and peers. Despite their apparent inability to accept the standards and values of the adult world, such youth seemingly do admire and hope to emulate many of the qualities valued by middle-class culture including responsibility, perseverance, and conscientiousness.

The adult who is effective in using humor can find it to be a powerful tool. Certainly, care must be taken that the humor is of the type that all can enjoy rather than depending on sarcasm or embarrassment of another. Generally, spontaneous humor arising out of mutually shared situations is more desirable than contrived funniness. One can tell a great deal about the relationships that exist between individuals by noting whether in natural situations they interact with humor. Unfortunately, adults who work with disturbed children are sometimes so concerned about losing control — or being the butt of humor — that they do all they can to extinguish laughter.

Perhaps the greatest single factor in enhancing the attractiveness of adults to youth is to show respect to young people. This is illustrated in an account by New York's first teacher-educator, David Page:

> Two teachers were once walking together in the streets of a large town in New England. Several lads whom they met on the sidewalks raised their caps as they exchanged the common salutations with one of their teachers. "What boys are these that pay you such attention as they pass?" inquired the other. "They are my scholars," answered his friend. "Your scholars! Why, how do you teach them to be so very polite? Mine are pretty sure never to look at me; and generally they take care to be on the other side of the street." "I am unable to tell," said his friend; "I never say anything about it. I usually bow to them and they are as ready to bow to me." The whole secret consisted in this teacher's meeting his pupils in the spirit of kindness (1885, p.66).

Finally, young people have more positive attitudes about staff who have positive expectations about them. The sociologist Robert Merton (1957) coined the term "self-fulfilling prophecy," noting that people generally act in a manner consistent with what they believe others expect of them. Charles Cooley (1918) had noted the same phenomenon much earlier and he called it "the vicious circle." Research shows what the practitioner always knew — that Pygmalion is alive and well in work with young people. Adults who convey a sense of futility to youth always seem to find their prophecy fulfilled, whereas those with great expectations likewise discover great potential in youth.

> A parent beats a child and finding him still recalcitrant, thinks he needs more beating; a teacher whose suspicious methods and appeals to fear have alienated his scholars is all for more suspicion and intimidation; an

employer, who having made no effort to gain the confidence of his men, finds that they are disloyal, is convinced that nothing but repression can solve the labor question. . . . We shall never get out of these vicious circles until we take our stand on the higher possibilities of human nature (Cooley, 1918, p. 135).

Or, as Floyd Starr often said, "If you really believe that these young people can be good, you will find that their badness will melt away like muddy snow in the sunshine."

There are many possible reasons why youth may be more responsive to adults who treat them in a positive manner. Perhaps the simplest explanation is that offered by Juul (1981), who notes the powerful motivating force of a sense of gratitude. He suggests that the highest form of influence that workers with disturbed youth have is when young people try to reciprocate to those to whom they feel grateful.

Minimizing Aversiveness

Most handicapped children (for example, blind or crippled young-sters) evoke sympathetic feelings that motivate attempts to help meet their needs. This is not so with the antagonistic, rebellious, behavior-ally handicapped youth. Instead, it is typical for teachers or counselors to be oriented toward controlling rather than giving. According to the British educator Laslett (1978), those who are most successful with maladjusted children are able to keep the idea of service and profes-sional commitment to children central in their approach. They are characterized by a sympathetic response to children's needs and a certain degree of selflessness, which has a great impact on the youth as well as on other professional colleagues who work with these young people.

Dreikurs (1964) has shown how easy it is to become involved in power struggles with difficult young people. Frequently these youth create such difficulties for adults that they evoke hostile, aggressive feelings and behavior. Such counter-aggression is always counter-pro-ductive because it validates the child's existing perception of the adult as a negative person. Aichorn's advice on his initial encounters with a conflict-prone youngster is an example of a therapeutic way of avoiding such contests:

If the child is in open conflict and expecting an attack, he is disappointed. I do not ask him what he has done, I do not press him to tell me what has happened and in contrast to the police or the juvenile court, I do not try to pry out of him information which he is unwilling to give. In many cases where I feel the child wants to be questioned so that he can come into opposition with me, I say that he may hold back whatever information he wishes; that I understand that one does not want to tell everything to a person who has met me for the first time. When I add that I would do likewise he is usually willing to fall into a conversation with me about something remote from his difficulties but in line with his interests. To describe my attitude from the moment when I let the boy feel some activity in me, I would say that I become progressively passive the more he expects an attack from me. This astonishes him, he feels uncertain, he does not know where he stands. He feels, rather than understands, that I am not an authority with whom he must fight but an understanding ally (1935, pp. 127–129).

The concept of *lex talonus*, eye for an eye and tooth for a tooth, is deeply rooted in both the human constitution and culture, but it must come under effective control in work with troubled youth. The junior author had the opportunity to be in attendance when Martin Luther King accepted the Nobel Peace Prize in 1964. King's statement on that occasion could well afford to be worn on wristbands by all who work with difficult youth: "We must evolve for all human conflict a method which rejects revenge, aggression and retaliation. The foundation of such a method is love."

Teachers and therapists are not uniformly positive about all youngsters over whom they have responsibility. Research suggests many ways in which teachers behave less favorably toward students whom they perceive as having low potential. These differences in behavior are summarized by McMillan (1980) and include less proximity with the child, less attention through smiling and eye contact, less verbal communication, more criticism and less praise, providing less feedback, and demanding less work and effort. Adolescents are very sensitive to indications that adults are insincere and respond angrily to situations in which adults express negative views about adolescents but fail to share them directly with the youth. Jones (1980) tells of an example in consultation in a school setting where the tone between staff and students was very negative. What emerged was that the teachers' lounge was located next to the photography laboratory and students would regularly overhear staff during their coffee breaks spewing forth negatively about the students. When these tales were carried through the youth culture, they served to poison the interpersonal climate.

Presumably, therapists who can concentrate specifically on their individual relationships with clients would be immune from such negativism. Nevertheless, as Strupp (1960) has shown, even highly trained therapists frequently show a surprising lack of positiveness toward those they treat. As with teachers who tend to reject the less promising students, therapists tend to reject patients with a poor prognosis or those whose troubled behavior is negatively valued by the therapist.

Generally, new workers in the human service professions are highly motivated and enthusiastic. But it is easy for old-timers to lose this positive outlook. Sometimes it is academic baggage of professionalism itself that draws adults away from relationships with young people. For example, the need for excessive documentation of educational or therapeutic activities sometimes makes de facto clerks out of those who would better spend their time working with youth. It is all too easy to become so swept up in a paper world of reports that one becomes involved in the care and feeding of documents instead of children.

Freudenberger (1975) outlines the problems of burn-out common among staff in treatment settings. Prolonged exposure to stressful crisis situations can take a cumulative toll and exhaust a person's ability to adapt positively. He notes that symptoms such as cynicism, negativism, and inflexibility are common. The worker may also seek to distance himself from emotional involvement, as is seen when workers discuss clients in terms that are intellectualized or replete with jargon.

Even before the currently popular label "burn-out" was applied to staff in human services, the importance of managing stress was well recognized. Torrance (1965) used the concept of fatigue, a term that is not fraught with the dangerous self-fulfilling prophecies implicit in the concept of burn-out. In contradiction to the optimism that is necessary in working with troubled youth, the concept of burn-out can be self-defeating, creating an impression that it is just a matter of time. Also, among some people, it can be self-congratulatory in the tradition of martyrs of the ages. Finally, it is conceptually misleading. It implies that too many demands are made on a person. Certainly it bolsters the notion common among laymen that work with this kind of youth must be debilitating: "I do not know how you can stand it."

In reality much burn-out is a problem of the system not properly organized or workers not matched to the particular challenges of the job (Gallery & Eisenbach, 1981). For example, it is common to talk about burn-out among child care staff in institutions, yet we frequently encounter situations in which staff are expected to work long hours for weeks on end with minimal opportunities for psychological or physical renewal. Summarizing the research of fatigue, Torrance says,

> Putting the signs of fatigue into plain language, classroom teachers and other school personnel should be sensitized to the following as signs of fatigue:
>   1. Diminished initiative, keenness and enthusiasm—a "so-what" or "let-it-drift" attitude
>   2. Tendency to shun others and sit alone

3. Quarrelsomeness
4. Tendency to criticize others
5. Restlessness
6. Increased use of props such as tobacco and alcohol
7. Drowsiness
8. Mechanical quality of movement
9. Loss of weight
10. Loss of confidence
11. Recklessness and boldness calculated to restore confidence
12. Carelessness about safety, even about death (1965, pp. 58–59).

Whatever it may be called, it should be obvious that staff with the foregoing behaviors are likely to be most ineffective in dealing with troubled youth.

The Problem of Oppression

Writing in *The Pedagogy of the Oppressed*, the Brazilian activist Paulo Freire (1970) notes that the most destructive and coercive relationships are often sweetened by a false generosity, a quality of paternalism that justifies one's actions as being for the good of the oppressed. Freire's message should cause us to keep vigilance lest what we presume to be our concern for others mutate into little more than coercion. What is there about the human condition that so readily causes the helper to be transformed into the oppressor? Because the weak are usually compelled to identify with the powerful, Freidenberg has concluded that "all weakness tends to corrupt and impotence corrupts absolutely" (1963, p. 48).

Special treatment programs designed as alternatives for troubled youth often assume elements of coercion and punitiveness (Mesinger, 1982). Even experienced professionals are totally insensitive to the manner in which they patronize, infantilize, or dehumanize the very people they are pledged to serve. They preside over organizations originally created for human service that evolve into institutions of human servitude. Thus, because of the bureaucratization of the schools, interpersonal relationships as a means of problem-solving have been replaced by elaborate systems of rules. In fact, the American Association of School Administrators touts formal codes of conduct in a student handbook as "the most important innovation of American schools in this century for the control and management of student behavior. . . . The effective code carries a clear message to the student: *This* you can do; *this* you cannot do; and if you do what you shouldn't, *this* is the price you pay" (Brodinsky, p. 4).

Legalistic bureaucratic mechanisms may be necessary if one accepts the premise of huge depersonalized schools. However useful such codes are for protecting the organization, they do not meet the needs of difficult youth. In almost all cases, the official response to repeated offenses (fighting, assaults, smoking, alcohol or drug use, theft, or vandalism) is suspension or expulsion.

Those who advocate student codes as "innovations" are mistaken. Such codes were quite common as early as the mid-19th century, even before the advent of the secondary school. Adolescents who were enrolled in academies and "colleges" of the day were subjected to rigid codes of discipline. Then, as now, the goal was to control all possible deviation by punishing or ultimately excluding youth who violate institutional rules. Typical of the era is this account:

> If any scholar shall be guilty of profaneness, or fighting, or quarreling—if he shall break open the door of a fellow student—if he shall go more than two miles from Athens without leave from the president, the professor or tutor—if he shall play at billiards, cards or any unlawful game . . . he shall be punished by fine, admonition, or rustication [banishment to the country] as the nature and circumstance of the case may require (Ross, 1976, p. 72).

As might be expected, students were resourceful in circumventing these rigid, paternalistic rules. The records abound with cases of poultry stealing, drinking, frolics, profane cursing, live snakes in tutor's chambers, cows in the chapel, and routs and noises for sundry nights in the college yard. When intolerant masters sought to enforce the codes that existed, the institution was in a state of constant tension; flexible and compassionate masters were able to set a better tone (Ross, 1976).

There is an almost inevitable tendency for youth-serving organizations to encumber human relationships steadily with a web of institutional regulations. Swept up in the myopic process of teaching rules, staff lose sight of the basic values, depersonalize their interactions, and cease to be significant figures in the lives of youth. A selection from a rule book in a children's institution (circa 1965) demonstrates this problem to the extreme:

> Canned cherries are eaten with the spoon. The pits are made as clean and dry as possible and then dropped into the spoon from which you are eating and placed at the edge of a plate. It is horrid, however, to see someone spit pits or skins into the spoon or onto the plate unless they are really dry and the lips are compressed. Another good way is to remove a pit from your mouth with the thumb and finger, having the thumb underneath, and very quietly and unobtrusively remove the pit from your mouth.

In addition to the fact that such rule-making probably impedes rather than facilitates control, the adult loses the opportunity to teach young people responsible behavior and values. Certainly, it is important that youth live in a world of rules and learn to submit to authority but, even more important, they need to learn to live in a world where rules are not always clear, where there will not always be someone watching them, and where they will someday be making the rules.

> An Ohio judge has a huge law library lining a wall of his chambers. On an adjacent wall is a sign which reads "Thou shalt love thy neighbor as thyself—all else is explanation" and an arrow points to the rows of books.

Too often our preoccupation with the explanations obscures the underlying values.

PROVIDING APPROPRIATE MODELS

Writing of his work in the Montreal educateur program, Gauthier (1975) concludes that it is essential that troubled children have a generally favorable orientation toward the program. Yet far too often schools and treatment centers for troubled youth are marked by strong negativism on the part of young people concerning adults and the program they run. It is imperative that these barriers be removed if adults are to become strong, positive role models for youth. This does not mean that relationships must or can be consistently pleasant or friendly or that the therapeutic relationship is one in which no demands are made. Fritz Redl often referred to those who seek to build relationships with troubled youth but place no demands on them as "friends without influence." Attempts to keep the relationship on a constantly pleasant level constitute one of the great sources of ineffectual helping; any relationship that can be destroyed because the adult has to be firm or confront the person with the real situation as it exists is not worth preserving (Keith-Lucas, 1972).

Research on effective educational environments has shown that students experience greatest satisfaction in classrooms where a personal student–teacher relationship exists in combination with expectations for hard work (Moos, 1979). We are able to affect the lives of young people most powerfully when we are able to integrate warm, human relationships with clear demands and task expectations. "The crowning achievement of education is to reach the child's heart to convince him of our fervent love at the very moment when we are pointing out mistakes and are seeking to break a bad habit" (Pestalozzi, 1951, p. 33).

An excellent discussion of the authority-versus-relationship controversy is provided by Dahms (1978). He points out that although there is general agreement that no treatment is possible unless these youths can be made responsive to staff authority, there is very little understanding about how to teach staff to exercise their authority skillfully. He attacks the notion common in helping professions that authority and relationship are two different matters. In spite of the fact that social work literature long ago conceptualized treatment processes as incorporating both relationship and authority (Prey, 1949), the myth continues that those who would be therapeutic cannot exercise authority.

> In fact that division between custodial and treatment, between authority and relationship may have been more responsible than any other thing for the continuing failure of residential treatment. Authority and relationship have to be viewed as part and parcel of the same fabric. To do otherwise is to deprive authority of a foundation. Authority without a relationship foundation is authority that is arbitrary and that has to be propped up by intimidation, fear, threats, and hostility (Dahms, 1978, p. 337).

Without a sound base in a relationship, no amount of force or strength will be sufficient. Tyranny will hold together only for a short time, inevitably evoking resistance and defiance and undermining quality treatment. Dahms argues that the effectiveness of authority is dependent on the perceptions of the group. Staff must screen or filter their actions, being aware of the impression they are having on the troubled young people in their care. Adults must take unusual precautions to see that they enhance the perception of themselves as caring, honest, fair, dependable, and reasonable. They must learn to show anger, affection, warmth, and firmness in ways that leave youth with no doubt about the quality of the relationship. More so than with ordinary youth, staff dealing with the delinquent and disturbed must planfully avoid actions that allow youth to infer that they are uncaring, dishonest, or unreasonable. Dahms (1978) puts forth a program of seven specific points to help workers to be perceived in a positive manner by troubled youth:

1. Building the perception of honesty. It is important that a worker never directly or indirectly lie to a youngster. It takes only a single instance of dishonesty to undercut the tenuous foundations of trust. There are matters that adults cannot share with young people, and it is better to indicate this directly than to lie.

2. Building the perception of fairness. It is not necessary that staff

treat all youngsters alike since young people readily understand that individuals are unique. Were this not true we would need only group treatment or education plans and no individualized plans at all. Yet there are many different rules and routines in which staff should expect a uniform response. Furthermore, staff can take precautions not to call undue attention to their individualization efforts with a particular youth.

3. Building the perception of caring. The most important thing you can offer kids is yourself. When a youngster is caught up in the joy of an experience, share his happiness; if he is lonely, reach out to him. Be particularly cautious of what you say when angry or this will poison all the positive exchanges that have gone before. These young people readily feel "you like me on the surface, but deep down underneath you really hate me." Problems should be carried through to a conclusion that will allow staff to again resume a caring posture.

4. Building the perception of rightness. Adults are powerful models about what is right or wrong by the way in which they conduct themselves. Those with careless or cavalier attitudes toward their jobs cannot demand high standards of behavior from young people. Staff should avoid jumping to conclusions lest they paint themselves into corners where they are wrong, thereby becoming weak and vulnerable. When wrong, admit it. Few things anger youth more than adults who insist they are right even when everyone knows it's not so. If youth are expected to admit their shortcomings, then adults also must acknowledge their imperfection.

5. Building the perception of reasonableness. It is important that rules, regulations, and instructions not be imposed in an arbitrary, authoritarian manner. Adults should have enough regard for youth to try to communicate why certain rules or consequences are necessary without, of course, being drawn into the defensive posture of needing to justify every action.

6. Building the perception of dependability. If youth cannot depend on staff to keep their personal commitments, to maintain regular work schedules, and to act conscientiously, they have nothing to build on. Staff should make no commitment to young people that they have no intention of keeping, for troubled youth desperately need the security of relying on the word of staff.

7. Building the perception of mutual support of fellow team members. Youth sometimes seem to have a special sonar that ferrets out conflict between significant adults in their lives. When students know that all staff will support one another, their ability to overpower weaker members of the team is lessened. Staff should never disagree in front of students. Although no one should lie to the youth about the fact that adults may have different points of view, adults must be seen as

determined to resolve conflicts successfully. For any staff member to "go public" and draw youth into a grievance with another member of the staff is to court program disaster. The absence of overt staff conflict will not establish a positive climate unless staff in verbal and nonverbal ways communicate a spirit of positive cooperation.

Overidentification

Any good thing can be carried to an extreme, and so it is with the process of relationship. Two different problems of overidentification are common in work with troubled youth. They are *overinvolvement* and *abdicating* the adult role.

Overinvolvement occurs when an adult forms an exclusive relationship with one youngster to the detriment of that child, the group, or the adult. There are limits to a professional relationship, and the adult who promises to be all things to a youngster is usually exceeding the capacity to deliver. The proper role is not to envelop the youngsters or to become their new parents, but to help them in their own search for self-actualization and independence. Perhaps the greatest risk of over-involvement in a group setting is that it fosters the perception of playing favorites. How can the teacher or youth worker justify encouraging the attachment to one child while keeping others at a distance? Certainly, the individual needs of children preclude treating everybody the same. Yet often the youngster who most needs the special interest of adults is the one whom most adults would rather avoid. Likewise, other children are skilled at seducing a number of adults into "adopting" them (in fantasy or in fact).

Much like the relationship of parents to all of their children, group workers must keep a balance in their attachments to individual youngsters lest they inadvertently foster strong feelings of jealousy and rejection. As the title of McDermott's (1980) book on sibling rivalry suggests, our responsibility is one of *Raising Cain (and Abel Too)*.

Adults must balance the capacity to mold youth with a deep respect for their integrity and with a commitment not to make the youngsters excessively dependent on them. Writing in 1840 in *Orphic Sayings from the Diad: The Teacher*, Amos Bronson Alcott notes, "The true teacher defends his pupils against his own personal influence, and inspires self-trust. He guides their eyes from himself to the spirit that quickens him. He will have no disciple." It is important, particularly with adolescents, that young people be given some breathing room in their adult relationships. As Perlman (1979) suggests, the push toward union with another must be balanced with a pull-back to ensure self-ownership, and this process will continue throughout our lifetime. Or, in the words of the poet Gibran:

You may give them your love but not your thoughts,
For they have their own thoughts.
You may house their bodies but not their souls,
For their souls dwell in the house of tomorrow which
     you cannot visit, not even in your dreams.
You can strive to be like them, but seek not to make
     them like you (1923, p. 17).

Abdicating the adult role in order to build relationships with youth is a second type of problem that occurs with overidentification. This is most often seen in novice workers who are not comfortable with the authority role and feel that their influence would be greater if they approached youth as a peer. As experienced workers know, the result is quite predictable. Such an adult cuts himself off from his or her peers and soon also comes to be rejected by the youth themselves, who have little respect for an adult whose personal identity is like a chameleon. The disastrous consequences of such overidentification are legend, as seen in this classic story shared by the pioneering British-American social worker, Alan Keith-Lucas:

The most difficult consultation I ever had was heralded by a phone call from the chairman of the board of a children's home. He indicated "while we were dedicating a new building, one of the house parents and two of the boys burned it down — and we think there is something wrong." Apparently a baseball game had been cancelled to make way for the dedication, which upset the boys and their house parent. Needless to say, this was not the core problem.

The Normalized Model

During the decade of the 1960's, there was a strong push to use indigenous workers in human service roles. The idea emerged that only delinquents could help other delinquents, only drug addicts could work with addicts, and there was no role for the well-adjusted (usually given the pejorative "middle-class") professional. As Perlman (1979) suggests, people with problems can make real contributions, but there is no evidence that these helpers are more effective or humane than those who entered the profession as a vocation. She states:

there are "naturals" among people with no training at all and also among highly trained professionals. There are those persons trained and untrained, whose characteristic warmth and genuineness of concern for others, whose interest in the individuality of each person, enable them to spark and develop good relationships spontaneously. And vice versa; there are persons whose professional trappings only serve to bolster their personal and relationship uncomfortableness, and those whose apparent likeness is scarcely a substitute for their lacking of compassion or tolerance for the other's difference (1979, p. 146).

Perlman notes that Plato's *Republic* grappled with this issue nearly 2000 years ago with the argument that the most skillfull physicians should not be those of robust health, but rather those who have had all manner of diseases in their own persons, thereby enhancing their knowledge of the art with practical experience. However, Plato was not consistent, for he believed judges should not have experience associating with criminals or they would be contaminated by evil habits.

Wolfensberger offers a unique rationale for placing well-adjusted, nondeviant individuals in most roles for the education or treatment of troubled people. He suggests that to do otherwise is to undercut the goal of normalization.

In order to accomplish the greatest amount of normalization, both by encouraging deviant persons to imitate nondeviant ones, as well as by shaping the stereotypes held by the public of various deviant groups, deviant individuals should have minimal exposure (or juxtaposition) to workers, volunteers, or other individuals who are perceived as deviant themselves by a significant portion of the public (1972, p. 35).

Certainly this has relevance to re-education. Common practice has been to provide a caliber of staff that would be unacceptable in dealing with normal, middle-class youth. Wolfensberger makes this point poignantly in his outrageously sarcastic piece entitled "The Ideal Human Service for a Societally Devalued Group":

You must go out of your way to find and employ stigmatized and devalued staff. Prime candidates are retired school teachers no longer able to cope with the able-bodied hellions in the regular grades, physicians who don't have licenses, preferably unable to communicate in English, and who, if they are not alcoholic, have wives who are. A great and creative modern favorite is to have prisoners teach scouting to handicapped children, by busing the children to the prisons—preferably with a non-ambulatory group of foster grandparents assisting. Isn't it remarkable what prisoners can do with handicapped people, as long as you keep them away from nonhandicapped ones! And as everyone knows, mentally retarded people make excellent workers in nursing homes for other people's decrepit mothers and grandmothers—as long as they don't lay their hands on my old mother or, God forbid, on myself in case I have to go to a general hosptial.

If you are a rehabilitation agency, then it is *de rigueur* to hire your own clients as staff, because if you didn't, no one else might. At the very least, you simply must have a few dedicated counter-culture adults who never cut a hair or beard, never comb, never bathe, or clean their fingernails, who dress awful, and smell worse—but boy, are they good with the kids! (1978, pp. 15–17)

REFLECTIONS ON THE POWER OF LOVE

> What power is real?
> To direct the actions of men and empires
> seems insignificant
> as compared to helping influence *one*
> learn to love.
> —Theta Burke

Perlman (1979) notes that we seem to have the fewest words to explain our deepest experiences; thus concepts such as love all but defy exposition. Outside of religious writings, probably the best-known definition is that attempted by Eric Fromm in *The Art of Loving* (1956). He suggests that love is not an affect but an action; a process of giving, not of feeling. According to his theory of love, four basic elements are common to all forms. They are care, responsibility, respect, and knowledge. *Care* is the active concern for the life and growth of the person who is loved. To be *responsible* means to be able and ready to meet the needs expressed or unexpressed of another human being. Responsibility could easily become domination were it not for the third component of love, respect. *Respect* is the ability to see a person as he or she is and to allow that person to develop without exploitation. Finally, love implies *knowledge*, not a superficial awareness of the person, but a knowledge that penetrates to the core so that one is aware of the other's feelings even if they are not readily apparent.

Speaking of the importance of loving human relationships, Urie Bronfenbrenner (1981) has proclaimed that every child needs at least one special adult who is fervently involved in his or her life, for only then can the child develop to full potential. Keith-Lucas challenges those who would reduce love to social reinforcement, to be employed as another tool for manipulating behavior. He sees love, acceptance, and understanding as *prerequisites* to behavior, not its reward: "One doesn't have to behave in order to be loved, but be loved in order to behave" (1981, p. 12).

Such strong statements about the importance of love are rare in the professional literature and, if present at all, are usually the expressions of successful practitioners rather than those who produce contemporary social science research. Among educational theorists, the concept of love becomes more alien at each successive level of schooling. It is not so unusual to encounter literature on early childhood education that speaks of the importance of love in the educational process, but teachers of adolescents — many of whom are plagued by behavior problems stemming from the lack of love — usually assign the blame to youth for their "lack of respect." However, direct efforts to instill respect in rebellious youth usually backfire. Genuine respect is not the product of instruction but of relationships in which children receive acceptance and are cherished as important people (Bills, 1969).

It has been suggested that schools might be able to develop a curriculum drawing on the humanities and designed to teach love in all its facets (Dyer, 1969). But if love is an action as Fromm suggests, one must be skeptical of the utility of cognitive instruction in love separate from interpersonal experiences. Love is not something that one adds to the curriculum like new math or consumer affairs. Rather, if love has any value at all in the re-educational process, it is because it permeates our actions.

We have chosen to conclude this chapter by relating a personal experience shared by the authors during a visit to Eagle Village, a small residential treatment facility for troubled youth located in a rustic setting near Hersey, Michigan. In the center of the wooded campus stands a small chapel, and on the wall of the chapel are colored portraits of two smiling boys. One picture is of Rick, a blond youth of about twelve, and the other is of Rosy, a black youngster of similar age. When the authors first encountered these paintings, we asked the director, Kermit Hainley, for an explanation. He shared a moving story, which, more than any other we know, represents the spirit of the human relationships permeating successful treatment of troubled youth.

A group of boys had been on a canoe expedition on Lake Superior and pulled to shore to make camp for the evening. Rosy, seeing something floating away on the water, pushed off in a canoe to retrieve it. Suddenly Rosy found himself being swept farther away by the strong, shifting winds and he was unable to maneuver the canoe back to shore. Quickly staff prepared two canoes to set out to rescue him. Twelve-year-old Rick, sensing the trouble his best friend was facing, insisted on joining with one of the staff canoes in the rescue attempt. But soon these canoes were also tossing about helplessly on the treacherous waves that can sweep so suddenly across Lake Superior. One by one the canoes capsized. The boys and the staff clung to their canoes with all their strength until finally each was ripped loose by the waves. Miraculously all of the staff were somehow swept to the shore nearly unconscious, but the two boys were lost in the depths of Lake Superior. A bronze plaque is affixed to the chapel wall between the pictures of these two boys. The engraving on that plaque stands as a testimony to the central value underlying our mission with children and to the value that we place on each young life. The inscription simply reads:

RICK, who loved enough to give his life for another.
ROSY, who was loved enough to have another pay that price.

REFERENCES

Aichorn, A. *Wayward youth.* New York: Viking Press, 1935.

Beard, R. Therapeutic intervention with black female adolescents. In B. A. Cooper, Jr., and F. H. Wood (Eds.), *Issues in education and mental health of Afro-American youth with behavior and emotional disorders.* Minneapolis, MN: University of Minnesota, Department of Psychoeducational Studies, 1979, pp. 67–101.

Biestek, F. *The casework relationship.* Chicago: Loyola University Press, 1957.

Bills, R. Love me to love thee. *Theory into Practice,* 1969, 8(2), 79–85.

Brodinsky, B. *Student Discipline: Problems and Solutions* American Association of School Administrators. Sacramento, CA. 1980.

Bronfenbrenner, U. Children and families: 1984? *Society,* 1981, 18(2), 38–41.

Bullmer, K. *The art of empathy: A manual for improving accuracy of interpersonal perception.* New York: Human Sciences Press, 1975.

Burke, T. *I've heard your feelings.* Ann Arbor, MI: Delafield Press, 1976.

Combs, A., Avila, D., & Purkey, W. *Helping relationships.* Boston: Allyn & Bacon, 1978.

Cooley, C. *Social process.* New York: Charles Scribner and Sons, 1918.

Dahms, W. Authority vs. relationship? *Child Care Quarterly,* 1978, 7(4), 336–344.

Dreikurs, R. *Children: The Challenge.* New York: Hawthorn Books, 1964.

Dyer, P. Love in curriculum. *Theory into Practice,* 1969, 8(2), 104–107.

Erickson, E. *Childhood and society.* New York: Norton, 1963.

Evertson, C., Anderson, C., Anderson, L., & Brophy, J. Relationships between classroom behaviors and student outcomes in junior high mathematics and English classes. *American Educational Research Journal,* 1980, 17(1), 43–60.

Fixen, D., Phillips, E., Baron, R., Coughlin, D., Daly, D., & Daly, P. The Boys' Town revolution. *Human Nature,* November 1978, 54–61.

Freire, P. *Pedagogy of the oppressed.* New York: Seabury Press, 1970.

Freudenberger, H. The staff burn-out syndrome in alternative institutions. *Psychotherapy: Theory, Research and Practice,* 1975, 12(1), 73–83.

Friedenberg, E. Coming of age in America. New York: Random House, 1963. (Reprinted in J. M. Rich [Ed.], *Innovations in education.* Boston: Allyn & Bacon, 1978.)

Fromm, E. *The art of loving.* New York: Harper & Row, 1956.

Gallery, M., & Eisenbach, J. Burnout: Myth or reality? *Counterpoint,* 1981, 2(1), 30.

Gauthier, P. *Modes d'adaptation sociale des anciennes eleves d'un centre de reeducation.* Montreal: Centre de Psycho-Education du Quebec, 1975.

Gibran, K. *The prophet.* New York: Alfred A. Knopf, 1923.

Ginott, H. *Between parent and child: New solutions to old problems.* New York: MacMillan, 1965.

Glasser, W. *Reality therapy.* New York: Harper & Row, 1965.

Gordon, T. *P.E.T.: Parent effectiveness training.* New York: Peter H. Wyden, 1970.

Guindon, J. *Les e'tapes de la re'education des jeunes delinquants et des autres.* Paris: Editions Fleurus, 1970.

Hall, S. *Lectures on school-keeping.* Boston: Richardson, Lord and Holbrook, 1829.

Hewett, F., & Taylor, F. *The emotionally disturbed child in the classroom: The orchestration of success.* Boston: Allyn & Bacon, 1980.

Hollis, F. *Casework: A psycho-social therapy.* New York: Random House, 1965.

Hunter, E. *The blackboard jungle.* New York: Simon and Schuster, 1954.

Jones, V. *Adolescents with behavior problems: Strategies for teaching, counseling and parent involvement.* Boston: Allyn & Bacon, 1980.

Juul, K. Presentation to the staff of The Starr Commonwealth Schools, Albion, MI, April 1, 1981.

Keith-Lucas, A. *Giving and taking help.* Chapel Hill, NC: The University of North Carolina Press, 1972.

Keith-Lucas, A. Report on coordinated child-care consultation. Paper presented to the Presbyterian Synod of North Carolina, Camp Caraway, Asheboro, NC, March 10, 1981.

Laslett, R. *Educating maladjusted children.* Denver: Love Pub. Co., 1978.

McDermott, J. *Raising Cain (and Abel too): The parents' book of sibling rivalry.* New York: Wyden Books (Harper & Row), 1980.

McMillan, J. *The social psychology of school learning.* New York: Academic Press, 1980.

Mesinger, J. F. Alternative education for behavior disordered and delinquent adolescent youth: What world—Maybe? *Behavioral Disorders,* 1982, 7(2), 91–100.

Merton, R. *Social theory and social structure.* New York: The Free Press, 1957.

Milburn, L. Ten Commandments for parents. Department of Child Care, Baptist General Convention of Oklahoma, Oklahoma City, OK.

Moos, R. Educational climates. In H. J. Walberg (Ed.), *Educational environments and effects.* Berkeley, CA: McKutchean, 1979.

Morse, W. Worksheet on life-space interviewing for teachers. In N. Long, W. Morse, and R. Newman (Eds.), *Conflict in the classroom.* Belmont, CA: Wadsworth, 1980.

Okun, B. F. *Effective helping: Interviewing and counseling techniques.* North Scituate, MA: Ducksbury Press, 1976.

Page, D. *Theory and practice of teaching.* New York: A. S. Barnes, 1847 (rev. 1885).

Perlman, H. *Relationships: The heart of helping people.* Chicago: University of Chicago Press, 1979.

Pestalozzi, J. H. *The Education of Man.* New York: Philosophical Library, 1951.

Phillips, E., and others. Achievement Place: Behavior shaping works for delinquents. *Psychology Today,* 1973, 7(1), 74–80.

Phillips, E. L., Phillips, E. A., Fixsen, D., & Wolf, M. *The teaching-family handbook: Group living environments administered by professional teaching parents for youth in trouble.* Lawrence, KA: University Printing Service, 1972 (rev. 1974).

Prey, K. The place of social casework in the treatment of delinquency. In K. L. M. Prey, (Ed.), *Social work in a revolutionary age.* Philadelphia: University Press, 1949.

Redl, F., & Wineman, D. *Controls from within: Techniques for the treatment of the aggressive child.* New York: The Free Press, 1952.

Rogers, C. *On becoming a person.* Boston: Houghton Mifflin, 1961.

Ross, M. *The university: The anatomy of academe.* New York: McGraw Hill, 1976.

Savicki, V., & Brown, R. *Working with troubled children.* New York: Human Sciences Press, 1981.

Schwartz, A. Behaviorism and psychodynamics. *Child Welfare,* 1977, 56(6), 368–379.

Schwartz, A., & Goldiamond, I. *Social casework: A behavioral approach.* New York: Columbia University Press, 1975.

Shalock, D. Research on teacher selection. In D. C. Berliner (Ed.), *Review of research in education*. Tucson: University of Arizona: American Educational Research Association, 1979, pp. 364–417.

Smith, M., & Smith, D. *Child management: A program for parents*. Ann Arbor, MI: Ann Arbor Publishers, 1966.

Spotts, J., & Spivack, G. Some possible determinants of adolescent admiration for adults in a residential treatment center. Paper published by the Devereaux Schools, Devon Schools, Devon, PA, undated.

Strupp, H. *Psychotherapists in action*. New York: Grune & Stratton, 1960.

Tagore, R. *The crescent moon*. New York: MacMillan, 1916.

Tagore, R. *Gitanjali*. London: MacMillan, 1959.

Thomas, B. The educateur in America. *Child Care Quarterly*, 1975, *4*(2), 108–111.

Thomas, L. Medicine without science. *The Atlantic*, 1981, *42* (April), 40–42.

Torrance, E. *Constructive behavior: Stress, personality, and mental health*. Belmont, CA: Wadsworth, 1965.

Towle, C. Factors in treatment. In *Proceedings of the National Conference of Social Work*. Chicago: University of Chicago Press, 1936, pp. 179–191.

Trieschman, A., Whittaker, J., & Brendtro, L. *The other 23 hours*. Chicago: Aldine, 1969.

Vorrath, H., & Brendtro, L. *Positive peer culture*. Chicago: Aldine, 1974.

Whelan, R. The emotionally disturbed. In E. L. Meyen (Ed.), *Exceptional children and youth*. Denver: Love Pub. Co., 1982.

Wolfensberger, W. (Ed.). *The principle of normalization in human services*. Toronto: National Institute on Mental Retardation, 1972.

Wolfensberger, W. The ideal human service for a societally devalued group. *Rehabilitation Literature*, 1978, *39*(1), 15–17.

The Group Culture: Responsible Youth Participation

LARRY K. BRENDTRO AND ARLIN E. NESS

> Ours is a culture where youth are
> excluded from responsible participation
> only to be blamed for their irresponsibility
> and belligerence.
> — Ruth Benedict (1938)

Peer group influence becomes important in the life of young people as soon as they enter school. In a typical developmental progression, the young person becomes steadily more responsive to age mates and correspondingly less responsive to adults as he or she moves through childhood and enters adolescence. Although peer group processes are influential at every age level, they are absolutely crucial during the junior and senior high school years.

We know that the transition from childhood to adulthood has always been difficult. Yet most other societies have created specific roles for young people and have developed "rites of passage" to help the young person bridge the gap from childhood to adolescence. In earlier days in a simple society, one needed only a simple ritual: the adolescent boy might be given a spear and sent from the tribe to live for 30 days in the wilderness; his return was cause for celebration as a boy had become a man. And, of course, girls were ordinarily drafted into the role of wife and mother at a tender—but biologically ready—age. In rural America it was easy for a young person to drop out from grammar school if this experience no longer met his or her needs and a ready role was available in farm labor. But, with urbanization and industrialization, adolescents could no longer be assimilated into the work force and thus they were kept from participating in adult roles.

THE YOUTH SUBCULTURE

Resigned from childhood but not allowed to enlist in adult society, young people are forced into their own youth subculture. This world apart is replete with its own norms, values, language, heroes, and uniforms. The adolescent peer group is an example of what sociologists call a reference group. As Sherif and Sherif state, "Those groups in which he wants to be counted as an individual which include the individual whose opinions make a difference for him, whose standards and goals are his, are his reference group" (1964, p. 180). Although this culture of the young can offer companionship, it seldom promotes a lasting sense of self-worth and often fosters values that seem destructive to concerned adults.

Parsons (1963) has pointed up the classic inconsistency of adolescents: at the same time that they compulsively oppose adult expectations and authority, they just as compulsively conform to their group code. The paradoxes and contradictions of adolescence are well described by Lerner:

> It is a time of rapid strides — physically, sexually, intellectually, emotionally — yet it is also a time of moratorium, of waiting and dawdling. It is filled with intense frustrations. It is a time when pent-up energies clamor for release but also one of passivity, of gawking, of hesitating on the brink of action. It is a time of hunting in single-sex packs, of huddling for warmth in closeness of the male or female bond but it is also a time of cross-sexual exploration, of reaching for intimate relations with outward boldness but inner timidity. It is a time of dawning skepticism when earlier love objects or identification models have lost their hold but it is also a time of hunger for something or someone to believe in and hold onto. It is a time for dreaming of honor, achievement, fame but also one of searching for an anodyne (alcohol, drugs) which will ease the terrible adolescent sadness of life, break the dullness of the school years and offer dreams against a reality that turns out differently from the ideal (1976, p. 114).

Among those working with troubled youth, it is a truism that the power of the peer group confounds our most valiant efforts. Regardless of the treatment strategy employed, those who fail to develop effective ways of dealing with this formidable force risk destruction of the program. Behavior managers have long been frustrated by the difficulty of locating reinforcers that can compete with the potent and pervasive power of the peers. Fritz Redl humorously described the potency of peers in counteracting treatment measures as being akin to counseling with the gang under the couch.

The classic adult response to the power of peer culture is conflict. "We'll show them who is boss," we say as we attempt to reinstill an obedience that works imperfectly even with tiny children. Certainly if all the resources of adults are mobilized, youth can be placed under at least superficial control. But forcing young people to submit to adult authority may only move their conflict underground. With enough hall monitors or guards, any public school can become quiet — even though youth may stash their weapons in the bushes as they enter the school "clean." Yet the use of police-state measures to protect participants in an educational community from one another is antithetical to the very purpose for which these organizations were established (Governor's Task Force on School Violence and Vandalism, 1979).

As a member of congress, Shirley Chisholm has said:

> Money to provide security for children and employees attending schools in districts with high crime rates will pay for the locks, fences, and alarm systems to separate us further from those who desperately need our services. These simplistic approaches alone will not prevent ongoing attacks on persons and vandalism on school property. . . . We must abandon traditional approaches which have failed, and seek new strategies and new formats for the delivery of educational services, if we are to survive the epidemic of violence and vandalism by youth in our communities (1980, p. 2).

Another approach to the youth subculture is to turn it loose. Those advocating the strategy of liberation say: "Well, go ahead. Do your own thing. You're old enough to decide for yourself." Even the most enthusiastic proponent of permissiveness, however, is likely to have some reservations about the ability of the young to meet the challenges in this complex society. Many adults who liberate the young do so out of desperation rather than choice, believing that "there is nothing I can do anyway; what's the use?"

A few adults decide to join the opposition, "going native," so to speak. Disguising themselves as teeny-boppers, grooming their hair and dressing as young people, learning the latest lingo, such adults hope to infiltrate the youth culture. But young people seem to know how to spot card-carrying adults, and they have little respect for such a disguised individual. The 40-year-old school teacher trying to be like the children that he or she teaches gains little more than ridicule.

There is one more strategy available to adults, a very powerful strategy indeed. Unwilling to become locked in conflict with peer groups or to capitulate to their power, adults may instead concentrate on enlisting and utilizing the power of peers. Outstanding youth workers from many eras and nations have developed effective programs for responsible peer involvement in the process of education or treatment. If the answer is this simple, then why is peer participation so seldom employed? Two principal reasons are the professional monopoly on helping activities and the pessimism about the potential of troubled youth to make significant contributions.

THE ADULT MONOPOLY ON HELPING

The increasing sophistication of the human service professions has given rise to a myth that only those with high degrees of training can be effective in teaching or treatment. Although it is commendable that the emerging professions have sought to improve the qualifications of practitioners, this emphasis has sometimes obscured the reality that young people can and usually do have more influence on one another than do adults.

In most programs for troubled youth, adults hog the helping. We even anoint ourselves "the helping professions." Deriving great satisfaction from our service, we rarely take a careful look at what it is like to be at the receiving end. Being forced into the status of a perpetual welfare recipient erodes a person's self-esteem; a person who cannot produce or give feels worthless. Inadvertently, those who strive to be the saviors of children may actually keep them small and helpless.

Among some it has become almost an axiom that a young person must want help in order to be helped. To be truthful, the authors cannot remember a single case among the thousands with whom we have worked in which a troubled young person came to us and asked, "Will you please rehabilitate me?" In fact, if we heard such a plea we would most likely think it was from a con artist or maybe even a youth who was beyond help. If educational and treatment programs are to build self-esteem in troubled youth, they must somehow design ways for young people to take greater charge of their own lives, instead of expecting them to cry out for our help.

In the past many have assumed that it would be sufficient if the adult would communicate to the young person that he or she was accepted. We tried in a myriad of ways to tell these young people that they were not as bad as they thought, that they were worthy as individuals, that they had many fine qualities, and that we accepted them. Instead of a cure, we found that many of these youth assumed that we were being nice to them because we felt sorry for them and probably we were getting paid to act this way. What we overlooked was that, in spite of how others treat a person, he or she may not feel *worthy* of acceptance. Troubled young people are quite aware that much of their behavior is irresponsible and damaging, that they have disappointed their families, their teachers, their friends, and themselves. They do not believe that they are making worthwhile contributions to life, and no amount of "acceptance" by the professional helper will, in and of itself, rectify this situation.

Preoccupation with the negative, the disturbance, with the weakness of troubled young people blinds one to the reality that many are immensely adaptable, resilient, and resourceful. They also happen to know more about what it feels like to be troubled than most adults in the helping professions. Those who have experienced and surmounted a problem have a special expertise in that problem. It is well known that alcoholics respond better to people who have been there. It is no secret that delinquents listen to other delinquents more carefully than to adults. When a new youth enters a program, it matters little what orientation talk might be given by the adult, for the real orientation will come when the young person goes to his or her peers and says, "Now, what is it really like?"

It is a great mistake to assume that difficult children are inadequate. In many ways they have learned to be stronger than youngsters blessed with a more tranquil life experience. Think of the strength it must take to be able to stand in defiance of parents, principals, police, and probation officers. In fact, the negative bravado of acting-out young-sters is frequently cheered (silently or otherwise) by so-called normal youth who would never think of acting like that but who derive im-mense vicarious gratification by seeing a daring peer insult the system.

If only our schools and youth organizations could figure out how to turn the strength of troubled youth around—but instead the typical response is to kick them out. Excluding a youngster never really solves the problem, for usually some understudy stands ready to move to center stage in the ongoing drama of "we against them" that character-izes much of America's education and youth work. Perhaps the reason that educators are so quick to remove troublemakers from programs is their awareness of the leadership power that such youth have to shape the behavior of their peers. Even the most highly trained helping professional must be humbled by the reality that he or she often wields less influence on a child than do the youngster's peers.

THE TYRANNY OF PEERS

No program of re-education for troubled youth can be effective unless it deals with this awesome power that young people can have over one another, a force that Pilnick, Elias, and Clapp (1966) once termed "the tyranny of adolescents." In *Cottage Six*, Polsky (1962) described the pecking order of power relationships that emerged among a group of delinquents in a residential facility. At the highest levels were leadership cliques composed of toughs and con artists. The middle ranges were occupied by youth who faded into the background and a somewhat lower-status clique of "bush boys" who did the bidding of others. In the lowest position were scapegoats who were fair game for physical or psychological harassment by any of the higher status groups. Although Polsky's observations are typical of what can happen in a group of troubled youth, such a structure is in no way inevitable. It should be noted that *Cottage Six* did not have any systematic program designed to influence the group process or group structure directly.

When no professional attention is given to the group process, it is probably inevitable that a group of aggressive young people will evolve group processes built on raw power relationships. The most severe examples of this are seen in captive populations of troubled youth residing in punitive or custodial group settings such as in many large correctional facilities. Large urban schools also produce patterns of ranking and territorialism as various cliques and factions divide up the school corridors, bathrooms, and assembly areas into turfs that are carefully avoided by out-group students (and frequently by principals and teachers as well).

Wynne provides disquieting examples of the conflict between peer loyalty and adult authority at both the elementary and high school level:

> Generally speaking, students do not report to teachers about significant violations of the rules by other students. I talked to ten students from different grades. The main thrust I got was that if a student was doing something that did damage to the school, nine times out of ten he wouldn't be reported to a teacher by any student (1980, p. 53).

> Five of the students told me of one student whom they believe keeps a gun in his locker in school. None of the five would consider informing the faculty about this weapon. The five also mentioned several other students who carry knives with blades over 4-inches long (1980, p. 53).

Perhaps no problem among youth has caused greater concern in the United States than use of illicit drugs. Richards (1979) notes that drug abuse has steadily reached younger groups of children, to the point where now drugs are available in elementary school. It has also extended from urban areas to small towns and has crossed social-class lines. Furthermore, girls are now as involved as boys in the use of a wide range of drugs. Johnson (1980) summarizes a large body of research that supports the central role of peer group influence in the problem of illicit drug use. Such young people generally have unsatisfying family relationships, feel alienated from many of their peers, and have a marked lack of self-control and self-esteem. They gravitate into peer subcultures that support such activity and actually indoctrinate them into the drug experience. Because of the difficulty in relying on the family for constructive socialization of such youth, Johnson concludes that peer group relationships, particularly through the schools, are the best avenue for facilitating positive social development.

Although teachers once filled a myriad of extracurricular roles and felt fully responsible for the well-being of their students, this stance no longer characterizes the typical teacher. Greater specialization and the addition of personnel have caused teachers to retreat into narrow academic responsibilities in their classrooms while the halls and playgrounds have become the responsibility of someone else or of no one else. Unfortunately, few seem to realize the pivotal role of transitions and unstructured time in shaping the student learning climate.

Many schools are organized (or disorganized) in such a manner that no staff members feel accountable for the behavior of young people who are not being directly supervised by them at the moment. Wynne offers this example:

> Both the administrators and the students felt that drugs are a problem and that there were at least four or five drug dealers on campus. One day as I was leaving the school, a group of boys were standing around in a circle outside the door and rolling a joint. They thought nothing of the fact that I was a stranger walking in their direction. When I mentioned this incident to other students, they said the reason why the students continued on with what they were doing was that all the students know who the "narcs" are (that is, plainclothes policemen). One student, Miss C, told me that in the spring the school lawn is covered with kids passing around joints and pipes and that no one stops them. She said she felt it was not really dealt with because there are just too many students out there to "single out" just a few (1980, p. 21).

Wynne notes that this lackadaisical attitude about school discipline is not new in its perspective on the violator, but rather in its lack of concern for the victim.

> Student drug dealers are selling drugs to other students. Student drug users are placing temptation before their peers and other students. Sexual attractions casually fostered in (and by) schools lead to illegitimate children being born to unprepared mothers. Teachers who become reluctant to enforce discipline (because they are not backed up) are then less able to help and protect law-abiding students. The fact is that for any significant violator—for example, a 14-year-old high school student whose locker can't be searched for a reputed gun without applying cumbersome safeguards—there are innumerable potential victims—students and faculty—who will experience fear, uncertainty, and temptation. Under such

circumstances it is not surprising that increasing proportions of students find disorder attractive. They may receive more "understanding" from the enforcement system as rule-breakers than they will as potential rule-abiders (1980, p. 153).

Even though young people are strongly influenced by their peers, we must not forget that they also derive their expectations about behavior from the adults in their environment. Adults who fail to intervene when everything is falling down around them communicate a clear message to young people. Likewise, as Rist (1973) notes, young people are heavily influenced in their treatment of peers by the way adults respond to these individuals. He found that the dominant group emulates the adult leader in ridiculing, belittling, and ostracizing certain young people, particularly those from disadvantaged backgrounds. "Thus the middle class students were learning to control the poor and the poor students were learning to shuffle" (1973, p. 245).

EFFECTIVE AND DYSFUNCTIONAL GROUPS

Although there is a wealth of research on the social-psychological process of groups, much of it is not available in a form useful to the practitioner. Loughmiller, reflecting on the lack of teacher skills in using the group process effectively within the educational setting, notes: "I believe one of the most neglected areas of teacher training is in the use of the class as a group. The students can do more to set reasonable limits on classroom behavior and to establish levels of performance in all areas than we can achieve in any other way I know" (1979, p. 72). Herstein (1977) points out that treatment programs for troubled youth have been dominated by the one-to-one model and thereby have minimized the group. The literature tends to feature the negative group phenomenon such as group contagion and ignores or depreciates the role of group process in treatment. Herstein concludes that many programs that provide a great deal of individualization to youth do so at the expense of a logical group culture and thereby contribute greatly to confusion and anxiety and offer a lure for narcissistic adventure by behavior-disordered adolescents.

Successful re-education requires attention to key factors associated with the development of effective groups. However, one can infer whether a group is effective only if one has some idea about the type of group he or she is seeking to develop. Combs, Avila, and Purkey (1978) have identified four major categories of groups. They are *conversational groups, exploratory groups, problem-solving groups,* and *instruc-*

tional groups. Some groups by their very nature are designed as open systems, that is, they operate without specific predetermined objectives. In this category we would see conversational groups (such as relaxed social dialogue or "bull" sessions) and exploratory groups that help individuals come to new and better understandings of themselves and their interrelationships. Problem-solving or decision groups focus on a particular question in search of a program of action or a solution. Instructional groups, in which the purpose is to show or tell participants something, are the most programmed of all groups.

As can readily be seen from this discussion, there is no single appropriate group because different tasks and situations call for different kinds of groups. For example, if our purpose is to teach a specific academic skill, one would assume that free discussion or brain-storming would be ineffective in reaching the desired end. On the other hand, if the purpose is to facilitate relaxed dialogue between group members or to explore the perceptions of participants, then a closed, didactic manner would be equally inappropriate. In practice, teachers and group leaders usually use various group processes depending on the needs of the moment.

It is difficult to specify exactly what makes up a successful group because of the wide variation in the definition of the purpose of groups. Nevertheless, there have been numerous attempts to distill the variables most often associated with effective groups as compared with those that are dysfunctional. Johnson and Johnson (1975) have highlighted a number of salient dimensions including the following:

> *Goals.* Effective groups attempt to harmonize individual and group goals. With ineffective groups, goals are imposed or competitively structured.
>
> *Communication.* Effective groups have open communication, and consensus is sought for important decisions. Ineffective groups are marked by one-way communication, and decisions are made by an authority with minimal group involvement.
>
> *Leadership.* This is distributed among group members in effective groups. High-authority members dominate ineffective groups.
>
> *Conflict.* Disagreement is seen as an opportunity to enhance communication in effective groups. Ineffective groups tend to suppress, avoid, or deny controversy.
>
> *Desirable traits of group members.* With effective groups these traits include interpersonal skills, self-actualization, and innovation. Ineffective groups seek people who desire order, stability, and structure.

Perhaps the most severe group problem faced by the practitioner is when a group totally falls apart. Frequently such distintegration is a result of prolonged stress, during which individuals become overwhelmed by tensions and cease adaptive behavior. Instead of binding together in times of adversity, group members become competitive, divided, and isolated. Torrance studied dysfunctional survival training groups where members completely abandoned trail discipline. In such groups, members lost confidence in their ability to proceed, abandoned even the most rudimentary principles of camp management, and lived like pigs. He observed that the opposite of *esprit de corps* is a lack of group esteem: "Lack of group esteem occurs when members feel that the group does not deserve to exist, that they would be better off without the group, and that they are no longer attracted to the group or influenced by it" (1965, p. 167).

According to Torrance, the well-functioning group can be distinguished from the distintegrating group on a number of critical dimensions. Of particular concern in the re-educational process are positive affective relationships within the group. Torrance offers the following checklist to differentiate effective and dysfunctional group processes (1975, pp. 169–175).

— Do members of the group help each other without being asked?
— Do members willingly teach each other when the group is learning new skills?
— When a group member is ill, troubled, or confused, are the others concerned?
— Is the joking in the group good-natured rather than vicious?
— Are the members able to disagree without losing their tempers and becoming emotional?
— Do group members get over their disagreements easily?
— Are all members included in group activities? Do all members share in the peculiar language and jokes of the group?
— Do all members want to remain in the group?
— Do members have pride in the group?

ISSUES IN GROUP MANAGEMENT

The deleterious effects of negative affective relationships in group process have been extensively studied by Scandinavian researchers. The problem of *scapegoating* (which is called "mobbing" in Sweden) has received much attention from schools and mental health authorities. Olweus (1973) studied almost a thousand children at the junior high level and found that 5% were victims of scapegoating and an equal percentage were the perpetrators. Victims were found to be generally physically weak and had personality characteristics that triggered the scapegoating. Some were passive, whereas others were provocative and drew hostility toward themselves. Socioeconomic and academic factors had little or no influence on the selection of victims. Leaders of scapegoating were found to be physically strong, prone to aggression, and attracted to violence. Although their own family relationships were generally poor, they did have some close peers as friends in the class. Scapegoating was found to be related to the accumulation of pressures and tensions inside and outside the school that activated individual and group dynamics in the classroom.

A particularly troublesome aspect of group management has been called *group contagion* by Redl and Wineman (1957). Contagion is the tendency for the behavior of one student to spread to other members of the group very rapidly. Redl and Wineman observed that the group status of the initiator in behavior has a great deal to do with whether the group will pick up on his or her action. For example, if a low-status member engages in crazy or threatening behavior, other group members will probably not follow this model. Strong peer leaders, however, have immense power to mobilize the behavior of their comrades. Although youth workers can readily think of many examples of negative behavioral contagion, Redl and Wineman make the point that contagion can also be positive:

> In a cabin of delinquent thieves who took great pride in their code, using rough language and swearing, one of the youngsters suddenly knelt down when the bugle sounded taps, pulled out his rosary, and started his evening prayers. Amazement temporarily paralyzed the rest of the group. As our religious hero also happens to be one of the most openly delinquent representatives of toughness and the delinquent philosophy of life, he was suddenly joined by three others, who knelt down by their bunks, while the rest simply stared in open-mouthed surprise (1957, p. 205).

The evidence is abundant both from research and from the practice of education, group counseling, and child care that when groups become excessively large it becomes more difficult to develop a positive cohesive climate. Johnson (1980), in summarizing the effect of *group size*, notes that the opportunity for individual participation and reward declines with larger groups. This is also true as the size of the school increases. Furthermore, large groups require more of the members' energies to coordinate and assemble contributions of individual members. In large groups absenteeism, conflict, and group dissatisfaction are more likely and individual members are less likely to be supported and liked. Although some studies of class size have suggested no difference, there appear to be a great many more studies whose findings favor smaller classes.

If the purpose of a group is to engage in problem-solving or meaningful personal discussions (as in counseling and therapy groups), then obviously there is a limit to effective group size. Johnson and Johnson have noted that "groups larger than ten may have problems of 'air time' in that all group members may not have enough time to express themselves" (1975, p. 90). Even in a small group, such as one with 10 members, there is an immense complexity of potential interactions. The Group Child Care Consultant Services (1977) note that a group of 10 contains 1000 possible sets of interpersonal relationships (i.e., every conceivable combination of two- to 10-way relationships).

Complicating the problem of developing a cohesive group ethic in many programs for troubled children is the problem of *high turnover of group members*. There is a professional tendency to move a youngster to a less restrictive alternative as soon as some progress has been made, which deprives groups of potentially stable members. Morrison describes this process succinctly as it applies to residential treatment:

> A group may have had 27 different children living within it in, say, a nine-month period. Aside from the difficulties this causes staff in relating to children, and to teachers who must cope with changing classroom populations, there is the very serious problem of destruction of a group dynamic (1976, p. 1).

Morrison notes that an unstable group is easily captured by the strongest individual or the individual longest in residence who has affixed his own dynamics merely by his familiarity with the "territory." Treatment programs have paid too little attention to the effect on the surviving members of rapid turnover of group participants. Since this instability can destroy the equilibrium of the peer culture, a planful effort must be made to control the rate of turnover. Loughmiller (1979) proposes that an arbitrary standard be established whereby no more than two students leave a treatment group during a given month. Although some might argue that an individual student who is ready to leave a group would thus be made hostage to the group process, one must also consider what obligation that individual might have to contribute to the group process even after he or she has received most of the benefit from the group. The alternative is to saddle the survivors with a deleterious group climate.

Youth workers are constantly called upon to balance the *needs of the individual versus the needs of the group*. Although many have voiced strong opinions as to which should have priority, Redl observes that "it's funny that, with two good things, our first thought should usually be how we can sacrifice one in favor of the other" (1966, p. 262). Some programs sacrifice the individual for the good of the group while others largely ignore the group in order to attend to the individual. Redl concludes that the group leader's responsibility is always to enhance the behavior and growth of both the individual and the group. Ideally we would employ intervention strategies to help either the individual or the group without harming the other. This is not always easy. For example, providing a great deal of individual attention to one child can lead to excessive rivalry among group members. As Redl suggests, it is frequently impossible to reconcile these differences, so one must deal in series with the needs of the group and those of the individual. The wild behavior of one youngster may require immediate authoritative intervention to avert a potential negative impact on the group; subsequently, this problem could be discussed with more understanding on an individual basis.

Kounin (1977) has extensively studied the process of group management as it applies to school settings. His research identifies a number of specific group management skills that include:

1. *With-it-ness and overlapping:* the ability both to communicate to the students that the teacher knows what is going on and to attend to more than one issue simultaneously.
2. *Smoothness and momentum:* the ability to manage movement during recitations and transition periods.
3. *Group alerting and accountability:* the ability to maintain a group focus during recitations rather than becoming immersed with a single child.

The complexity of attending to group process may seem overwhelming to practitioners, who might feel that the problems of dealing with troubled youth as individuals are themselves sufficiently complex. Nevertheless, as Garner (1982) suggests, the question is not whether there will be a strong peer dynamic at work within a particular program. That is given. The real question is whether program staff will manage the group process in such a manner that the group contributes to rather than interferes with the goals of re-education.

INVOLVING CHILDREN AND YOUTH

Interest is re-awakening in using students to influence the behavior or learning of their peers positively. In addition to abundant philosophical reasons for having youth participate in the re-educational process, the economic argument should not be underestimated. Programs for peer involvement may be among the few innovations affordable when school systems are in financial difficulty and citizens carefully monitor expenditures. Adults have regularly been surprised to discover that youth are capable of performing many functions that once were thought the exclusive province of paid adults. Youth participation is a sleeping giant that offers great potential for innovation and increasing productivity without increasing program costs. Below, we shall highlight examples from three promising areas of peer involvement: cooperative learning, peers as tutors, and peers as agents of behavioral change.

Cooperative Learning: A More Effective Way?

Cooperation (working together), competition (working against one another), and individualization (working alone) are all legitimate strategies in the re-educational process. Traditionally America's educational programs have emphasized competitive processes at the expense of cooperation. The fields of special education and treatment have stressed individualization as a response to the widely variant needs of exceptional individuals. Johnson and Johnson (1975) point out that although specific benefits are gained by using competitive and individualistic goal structures, the cooperative approach should be used much more frequently within the classroom. Somehow the emphasis on individualized instruction has been misinterpreted to mean that we should individualize all teaching. We cannot ignore the fact that a youngster in the most individualized curriculum is usually still a part of a group. As Bryan (1980) indicates, to the extent that children really need individualized teaching, we shall fail for the lack of human resources. If remediation can be directed toward the group structure, we are able to help more children.

For all teaching except the most specific instruction in skills, cooperative learning seems to be preferable to either competitive or individualistic learning (Johnson, 1980). Greater emphasis should be placed on reinforcing the action of the collectivity rather than that of the person (Slavin, 1977). Individual rewards can break down friendships and set up dissension and competition. Although many would question Bryan's (1980) assertion that individual reinforcement should only be used in a group setting when all else fails, educators have probably paid too little attention to the importance of group contingencies. Johnson and Johnson proposed a general scheme in setting up group contingencies:

> There are times when a teacher may wish to reward students using extrinsic reinforcements such as tokens or privileges within the school. When extrinsic reinforcements are used they are made contingent upon certain behaviors and level of performances of students. There are three basic alternative group contingencies that may be used to promote cooperative behavior and achievement. The first is the average performance group

contingency; all members of a group are reinforced on the basis of the average performance of all of the group members. Alternatively, the group may be reinforced on the basis of the high performances in the group. Thus, the highest scores of one-quarter of the group may be used as a basis for determining reinforcements. This procedure is referred to as a high performance group contingency. Finally, a group may be reinforced on the basis of the low performances in the group; the lowest scores of one-quarter of the group are used as a basis for determining reinforcements under a low performance group contingency. Research on the use of these three types of group contingencies indicates that the most fruitful is the low performance group contingency. The performance of poor students is greatly raised, both through increased motivation to help their group and through tutoring by the more gifted students. The performance of the more gifted students is not hampered by the use of this group contingency. The overall performance of the group will be highest when the low performance group contingency is used (1975, p. 91).

Although cooperation would certainly be desirable in classroom groups, it is not sufficient just to tell the youngsters to work together. Fortunately, a wide range of materials is now available for use by teachers who wish to develop a cooperative approach to the curriculum. Typically such an approach would use small subgroups of five or six students who work together on structured tasks. Materials designed for this purpose are highly motivating; frequently built on formats such as academic games, tournaments, or projects, they require participation of all group members (Slavin, 1980).

Research on the outcomes of cooperative learning suggests a wide variety of positive effects. Slavin (1981) documents advantages in academic achievement, intergroup relations, mainstreaming, and self-esteem. He reports research suggesting that emotionally disturbed adolescents involved in cooperative learning improved their interactions with other students. Furthermore, cooperative learning shows particular promise in group situations where ethnic and racial tensions permeate the group climate. Since cooperative learning groups are designed with a mixture of students from various backgrounds rather than relying on natural cliques or friendship groups, they have the effect of bringing together in common pursuit young people who previously may not have had much in common. Thus cooperative learning can systematically break down the barriers that ordinarily impede the development of friendships outside of one's racial or ethnic group (Slavin, 1981).

Johnson and Johnson (1979) note positive effects of cooperative learning on the student's self-esteem, in contrast with the effects of competitive or individualistic methods. Cooperation enhances self-esteem among students at elementary, junior, and senior high levels. Competitiveness is generally unrelated to self-esteem, whereas individualistic attitudes can produce feelings of worthlessness and self-rejection. In summary, the research on cooperative learning suggests that cooperative strategies have decided advantages over competitive and individualistic structures when appropriately employed.

Peers as Tutors: Reviving a Tradition

The use of children to teach other children has a rich history going back at least to first-century Rome. The 17th-century educational reformer Comenius spoke out against harsh methods of teaching and advocated using students to tutor one another, noting that "he who teaches others, teaches himself" (Ely & Larson, 1980, p. 11). In 1791, Englishman Andrew Bell, who was superintendent of a boys' orphanage in India, developed a peer tutoring system that subsequently was adapted by Joseph Lancaster for use in a school for London's working class children (Allen, 1976).

Peer tutoring had an important place in the education and socialization of youth in early America. The large families common in the frontier era demanded that heavy responsibility be assigned older children for teaching their younger siblings. Likewise, in one-room country schools it was expected that the older youth would assist the smaller children. But the advent of small families and large schools decreased opportunities for peer teaching and learning. The modernization of education brought strict age-grading, and the use of peer tutoring systems fell into demise. Children came to be disconnected from the rich relationships of cross-age peer contact. The very design of educational institutions served to preserve the child's isolation. The school became "the agency of rigid age segregation, with children marching through their lives in phalanxes one year wide" (Kessen, 1980, pp. 4–5).

Goethe once observed that everything has been thought of before, but the difficulty is to think of it again. This certainly is true of peer tutoring, which is showing signs of a revival. As schools confront the problem of limited resources, peer tutoring will seem much more attractive. Inherently, however, the rationale of peer tutoring has a validity of its own, as it breaks down the artificial barriers that too often separate the process of teaching from the process of learning.

Cross-age and peer tutoring have been particularly useful in resource rooms for the handicapped, as is seen from the following report of a special education teacher:

The most crucial thing that happened to me when I had tutors was that all the children, smart or slow, wanted to come to the resource room. It seemed to lose any connection with students who had problems. The top kids came as tutors and as teacher-helpers, and the low kids came for help. We all worked, made progress academically and socially, and loved every minute of it. We had the school totally confused (J. Walker, cited in Jenkins & Jenkins, 1981, p. 14).

Although many programs for peer tutoring use older students to teach younger students, there is of course no reason that peer tutoring cannot be effective with students of the same age or even, in certain situations, with younger students teaching older peers. Research is emerging that suggests that peer tutoring programs can produce significant learning gains for both the tutor and the learner (Jenkins & Jenkins, 1981). As this field is still rather unexplored, there is wide opportunity for experimentation by those seeking to enhance the learning or behavior of children with special needs.

Peers as Agents of Behavioral Change: A Cross-Cultural Perspective

Contributors with various orientations have enriched our understanding of ways in which young people can positively influence the behavior of their peers in educational, counseling, and group care settings (Glasser, 1969; Rose, 1972; Strain, 1981; Whittaker & Trieschman, 1972). The use of peers for shaping behavior is not a new idea, and such programs cross all philosophical, cultural, and programmatic boundaries. Although there is a rich diversity in these approaches, they all share the goal of gaining the participation of young people in governing the program. In the remainder of this chapter we shall seek to portray this diversity and commonality by looking briefly at three distinct programs, each of which operates in a totally different cultural milieu. These examples are (1) the permissive Summerhill philosophy developed by Neill in England, (2) the highly structured, group-oriented discipline developed by Makarenko and practiced in Russia, and (3) a peer-oriented approach for reclaiming homeless street urchins developed by Father Javier de Nicolo in Bogotá, Colombia. These models are presented to broaden perspectives and stimulate an awareness of the potency of youth participation. Naturally these models should not be copied directly by programs designed for other populations and cultural settings, which must be tailored to their own specific educational or treatment needs. We present a model for peer group participation in re-educational settings for troubled children in Chapter 7.

Neill's Self-Governance

It is probably unfortunate that when one thinks of self-government of youth, the name that comes first to mind is that of A. S. Neill, the apostle of permissiveness. Neill gained wide international recognition for his residential school for troubled youth in England called Summerhill (Neill, 1960). Neill was heavily steeped in psychoanalytic thinking, had a deep faith in the goodness of children, and believed that most of their evil resulted from the imposition of adult authority. With a highly idiosyncratic method that seemed to work well for him (but which frequently would blow up when others tried to reproduce it), Neill created a permissive group climate in which children shared equally with adults in the operation of the school.

In Neill's totally democratic model every member of the staff, as well as each child regardless of age, had the same weight: one vote. The entire school body met each Saturday night in a general school meeting. This mechanism of self-government resolved everything connected with the social or group life including setting the rules and determining consequences for social offenses. We are indebted to Alan Keith-Lucas for sharing some of his early personal experiences with Neill and with Summerhill:

> In Summerhill the *Schulgemein* had all significant decisions. An example of the commitment of young people to such self-government is seen in the example of a cricket match which was scheduled with a visiting school, the headmaster of whom was a clergyman. Summerhill students determined that swearing would be forbidden during the time the visitors were on campus and that a five-shilling fine would be levied for any violator. The only one caught during the entire afternoon was Mrs. Neill.
> Neill himself was marked by an incredible honesty and directness. Once when I wrote him a letter asking whether I should bring two students who were being transferred from my school to his and whose parents lived across England, he responded with a handwritten postcard on which were penned only the words: "Good, bring brats." In contrast to Neill's personal approach, most of his imitators indulged the children. Not Neill. If the *Schulgemein* would determine that they wanted the staff to help them prepare a Roman banquet, Neill followers might indulge such nonsense whereas Neill would counter this simply by telling the young people that they were crazy.
> It is a misconception to assume that Neill did not have any values

underlying his program, for in reality he assigned full responsibility to young people for their behavior. For example, it seemed apparent that two adolescents were becoming excessively romantically involved; Neill approached them and told them that while he understood that what they did with themselves probably was their business, he hoped they "didn't wreck this place by having an illegitimate child," and he placed upon them the considerable responsibility for seeing that this did not happen.

Nevertheless the visitor to Summerhill would more than likely notice the permissiveness rather than the responsibility. I recall my first impression of seeing an eight-year-old come walking down the staircase with a cigarette in his mouth and upon passing the wife of the headmaster told her to get out of the bloody way.

Typically Neill would ignore any visiting dignitaries upon their first visit, leaving them to the mercy of the children. If their interactions with the young people went well and they decided that they would come back another time, then Neill would communicate with them upon their return visit. However, many influential people never made it past the first visit. Some of the greatest psychiatrists in England were thrown out by the kids.

Makarenko's Group Discipline

Equally committed to responsible youth participation but operating within a totalitarian society was Russia's Makarenko. This account of Makarenko's philosophy as it is practiced in the Soviet Union has been provided by Bronfenbrenner (1962).

Makarenko, a young school teacher in the 1920's, was assigned responsibility for establishing a rehabilitation program serving children who were roaming the Soviet Union after the civil wars. Makarenko relied on a group-oriented discipline technique that developed a strong sense of group responsibility and commitment. Although Makarenko felt that parents had an important obligation to give love and joy to their children, this responsibility was seen in the context of its contribution to the Soviet state.

Following Makarenko's principles, Soviet education seeks from the youngest age to build a sense of group identity in students. Thus a teacher first encountering students in a classroom does not direct individual children to sit straight in their chairs, but rather challenges them to see which row can sit the straightest. By systematically arousing a spirit of *competition between subgroups,* youth are taught from the primary grades upward to monitor carefully the behavior of their comrades and to correct those who forget or ignore the teacher's rules. As Bronfenbrenner notes, "teacher soon has helpers" (1962, p. 552).

In all areas of academic achievement and deportment, the emphasis is on which group is best. Great charts cover the walls of schools showing the performance of each row unit in every type of activity. Teachers delegate to young people the responsibility for monitoring rows rather than assuming this as an adult responsibility. When a student is chronically late, this problem is translated into a group responsibility and other students are usually eager to volunteer to stop and pick up the late-comer on the way to school. If a young person fails to act responsibly or help another, this becomes further opportunity for instructing group members in their peer responsibility. By the third grade, students are expected not only to monitor one another but to state their criticisms publicly. This behavior does not come off as "tattling" since control through social criticism is seen as a constructive rather than negative process, and great emphasis is placed on recognizing and appreciating the contributions of the various groups of young people rather than dwelling on the limitations.

In summarizing this process, Bronfenbrenner concludes that:

1. The peer collective (under adult leadership) rivals and early surpasses the family as the principal agent of socialization.
2. Competition between groups is utilized as the principal mechanism for motivating achievement of behavior norms.
3. The behavior of the individual is evaluated primarily in terms of its relevance to the goals and achievement of the collective.
4. Rewards and punishments are frequently given on a group basis; that is to say, the entire group benefits or suffers as a consequence of the conduct of individual members.
5. As soon as possible the task of evaluating the behavior of individuals and of dispensing rewards and sanctions is delegated to members of the collective.
6. The principal methods of social control are public recognition and public criticism, with explicit training and practice being given in these activities. Specifically, each member of the collective is encouraged to observe deviant behavior by his fellows and is given opportunity to report his observations to the group. Reporting on one's peers is esteemed and rewarded as a civic duty.
7. Group criticism becomes the vehicle for training in self-criticism in the presence of one's peers. Such public self-criticism is regarded as a powerful mechanism for maintaining and enhancing commitment to approved standards of behavior, as well as the method of choice for bringing deviants back into line (1962, p. 555).

Most Americans would be uncomfortable with the degree of group-think characterized by Russian education. However, we tend to forget that peer groups in American schools often wield totalitarian control over individual member's behavior. Children and adolescents are well known for their ability to launch intense, even scathing, attacks on members of their peer group who deviate from a particular standard. By their indifference to peer processes, American educators allow peer social criticism to exist outside the realm of the educator's influence, whereas Russians consider it important to mold peer influence in a responsible direction. Another observation that can be gleaned from Bronfenbrenner's work is that great potential for using the peer group process to influence behavior exists at every educational level. It has been a common assumption in this country that peer group influence is a largely adolescent phenomenon, but the Russian experience suggests its potency with much younger children.

Father de Nicolo and the Street Urchins

Perhaps the most creative uses of peer group influence are those emerging from the underdeveloped nations. In such cultures it is taken for granted that paid professional adults will never be sufficiently available to carry out many tasks, so any success must depend on the involvement of indigenous participants.

A stirring example of a peer group program in an underdeveloped nation was provided to the authors by Carlos Canón, an educational psychologist from Bogotá, Colombia, who has dedicated his career to working with the *gamines*, homeless street urchins that plague this capital city. Bogotá has the highest crime rate in the world, largely due to the thousands of these *muchachos de la calle* (boys of the street), who live a dead-end existence that leads from juvenile to adult crime.

By day these *gamines* as young as five or six are found roaming the city in small groups of peers, which are termed *galladas*, literally "flock of roosters." They exist in a climate of almost total freedom, support themselves by theft, and very early come to be exposed to a wide range of social evils including illness, abuse, and drug problems.

The daytime peer group or *gallada* is insufficient protection when night settles upon the city. Each evening the *gamines* regroup into cross-age living cells called *camadas* or "dens of kittens." Each *camada* is headed by an older veteran of the streets called the *jefe* and he provides a type of protection to the younger children in return for sexual and other favors. Sociologists have been able to map out the precise boundaries of each *camada*, and they are well organized with all *jefes* reporting to a city-wide *jefe* of *jefes*.

Broad social problems render police helpless to eliminate the *gamine* subculture which, according to historians, has persisted for over 200 years in Colombia. The *gamines* are at the very bottom of the ladder, outcasts in a very hierarchial society. Yet those working with them are amazed at their camaraderie, their fierce pride, and their sense of independence and group identity. Any attempt to reach such young people obviously must be able to tap this peer culture.

An exciting program to salvage these street children is Bosconia-La Florida, directed by a Catholic priest, Father Javier de Nicolo. The initial point of contact with these young people is to reach out to meet their simple basic needs. A patio off a busy street provides a place for the boys to come during the day for medical attention, to launder their clothes, and for recreation with their *campañeros* in an atmosphere removed from the scrutiny of police. Staff seek to build a relationship within the daytime *gallada* subculture before they make inroads in the evening group.

After several months of contact during the days, boys are invited to join with their *campañeros* in an evening program that runs for 30 nights from suppertime through breakfast. In this residential experience, young people receive food, shelter, and rich involvement in group activities, arts, and recreation. Spirited singing and chants foster a group cohesiveness, as even the most reserved of the youth are swept up into enthusiastic refrains of "MARI-I-JUAN-A — NO! TRA-BA-JAR [work] — SI!" After 30 nights the program ends and the boys are sent out to the streets. They are to return to their old haunts for the purpose of making a decision about what kind of life they wish to live. If after 3 days and nights living in their old ways they decide that they desire a new life, they are welcome to return to permanent residence.

Those boys that return to start a new life make their commitment manifest by a rite of passage (*el rito de ingreso*). In a striking ritual, all of their clothing is thrown onto a pile and burned as they are given a bath and new clothes by their new brothers. The youth then enter into a residential group care experience designed to develop their new identity. Former street youth who are more advanced help to teach the new arrivals both social and academic skills. The elementary school is entirely staffed by older youth. As young people progress, they take on more responsibilities including going out to the streets to recruit their former companions to join in this new life. As the program has proliferated, a number of residences have been established throughout the city, and these are largely operated by former street youth. In his book *Colombia Amarga*, the prominent Latin American journalist Castro Gaycedo (1977) writes of the remarkable talents and resourcefulness of these outcast children, concluding: *"El gamine es un ser superior"* [the *gamine* is a superior being].

The saga of the Colombian street urchin portrays in bold relief the landscape of troubled children everywhere. Here we see in exaggerated form the dynamics of deviant behavior in a deviant ecology, the stigma of labeling, the resilience of the rejected, the power of peers, and the need for Pygmalion optimism in the face of staggering odds. Whatever difficulties we face in developed nations seem insignificant when we comprehend the magnitude of the problems being faced by those in the underdeveloped nations. Yet we have much to learn from these people for they are demonstrating the rich human resources that lie untapped in the very people in need of help.

REFERENCES

Allen, V. The helping relationship and socialization of children: Some perspectives on tutoring. In V. Allen (Ed.), *Children as teachers: Theory and research on tutoring.* New York: Academic Press, 1976.

Benedict, R. Continuities and discontinuities in cultural conditioning. *Psychiatry,* 1938, *1,* 161–167.

Bronfenbrenner, U. Soviet methods of character education: Some implications for research. *American Psychologist,* 1962, *17*(8), 550–564.

Bryan, J. Social experiences of learning disabled children. Paper presented to the 10th Annual Invitational Conference on Leadership in Special Education Programs, Minneapolis Public Schools, Minneapolis, MN, November 24, 1980.

Chisholm, S. Children and violence in American society: The social costs. *Discipline,* 1980, *1*(1), 1–2.

Combs, A., Avila, D., & Purkey, W. *Helping relationships.* Boston: Allyn & Bacon, 1978.

Ely, S., & Larsen, S. *Peer tutoring for individualized instruction.* Boston: Allyn & Bacon, 1980.

Garner, H. Positive peer culture programs in schools. In D. Safer (Ed.), *School programs for disruptive adolescents.* Baltimore: University Park Press, 1982.

Gaycedo, C. *Colombia Amarga.* Bogotá: Carlos Valencia Editores, 1977.

Glasser, W. *Schools without failure.* New York: Harper & Row, 1969.

Governor's Task Force on School Violence and Vandalism: Report and Recommendations. Michigan Office of Criminal Justice, Lansing, MI: November 6, 1979.

Group Child Care Consultant Services. The child care worker: The group. Chapel Hill, NC: University of North Carolina, 1977.

Herstein, N. Reflections on the primacy of the one-to-one model in residential treatment. *Child Welfare,* 1977, *56*(5), 311–320.

Jenkins, J., & Jenkins, L. *Cross age and peer tutoring: Help for children with learning problems.* Reston, VA: Council for Exceptional Children, 1981.

Johnson, D. Group processes: Influence of student–student interaction on school outcomes. In J. McMillan (Ed.), *The social psychology of school learning.* New York: Academic Press, 1980.

Johnson, D., & Johnson, R. *Learning together and alone: Cooperation, competition and individualization.* Englewood Cliffs, NJ: Prentice Hall, 1975.

Johnson, D. & Johnson, R. Cooperation, competition, and individualization. In H. Walberg, (Ed.), *Educational environments and effects.* Berkley, CA: McCutchan Pub. Co., 1979.

Kessen, W. Our disconnected child. In H. E. Fitzgerald (Ed.), *Human development 80/81.* Guilford, CN: Dushkin Pub. Group, Inc., 1980.

Kounin, J. *Discipline and group management in classrooms.* Huntington, NY: Robert Krieger Pub. Co., 1977.

Lerner, M. *Values in education: Notes toward a values philosophy.* Bloomington, IN: Phi Delta Kappa Educational Foundation, 1976.

Loughmiller, C. *Kids in trouble: An adventure in education.* Tyler, TX: Wildwood Books, 1979.

Morrison, I. Child care: The guardian's dilemma. *Residential Group Care*, 1976, *1*(2), 1.

Neill, A. *Summerhill: A radical approach to child rearing.* New York: Hart Pub. Co., 1960.

Olweus, D. *Hackkycklingar och oversittare—Forskning om skolmobbing* [Bullies and whipping boys—Research on mobbing in schools]. Stockholm: Almquist Wiksell, 1973. Cited by Juul, K. and Linton, T. European approaches to the treatment of behavior disordered children. *Behavioral Disorders* August 1978, *3*(4), 232–249.

Parsons, T. Youth in the context of American society. In E. H. Erickson (Ed.), *Youth: Change and challenge.* New York: Basic Books, 1963.

Pilnick, S., Elias, A., & Clapp, N. The Essexfields' concept: A new approach to social treatment of delinquents. *Journal of Applied Behavioral Science*, 1966, *2*(1), 109–125.

Polsky, H. *Cottage Six: The social system of delinquent boys in residential treatment.* New York: Russell Sage Foundation, 1962.

Redl, F. *When we deal with children.* New York: The Free Press, 1966.

Redl, F., & Wineman, D. *The aggressive child.* Glencoe, IL: The Free Press, 1957.

Richards, L. Useful drug use. In R. Depert *et al.* (Eds.), *Handbook of drug abuse.* Washington, DC: United States Government Printing Office, 1979.

Rist, R. *The urban school: A factory for failure.* Cambridge, MA: M.I.T. Press, 1973.

Rose, S. *Treatment children in groups: A behavioral approach.* San Francisco: Jossey-Bass, 1972.

Sherif, M., & Sherif, C. *Reference groups.* New York: Harper & Row, 1964.

Slavin, R. Classroom reward structure: An analytical and practical review. *Review of Educational Research*, 1977, *47*, 633–650.

Slavin, R. *Using student team learning* (rev. ed.). Baltimore: The Johns Hopkins University, Center for Social Organization of Schools, 1980.

Slavin, R. Synthesis of research on cooperative learning. *Educational Leadership*, 1981, *38*(8), 655–659.

Strain, P. A. *The utilization of classroom peers as behavior change agents.* New York: Plenum, 1981.

Torrance, E. P. *Constructive behavior: Stress, personality, and mental health.* Belmont, CA: Wadsworth Pub. Co., 1965.

Whittaker, J. K., & Trieschman, A. E. (Eds.). *Children away from home: A source book of residential treatment.* Chicago: Aldine, 1972.

Wynne, E. A. *Looking at schools: Good, bad, indifferent.* Lexington, MA: Lexington Books, 1980.

The Organizational Ethos: From Tension to Teamwork

4

LARRY K. BRENDTRO AND
MARTIN L. MITCHELL

> Many times a day I realize
> how much my own outer and
> inner life is built upon the
> labors of my fellow man, and
> how earnestly I must exert
> myself in order to return as
> much as I have received.
> —Albert Einstein

The success of any complex organization depends heavily on the way it is structured and managed. It is a mistake to assume that only administrators, and not practicing professionals, should be knowledgeable about principles of organizational design. Unless the teacher or treatment worker is aware of organizational dynamics, he or she may not even recognize the profound impact these factors can have on the process of re-education. Here we shall examine what we believe to be the crucial organizational variables that underlie the creation of effective child-serving programs. We have drawn from our experiences in administering schools and treatment programs and from organizational literature to identify those issues of greatest relevance to the mission of re-education.

In this chapter we shall note how the task of socializing children became embodied in formal organizations. Many of these organizations are no longer achieving their intended mission. We shall examine the symptoms of dysfunction in child-serving organizations and shall compare two competing organizational models: participative and hierarchical/authoritarian. We hope to show how the participative model can provide an organizational technology that is matched to the specialized enterprise of re-educating troubled children. A number of concrete suggestions will be made on how programs can be restructured to establish teamwork as the highest administrative objective. We shall underscore the importance of involving parents in this teamwork process and discuss factors that impede their full participation. In the final analysis, the effective organization is one which can bind together a diverse group of children and adults as they work toward a shared common mission. We believe that the attainment of such an *esprit de corps* is an essential component of re-education.

THE RISE OF THE BUREAUCRACY

Many early pioneers in education and treatment developed powerful programs, not because of effective organizational design but because of the dynamism and charisma of their personalities. Pestalozzi, Korczak, Aichhorn, and other such giants did not just direct their programs; they were the programs. The limitations of this "great man" approach are most obvious when such a leader departs, for often the organization then has great difficulty continuing to thrive. One of the strongest rationales for the creation of bureaucratic systems has been to ensure the survival of the organization in the absence of any particular leaders.

During the nineteenth century, bureaucratic models of organization were created to meet the needs for socializing children that in earlier civilizations had been met by the extended family or the tribe. By the early 1900's the role of formal organizations in the education and socialization of children was well established. Carney (1912) could have been speaking for the entire twentieth century in declaring that education had been broadened until the school found itself taking over many of the duties of the home, church, and other social institutions: "Manifold tasks are put upon the school because, of all social institutions, it is most adaptable and most capable of serving numerous and varied ends. Thus it has come about that any neglected or unprovided condition of society is usually relegated to the schools for correction" (pp. 133–134).

During the same period, Cooley (1918) noted that the school was second only to the family in socializing children because it offered the only other significant primary group relationship. Yet already at that early date, schools and children's institutions were systematically abandoning their primary-group status. New ideas of scientific management that had revolutionized American industry were now having a similar effect on education and social service.

Just as industry found that the craftsman could be efficiently replaced with the assembly line worker, so people-serving organizations were designed around bureaucrats with highly specialized functions. Educational administrators have been enamored for more than a century with the virtues of greater and greater specialization. This glowing endorsement of Taylor's principles of scientific management was written by an early school superintendent, William Payne, in 1875:

> It is an application to the work of instruction of the great law of the division of labor. By this means a teacher's time, talent and attention are concentrated on a prescribed range of duties, which become easy by repetition, and hence are likely to be performed in a thorough manner. . . . The work of teaching thus followed the law which prevails in all well-regulated industries. This general movement is characteristic of a growing civilization (pp. 83–84).

This enthusiasm for mass-production technology reflected the acknowledged purpose of schools of the period to produce conformity among children (Ponder, 1976).

Once established, these bureaucracies serve to perpetuate themselves; the basic structure of America's educational organizations has changed very little since they were first formed around the bureaucratic assumptions of the late nineteenth century (Katz, 1971). The only change that has been consistent over time has been an increase in the size and complexity of organizations. Urban schools grew larger as cities grew. Small rural schools were swept aside in favor of the magic of consolidation. Children's institutions expanded their capacities until many became virtual warehouses for troubled persons. Departments became more numerous and more specialized as schools and institutions adopted the assembly line model. Layers of middle management, coordinators, and specialists proliferated. Formal rules, regulations, and procedures replaced cooperative, informal working relationships.

The trend to bureaucratic educational organizations was not without its vocal critics (Mumford, 1938; Veblen, 1918). Lewis Mumford attacked the production-line school:

> The notion of making education "economical" or "comprehensive" by creating megalopitan school buildings holding from 1500 to 3000 pupils, and then expanding the scale of the neighborhood so that it can bestow a sufficient number of children on these buildings may be dismissed as a typical megalopitan perversion. A neighborhood should be an area within the scope and interest of a child, such that daily life can have unity and significance for him (1938, pp. 472–372).

Mumford argued instead for a series of small units framed to the human scale. These organizations would restore face-to-face cooperative behavior as an alternative to mass regulations and mass decisions imposed by ever-remoter leaders and administrators. Mumford impugned the bureaucracy for its vast mechanical administrative overhead and its inability to provide for the special needs or capacities of individuals. But pleas such as this went largely unheeded in the face of the impregnable bureaucracy, and the machines of progress continued to mow down and plow under the small organization (Dunathan, 1980).

After a century of bureaucratization in child-serving organizations, it would be easy to become discouraged about the future. However, there are indications that this trend is being increasingly questioned, checked, and sometimes reversed. Among the strongest challenges to the bureaucratic model are the press for accountability and the shifting mission of schools and children's institutions.

> Community resources are absorbing larger and larger numbers of younger, less disturbed, or less retarded children who can be cared for while living at home or in foster homes. In turn, this means that the more severely retarded children are squeezed to the top and referred to institutions. Since these children have more complex treatment needs, institutions are being asked to provide more specialized care and treatment (Gula, 1958, p. 4).

As long as institutions could serve only children with modest problems or provide only routine physical custody to the seriously handicapped, then the bureaucracy could continue to exist. As long as schools could shuck off children whose handicaps or behavior gummed up the machinery, then the system was not seriously threatened. Society now expects more of its schools and treatment institutions. Schools no longer have the power to exclude troublesome children arbitrarily, and residential institutions no longer have the luxury of selecting "workable" clients. Kicking out troublemakers or warehousing them in segregated institutions is no longer acceptable. Increasingly the public demands that schools actually educate children — all children — and that children's institutions provide effective treatment. Organizations are being confronted with strong pressures for accountability. And there is probably no greater force for change than parents who want the best for their children. If they feel they are being cheated, parents can rise to a fury and demand a response to the ultimate question of accountability: "We have given you our children; now what have you done with them?" (Lerner, 1976, p. 84).

THE DYSFUNCTIONAL ORGANIZATION

The picture that is emerging is of a child-processing bureaucracy that is neither effective nor accountable. A publication of the National Association of Social Workers concludes: "The system is characterized by overbureaucratization, fragmentation, inability to adapt to changing conditions, tremendous pressures of size, racism and ideological conflict, lack of adequate resources, and feelings of alienation, indifference, and powerlessness on the part of those who are most deeply affected by the system" (Sarri & Maple, 1972, p. 28).

Goffman (1961) documented how total institutions could become coercive and destructive, but it has become increasingly clear that his observations do not apply merely to residential institutions. In many ways, public schools have acquired the characteristics of total institutions and thus can subject students to the same potential abuse of "inmates." Schalock (1979) comments on the large and diverse literature supporting the idea that the nature of the school organization and climate has a profound effect on the outcome of the educational effort. He cites research by Brookover and others which suggests that different schools have their own characteristic climates, and those that fail are marked specifically by a sense of futility. In such an environment, teachers do not seem to care whether students succeed or not, children feel that they have no control over their success or failure, and the peer group negatively sanctions success. Although this sense of academic futility was particularly strong in urban schools where the majority of students were black, Brookover found that the climate of the organization itself was the most powerful predictor of success or failure, independent of the race or socioeconomic status of the children.

In order to comprehend the forces at work within the organizational environment, one must examine a number of interrelated variables. Among these key factors are patterns of authority, staff relationships, status and role definitions, and the size of organizational units (Brookover, 1980), as well as goal clarity, commitment to organizational mission, and participation in governance (Newman, 1981). The manner in which these variables are interrelated can result in either a cohesive or a dysfunctional organization. Among the more prominent symptoms of a dysfunctional organization are depersonalization, stagnation, negative youth and staff climates, and ineffective communication.

Depersonalization

Typically, as organizations increase in size, they become more depersonalized. Bonds between members of the organization are less meaningful; individuals do not feel that they matter, and there is a corresponding lack of commitment to the organizational mission. The problem with many large organizations is not that they are large but that, given their size, they are not structured so as to make primary relationships possible. Nesbit (1953) noted that no large association will remain an object of personal allegiance, however compelling its goals, unless it is sensitive to the crucial relationships of which it is really composed. He concludes that most successful enterprises are those that regard themselves as associations of groups, and not of separate individuals.

Throughout most of the twentieth century, largeness in organizations was more likely to be seen as an asset than a liability. Harvey Cox (1965) in *The Secular City* argues that living anonymously amidst a mass of persons actually enhances humanity by giving an individual greater privacy, mobility, and freedom of choice. Cox readily agrees that the large, complex setting causes people to deal with each other in compartmentalized roles; unlike life in simple communities in early America, relationships are predominantly secondary rather than primary. Most relationships are in fact impersonal, superficial, transitory, and segmented. Yet rather than seeing this depersonalization as a human problem, Cox considers it a human solution. Mankind is "immunizing" itself from the potentially overwhelming complexity of mass society in order to preserve privacy, freedom, and humanity. Although it is understandable that many adults might pursue such a lifestyle, it is hard to fathom how institutions for socializing children can possibly succeed when built around transitory, shallow, and segmented relationships. One would expect that these relationships would be satisfying neither to the children nor to the staff who care for them. Such is precisely the pattern in oversized and anonymous educational and treatment institutions.

Stagnation

Organizational theorists suggest that there is a natural tendency for a closed system, such as a bureaucracy, to move over time toward entropy, a state of decline and decay. Therefore a central goal is to reverse this decline, to create organizational renewal, by maintaining vitality, creativity, and flexibility (Argyris, 1971; Gardner, 1965; Lippit, 1969). The stagnation of an organization is often reflected in the care and upkeep of physical facilities. Frequently the entire physical environment communicates the lack of value that participants place on the program, and perhaps on themselves. The relationship between deteriorating facilities and dysfunctional programs is captured in this characterization of many public junior and senior high schools in large U.S. cities:

> The school buildings themselves are described as unpleasant environments at best. Those under strict controls generally have armed guards patrolling the halls; doors, behind which teachers confront skeleton size classes, are locked.
> Where such security measures are not in force, the scene is often pictured as mayhem. Graffiti besmears the walls, filthy bathrooms reek of nicotine and marijuana, class sessions either exude boredom or reduce themselves to marathon talk sessions (Parsons, 1980, p. B-3).

Such depressing climates are common in dysfunctional schools and treatment programs for troubled children and youth. Frequently staff blame deteriorating facilities on inadequate budgets, poor maintenance departments, or destructive children. The authors have even encountered isolated treatment professionals who rationalize that chaotic and disheveled physical environments are "therapeutic" and avoid the obsessive cleanliness and order that characterize many custodial children's programs. More likely, such climates signal the probability that participants are not committed to the organization. The physical setting for any program of re-education should communicate to students the message: "This is for you; you are of value." The lack of self-esteem of troubled children should not be reinforced with a physical atmosphere of decay.

Youth in Conflict

Dysfunctional educational and treatment organizations are marked by negative youth subcultures. Such climates increase the level of aggressive or avoidance behavior among young people. Thus one encounters a great deal of internal ranking among young people, scapegoating of weaker members by dominant peers, fighting, stealing from one another, name-calling, and similar signs of peer conflict. Sometimes the aggression is directed at staff, either through overt defiance and rebellion or through more passive-aggressive resistance and sabotage of the program. Many troubled youngsters respond to the tensions of the dysfunctional organization by flight rather than fight; absenteeism, truancy from schools or institutions, and dropping out are all examples of this reaction.
Not infrequently, a dysfunctional program is virtually taken over by

the youth themselves. The youth subculture may be more sophisticated at communication than is the staff bureaucracy. For example, delinquent boys in one group may be able to determine whether the new youth in another group can be trusted with the secret that students have the keys to the school station wagon and are planning on stealing it later that night. Programs in which students are better organized than staff can easily be captured by a negative youth subculture.

Staff in Conflict

Dysfunctional organizations are also marked by excessive fight or flight among staff. The intensity of conflict between various staff groups or between staff and administration is well known to those who have worked in large educational or treatment organizations. Staff dissatisfaction is not always shown in direct conflict but can also be expressed indirectly. For example, a union can become a conduit for general negativism rather than a channel for improving communication. Staff resistance in bureaucratic organizations can include "covering," that is, blocking communication about problems, and "satisficing," or doing just enough to get by. The latter term was popularized by Herbert Simon, a 1979 Nobel Prize winner in economics for his work in rational decision-making. Satisficing simply means that when there is an opportunity, staff will frequently take the easiest way out, make the easiest decision, and fail to contribute creatively to the organization.

The flight of staff from dysfunctional organizations is of great concern to youth service professionals. Symptoms of burn-out, including high rates of turnover, are clear signs of a dysfunctional organization. Equally problematic is the staff member who chooses not to leave but to withdraw into his or her own narrow territory and avoid relationships or tasks beyond those strictly required.

Ineffective Communication

Garner (1982) observes that the dysfunctional organization is marked by blocked, disruptive, erratic, or absent communication between various employee groups. Since the nature of the re-educational task requires collaboration, young people suffer from this confusion and conflict. Organizations often develop layers of middle managers separating front-line staff from those responsible for ultimate decision-making, thereby greatly impairing communication. Thomas aptly describes this phenomenon as it occurs in bureaucratic organizations:

> The direct care worker is placed three to ten levels beneath the level of the persons who actually make decisions affecting the daily operation of the unit. Communication is all one way, with orders flowing down the hierarchy but without information flowing back up, other than official reports on selected data. Each level communicates the information that is to that person's benefit. Problems, especially serious problems, seldom benefit the person reporting them, so they are not reported. Yet, the person at any level is responsible for reporting significant problems. The solution to the dilemma is to encourage, subtly, persons lower in the hierarchy not to report problems to the person at a higher level. After all, one cannot be held responsible for reporting some problem one never heard about (1981, p. 15).

THEORIES OF ORGANIZATIONAL BEDLAM

The foregoing state of affairs has been described by Garner (1982) as organizational bedlam. He notes that sundry theories are advanced to explain bedlam including:

> *Lack of clear philosophy.* The implication is that if administration would only lay down some policies and procedures, the confusion would clear up.
>
> *Lack of staff training.* This theory assumes that there is a specific knowledge base which should be taught to staff so that they will embrace the proper approach.
>
> *Relationship hangups.* The assumption of this view is that if only people could be open in their communication with one another, then organizational difficulties would disappear. Everything from encounter groups, coffee klatches, or beer parties is suggested as a solution to communication problems.
>
> *Problematic personalities.* Here the assumption is that those involved in conflict are troublemakers, and if their behavior could be modified (or, preferably, if they could be eliminated), the organization would function smoothly.

Another theory of bedlam is the common assumption that the frustrations experienced working with children are simply the result of *insufficient resources*, namely, money or people.

> If a bad educational system exists, saturate it with more of what it already has: new buses are better than old; new texts better than old; new buildings better than old; what one teacher can do well, three can do better; what two administrators can do adequately, twelve can do better (Barth, 1972, pp. 169–170).

Still another way to explain bedlam is to project the blame somewhere entirely outside of the organization. It is popular to attribute the fault to pathological children, parents, or communities. Whether or not such factors exist, these rationalizations avoid accountability and serve as a cop-out for professionals who should be re-examining the effectiveness of their organization.

In the face of such diverse theories of bedlam, it should not be surprising to find a potpourri of proposed solutions. Examples of such stop-gap measures have included the following:

—An elaborate system of crisis back-up support was designed in a children's institution so that teachers and child-care workers could always receive support. When staff dialed 11, radio-dispatched disciplinarians would sweep into action and rescue the staff member from the crisis. Successful staff members prided themselves on practically never calling for help. Weak staff members were made even weaker by habitually falling back on this crutch.

—A specialized school for troubled children has experienced a parade of programs touted as panaceas. A new swimming pool was built with the rationale that it would cut down truancy. Encounter groups were organized for a time but failed to establish a trusting atmosphere. Finally, students were shipped off to a "scared straight" experience at a nearby prison under the assumption that this strategy would have a significant impact on the school's problems.

—A residential treatment center sought to increase communication between different staff groups by a series of approaches. Informal receptions were arranged, but the various occupational groups segregated in different corners of the room. Social workers were asked to spend one night a week "down at the cottage." But several of the social workers said that this was a waste of time and that the child-care staff didn't want them there anyway. Finally, the institution reorganized on a unit system under which social workers were assigned to specific cottages. However, the departmental structure continued to exist and allegiance was still to the particular professional discipline.

Partial theories of bedlam and piecemeal approaches to reform are inadequate responses to the dysfunctional organization. Changing entrenched patterns in order to create bona fide organizational reform is not an easy undertaking. As Sarason and Doris warn: "Beware of those who, in claiming the birth of a new world, blithely assume that the old world will lie down and die; tradition, custom, and practice are not easily unlearned" (1979, p. 1). Probably most attempts to change dysfunctional schools or youth organizations fail because they are piecemeal. Newman (1981) notes that it has been common for educational reformers to limit themselves to a specific issue such as school vandalism, integration, or competency testing. Preoccupation with such narrow topics deflects attention from more comprehensive strategies to achieve a functional organization.

Because of the difficulty of reorganizing institutional structures, some believe that the only appropriate response is to eliminate them. This attitude is evident in Ivan Illich's (1970) call for "deschooling" as well as in the considerable literature on "deinstitutionalization." Although such approaches have a simplistic attractiveness, the solution is not likely to be found in removing all organization. Rather, our goal must be to identify the structures essential for creating effective organizations.

HIERARCHICAL VERSUS PARTICIPATIVE ORGANIZATIONS

Discussions on philosophies of leadership frequently categorize styles as authoritarian, participative, or democratic. Because a purely democratic system of government (every person having one vote) is not ordinarily thought to be an effective way of operating a complex organization (even in a democracy), we shall confine our comparison in this section to two competing models of organizational leadership, namely, the hierarchical/authoritarian, and the participative.

Participative models of leadership are not original to Western civilization. Miller (1955) noted that the French military officer Baren de LaHontan, observing American Indians in the seventeenth century, was amazed to discover that the tribal leaders did not exercise authoritarian control over their villagers. The Fox Indians who populated the Great Lakes region in the 1650's believed that leaders should never order anyone to do something they would not themselves do. One man was seen as being as much a master as others since all were made of the same clay. Believing that each individual derived power directly from the deity rather than from intermediaries, they developed a remarkably progressive concept of leadership:

—Power was seen as being equally available to all.
—Power was considered temporary, not a personal possession, and not able to be gained or lost since it was dependent on a successful performance in a specific situation.
—Demonstrative power did not give its possessors any right to control the action of others.
—Since power was seen as contemporary and contingent, it could not be properly distributed on a hierarchical basis.
—Those who sought to control power were believed dangerous, to be feared, not admired.

It is interesting to note the contrast between this concept of power and the traditional notion of power that emanates from Western civilizations. Harking back to the philosophy of the divine right of kings, the person in authority was originally assumed to have some special connection with God; one's worth was determined by how close he sat to the throne of power. Miller suggests that the entire structure of our thinking about power has been shaped by this history. We describe people who are getting ahead as "on the way to the top," "being elevated," "rising," "climbing the ladder of success." Ours is a culture that rewards those who overpower others through authoritarian means.

Table 4-1 contrasts hierarchical/authoritarian organization with one using a problem-solving technology. As seen in Table 4-1, the hierarchical organization is characterized by formal systems of rules and regulations, centralized decision-making at the top, a standardized repetitive function, and a departmental structure with specialized tasks. In production-line technology, one can increase efficiency by increasing size (economy of scale) until one reaches a point of diminishing returns. The knowledge base for production-line technology is complete — that is, one applies known principles to a closed system to execute a highly prescribed task.

By way of comparison, a problem-solving technology uses participative models of leadership based on collegial relationships and norms. The task of such an organization is customized, and decision-making is relatively autonomous with many problems being solved in a decentralized way, typically at the bottom of the organization. Although staff

Table 4-1. Comparison of Hierarchical/Authoritarian and Problem-solving Organizations

	Production-line technology	Problem-solving technology
Example	A factory	A professional organization
Leadership	Hierarchical, formal authority and rules	Participative, collegial relationships and norms
Nature of task	Standardized, repetitive production	Customized, creative problem-solving
Decision-making	Centralized (at top)	Autonomous, decentralized (at bottom)
Organization	Separate departments, specialized functions	Interdependent teams, working on common goal
Size	Efficiency may increase with size because of economy of scale	Efficiency may decrease with size because of breakdown of interdependent relationships
Knowledge	Complete, applying known principles to a closed system	Incomplete, exploring unknown, seeking feedback

Adapted from Smucker, 1975, and Duke, 1978.

may have specialties, they work in a highly interdependent manner toward a common goal. In such organizations efficiency may decline with increased size because of breakdowns in relationships. The knowledge base of the problem-solving organization is incomplete, since much of the activity involves exploring the unknown and seeking feedback in an open system.

Eisner (1979) notes that the dominant image in American education has been the factory model. The emphasis is on control, quality assurance, producing measurable products, and clearly differentiating the tasks of labor and of management. Such an organization is unfitted, according to Eisner, to educational tasks because in such a system creativity, surprise, ingenuity, and serendipity are viewed as noise that disrupts the authoritarian organization.

Authoritarian and nonauthoritarian managers may have different views of human nature and thus may approach the leadership task differently.* McGregor (1960) identified these extremes of style with the labels Theory X and Theory Y. *Theory X* managers operate with the following assumptions:

1. People will avoid work if they can, and they need the security of being controlled.
2. People respond best if closely monitored and directed.
3. Economic incentives, coercion, and the threat of punishment are the key means of fostering productivity.

On the other hand, *Theory Y* managers assume that:

1. People will enter willingly into work if committed to the organizational goals.
2. People are capable of assuming self-control and responsibility.
3. External controls are not the only means of fostering productivity; people also will work for social satisfaction.

Of course, this polarized scheme is an oversimplification, and most managers show elements of both Theory X and Theory Y. Still, McGregor demonstrates the dramatically different approaches that can be taken to leadership.

Another useful distinction between management systems is the relative emphasis placed on indirect versus direct control (Koontz & O'Donnell, 1978). *Indirect controls* are the checks that managers install to ensure proper performance by those whose capabilities to perform

* Although the terms "leadership" and "management" are sometimes used interchangeably, there is a formal distinction as noted by Hersey and Blanchard (1977). Leadership occurs whenever one attempts to affect the behavior of an individual or group regardless of the reason. Management presumes a more specialized kind of leadership geared to the accomplishment of organizational goals. Typical management functions might involve planning, staffing, motivating, problem-solving, controlling, delegating, and decision-making.

are not fully trusted. *Direct control* involves assigning a task to a person who can be expected to complete the task successfully. When this distinction is applied to re-education, the key to quality programs is not in proliferating indirect controls, but rather in retaining direct control through full professional competency.

Hersey and Blanchard (1977) propose a model of situational leadership that allows for different management behavior under differing circumstances. At certain points in the life of an organization the leader may be required to operate in a relatively authoritarian task-oriented manner, or by *telling;* at other times the leader will be *selling,* which is still directive, by seeking through two-way communication to gain some support from subordinates. A third style is *participating,* in which the leader shares with followers the task of decision-making by basing it on two-way participation. Finally, a leader may use a style of *delegating* because workers have sufficient maturity and skill to run their own show.

A common misassumption is that one can "delegate responsibility." Although *authority* can be *delegated* to subordinates ($\downarrow$), *responsibility* is *owed* to superiors ($\uparrow$). Thus authority and responsibility have very different meanings: authority is a right whereas responsibility is an obligation.

Much recent literature on leadership in organizations has stressed the advantages of *participative* models of management in which employee groups share in decision-making. Likert (1976) and colleagues have conducted numerous well-researched studies of this approach, which they call *system 4 management.* Ouchi's (1981) popularized account of Japanese industrial organization, *Theory Z,* is also representative of this tradition.

Advocates of participative organizational technologies frequently cite Maslow's (1954) hierarchy of human needs to support that model. Maslow classified needs into five levels. Meeting needs at the most basic levels enables the person to focus on higher-order needs. These levels are: (1) physiological needs; (2) safety needs; (3) love and belonging; (4) self-esteem; and (5) self-actualization. The participatory organization better allows workers to meet higher-level, psychosocial needs, because involvement in governing the organization allows their opinions and contributions to be valued directly.

Research by Herzberg (1959) and colleagues suggests that employees who are dissatisfied with their work usually complain about physical needs such as pay, working conditions, or hours. Nevertheless, removing these *dissatisfiers* does not necessarily create satisfied or motivated workers. *Satisfiers* are of a higher order; they include being challenged, being recognized for one's accomplishment, and having one's opinion respected. In a later work, Herzberg concludes:

The manager must find ways for workers to serve but they cannot serve if their work does not permit them to fill their needs for personal responsibility, personal productivity and personal development. . . . Management must realize that using animal training techniques to manipulate security needs will teach workers to spend more of their time and energy avoiding the pains of insecurity—avoiding failure, not seeking success. Manipulating security needs cannot result in personal or organizational development (1979, p. 63).

ORGANIZING FOR TOTAL TEAMWORK

Rhetoric about teamwork abounds in educational and treatment organizations. However, discussion has seldom been matched with action because of limited commitment by both staff and administration to communicate fully within a teamwork process.

In many programs for troubled youth, it has become almost a truism that one should employ representatives of numerous professional disciplines in order to gain an interdisciplinary perspective. Although this goal is appropriate, the practical result can be a staffing model fraught with role conflicts, confused communication, and inefficiency. An example is the field of residential group care, in which much of what has been described as specialized treatment is in reality a costly treatment veneer. A full complement of highly trained therapists and consultants is of little value if those who work *directly* with youth are not doing things right. As Kahn has said, many such programs "could become more useful if they invested less heavily in what are thought of as formal 'treatment' resources and built up their capacity for wholesome child rearing" (1973, p. 304).

Doing Staffings

The anthropologists Buckholdt and Gubrium (1979) studied what actually happens in multidisciplinary professional staffings. Such programs place great faith in the value of bringing various perspectives together to create a "true picture" about a child. Yet these researchers suggest that the content of such meetings is actually a caricature of reality. This is seen in the following observations by Buckholdt and Gubrium of a behavior modification program; however, the process of "doing staffings" can be equally dysfunctional under any treatment philosophy.

The staffers have been discussing recent changes in a child's behavior. The consulting psychologist asks the teacher to report her counts on fighting:

Teacher: If you look at this [chart], he is doing pretty well. I've only gotten two fighting episodes each of the past three days. His baseline was twelve, twelve, and fifteen.

Psychologist: He does seem to be doing better.

Ass't Teacher: I don't really see the change. He still seems to be fighting a lot. I think he knows when you're counting and lays off. He's really sneaky, ya' know. He punches kids on his way by and we don't see it.

Childcare Worker: He's still fighting in the cottage. I'm not counting that, but I know he's still causing a lot of problems with the rest of the kids. [Elaborates]

Teacher: Should I change my counts?

Psychologist: Well, if he hasn't changed much, your data should show that.

Teacher: What should I put, 12 or 15 or so?

Ass't. Teacher: I think 15 would be pretty close for a day.

Teacher: O.K. 15. [Changes her measures]

Psychologist: Watch him more closely, when he isn't aware of what you are doing. See if 15 is about right. It may be even higher. The actual number isn't so important as long as we have some reading on changes or trends.

                                                           (1979, p. 263)

As seen by these trained observers, such meetings can be marked by total confusion about the importance of a problem or whether a problem even exists. Unimpressed, the anthropologists called this process "doing staffings" and suggest that they are but hollow trivial rituals that better describe the activities of professionals than the behavior of those they purport to serve.

In reviewing literature on teamwork, one finds a growing consensus that this management structure best matches the needs of human service organizations. Teamwork studies typically identify variables correlated with team functioning and relate them to program outcome. For instance, Lacks, Landsbaum, and Stern (1970) designed a study that investigated a communication process with teams in a children's psychiatric unit. Their results suggested that improving communication skills may result in better team performance. Presumably, better teamwork leads to more positive treatment and thus better client outcomes. Stone (1970) states that critical components of team success include: (1) freedom of communication; (2) shared leadership and decision-making; (3) respect for individuals; (4) congenial interpersonal feelings; and (5) continuous evaluation in light of shared reality.

Summarizing studies on teamwork, Wagner (1977) suggests that teams provide a more holistic response to clients, and team members are inclined to make bolder decisions than are practitioners who are not operating on teams.

Smucker (1975) conducted organizational research on 30 residential treatment centers for children. Extrapolating from his studies, we can predict that teamwork would be facilitated by increased frequency of interaction and increased interdependence of staff. Specific adjustments to improve teamwork may include:

Informal interactions: Lower the social distance between groups of staff, increase the homogeneity of staff, and increase the physical proximity of working arrangements.

Formal interactions: Increase the frequency of formal meetings so that conflict must be accommodated.

Decision-making: Decentralize significant areas of decision-making to increase participation.

Interdisciplinary cooperation: Decrease departmental ties by making the work team the primary group.

THE TEAMWORK PRIMACY MODEL

A model for total teamwork called *teamwork primacy* was initially developed in residential centers (Vorrath & Brendtro, 1974) and has subsequently been extended to other settings including public schools (Garner, 1982). Although a team model is actually a simplification of a complex organization, it does represent a significant departure from how most human service programs are currently organized. The effect of a team model is to maximize primary group relations among co-workers. The following are central assumptions of the model as identified in these sources:

1. Teamwork becomes the highest administrative priority, and other administrative objectives are secondary.
2. Staff teams should be organized around discrete groups of children. Included on each team would be all staff who provide direct services to that particular group of clients on a regular basis.
3. In order to maximize primary group relationships, one must minimize the total number of adults who serve each group of children.
4. The teams become the new organizational unit with the responsibility and authority to plan and implement the program. Departments are replaced by these program units or become subordinate to them, since the new loyalty becomes the group of children rather than the departmental discipline.

5. A team approach must invest *all* team members with both power and responsibility. Thus, teams function best with the least internal hierarchy possible. Ideally the team would relate to one higher authority who is not a member of the team per se; generally this is the program's director.
6. The team model will minimize or eliminate the need for middle-level management or coordinative personnel.

Embodying these assumptions, the following series of procedures can be used to organize a teamwork structure:

1. *Create a self-contained program unit.* The program is reconceptualized as a number of smaller self-contained groups or units, each no larger than can be served by a team of 10 or fewer staff. More than 10 staff on a team usually leads to fragmentation. Teams with fewer than five members may have difficulty remaining dynamic.
2. *Form an interdisciplinary team.* The program director is responsible for constituting a balanced team consisting of all individuals with significant regular contact with the youth in the program. For example, in a school such a team might include a group of teachers and the counselor who share primary responsibility for a grade level of students. In a residential treatment center, the team might include all teachers, counselors, and clinicians who work with one self-contained cottage-classroom. Staff who work with students on a limited basis will meet with the team only as their specific consultation is needed (e.g., the school nurse). Parents may meet on a periodic basis when specific planning about their child is scheduled.
3. *Establish a meeting structure.* Each team member's working hours must be arranged so that he or she is available for a weekly team meeting of one to two hours. Alternative coverage of students must be arranged, if necessary, so that all can attend. In monthly rotation, all team members take turns serving as secretary and as chairperson of the team. The secretary records minutes of the meetings, which are then provided to all team members and to administration. The chairperson is responsible for seeing that the group uses the allotted meeting time efficiently, adequately covering the agenda items. The chairperson may also serve as a liaison between the team and administration between meeting times.
4. *Employ administrative–team channels of communication.* The director of the program rotates among team meetings to monitor functioning, impart information, and respond to issues raised by teams. All team members thus have regular direct contact with the program director. One director can ordinarily assume re-

sponsibility for two to five teams depending on the size of the teams, stability of the program, and other administrative support available. The director does not run the meeting and usually will not stay for the entire time lest his or her continual presence serve to undercut the team's need to function with sufficient autonomy. When the program director is concerned about some problem with the staff or students, he or she, insofar as possible, works through the team, placing responsibility on it to deal with these problems. When the team feels that policy or administrative changes are needed, it conveys its recommendations (during the meeting or through the minutes) to the director, who either accepts the recommendation or declines it with an explanation.

5. *Develop a sense of shared responsibility.* The measure of the importance of a team member is not one's credentials or the ability to control others, but rather the ability to develop competence and strength in other team members. A significant portion of each team meeting should be allocated to team development. If one team member continually leads and dominates team functioning, he or she is a liability, not an asset. If one team member fails to do his or her part, all members of the team are responsible for helping the person overcome this failure. Teams do not, however, have authority to discharge an ineffective employee, which remains a function of administration.

6. *Participate in the management of the program within an agreed framework.* Any issue affecting the program, be it treatment, administration, or personnel, is an appropriate topic for the team. Since teams have been delegated their authority by administration, the extent of that authority will have to be defined through experience. Realistically, there are limitations to any team's power because administration will have to consider other factors (such as financial, legal, or board policy). However, if the director should decide to override the team or reassume authority earlier delegated, he or she would communicate with the team directly.

7. *Strive for a consensual model of decision-making.* Team members should see conflict between various points of view as an opportunity for constructive and creative solutions. Insofar as possible, simplistic conflict-avoidance techniques, such as the majority vote, should be avoided in preference to a consensus model of decision-making. A conflict is considered to be resolved only when all opposing parties are satisfied with the outcome; if any party is still dissatisfied, the conflict remains unsolved (Likert & Likert, 1976). By achieving a consensus, all points of view will have been considered and all team members will thus be more willing to support the final decision (Ouchi, 1981).

Garner (1982) notes that the adoption of a team model has a significant impact on the re-educational process in three principal ways:

1. *Conflict reduction.* The team model provides a framework for
   resolving dysfunctional interdisciplinary conflict and tension.
   Thus the conditions are created in which proactive leadership
   can flourish.
2. *Increasing accountability.* By making a specific group of staff
   responsible for a specific group of students, one establishes the
   prerequisite conditions for accountability. Responsibility can no
   longer be defensively shifted elsewhere, since the problem and its
   solution both lie somewhere within the team.
3. *Responding holistically to children.* A fragmented and inconsistent structure is replaced with a unified response to the needs of
   children. A variety of approaches can be better tailored to the
   specific needs of the children because those who carry out the
   program are instrumental in designing it.

Implementing teamwork is not without its complications. Certain
staff who have learned to succeed as individuals may be initially
uncomfortable with the expectation that they will share responsibility
with and for others. For instance, teachers are accustomed to working
solo behind closed classroom doors and may lack teamwork skills;
even so, teachers know that classrooms are not in reality isolated, for
one teacher's failure becomes the next teacher's frustrations. Most
professionals are willing to participate in a team model if they honestly
believe that the team will be given some power and authority.

Another complication of teamwork results from the fact that if
teamwork is prime, then *anything* that competes with teamwork must
be subordinate. Yet professionals seldom give any thought to the effect
of proposed program changes on team functioning. Ecology groups
stress the importance of an "environmental impact study" before
making significant changes to a habitat. Similarly, we believe that
organizational changes should be evaluated in light of a "teamwork
impact study." An outline for a teamwork impact study is given in
Table 4-2.

Tight team models have been criticized by some who distrust institutional authority. According to this view, cohesive staff organization is
inherently more monolithic — and thus potentially more destructive in
a coercive institution (Eisikovits & Eisikovits, 1980). This is a reasonable point, for increasing the power of punitive staff can hardly be seen
as progress. We would conclude, however, that eliminating destructive
staff or destructive institutions is preferable to perpetuating organizational bedlam.

One final caveat is needed: "teamwork is a learned behavior; it is

Table 4-2. Teamwork Impact Study: A Checklist for Evaluating the Effect
of Proposed Program Changes on the Primary Organizational Goal
of Teamwork

---

1. *Responsibility without authority.* Would the change deprive the team of sufficient authority to carry out its responsibilities?
   Example: Requiring that day-to-day decisions be "cleared" with a supervisor
2. *Authority without responsibility.* Would the change give major authority for children's programs to people not responsible to the team?
   Example: Arranging for a free-lance therapist to "treat" a child in isolation from the team's treatment goals
3. *Ineffective size.* Would the change make the staff team too large or too small to function effectively?
   Example: Putting 15 people on a team
4. *Competing loyalties.* Would the change shift staff allegiance from the team to a department or professional discipline?
   Example: Setting up regular departmental meetings on topics that overlap team discussions
5. *Social distance.* Would the change create unnecessary hierarchial or status relationships within the team?
   Example: Designating certain team members as subordinate to others
6. *Decreased informal interactions.* Would the change reduce informal unstructured contact among team members?
   Example: Moving certain team members to anoher building
7. *Decreased formal interactions.* Would the change reduce formal structured contact among team members?
   Example: Curtailing the frequency, length, or regularity of team meetings
8. *Decreased staff–administration contact.* Would the change interfere with the direct communication between staff and the program director?
   Example: Add a middle administrator in the line and require the team to "go through channels"
9. *Decreased staff–parent contact.* Would the change interfere with direct communication between staff and parents?
   Example: Drawing children from too broad a geographical area
10. *Decreased interdependence.* Would the change decrease the interdependence and cooperation of individual team members working toward a common mission?
    Example: Allowing a certain "independent" team member to operate in an unchallenged private turf

---

learned slowly over one's personal and professional development" (Garner, 1982, p. 1). Teamwork requires *technical skills* such as translating specialized terminology to a common vernacular, generating ideas (e.g., "brain-storming"), setting priorities, identifying central issues, managing meeting time effectively, making decisions, assigning responsibility for action, and evaluating performance. Teamwork also requires sophisticated *interpersonal skills* such as active listening, asserting one's view, accepting criticism, confronting with concern, tolerating conflicting views, and being able to compromise. Only as staff have the opportunity to learn together for a period of months will they begin to see the full potential of a team model. However, by making the decision to commit the organization's administrative technology to a participative model, one has made a major humanistic value statement. Staff are pledged to deal with one another, not through status or intimidation, but in a spirit of sharing and cooperative problem-solving. Is this too much to expect of professionals whose mission is to teach these same behaviors to children?

PARENTS AS PARTNERS IN TEAMWORK

There has been a surge of interest in work with parents, particularly since national policies have mandated their inclusion in the educational and treatment process. Ironically, the demand for parental involvement comes at a time when parents are seen as less responsible than ever before, when family instability is heightened, and when the quality of parenting is widely assumed to have deteriorated. Nevertheless, despite dramatic changes in the family, the most formidable external influence on the development of youngsters continues to be their parents. As the child's first and most powerful teachers, parents can make potential contributions to re-education that cannot be surpassed by any other team member.

Our current focus on the family is in many ways a reaffirmation of what the earliest teachers knew—that theirs should be a partnership with parents. Despite much lip service about partnerships with parents, most contemporary efforts fall short of this goal. Sonnenschein (1981) charts the prevailing roles that parents play in relationship to professionals. These roles include the parent as *client,* or *patient;* the parent as *responsible for the problem;* the parent as *inferior* or *unintelligent;* and the parent as *resistant* or *adversarial.*

David Page's *Theory and Practice of Teaching* (1847, pp. 197-203) held a unique place in the education literature for half a century. He offered four guidelines for relations with parents.

1. *Seek frequent opportunities of intercourse with parents.* Taking the world as we find it, the teacher must lead the way. He must often introduce himself uninvited, calling at their homes in the spirit of his vocation, and conversing with them freely about his duty to their children and to themselves. It may be very useful to have an interview with such parents as have been disturbed by some administration of discipline. If there could be a meeting of

the parents as men, gentlemen, as Christians, as coadjustors for the child's welfare, it would always be attended with good results.

2. *Be willing to explain all plans to the parents.* If they had implicit confidence, then this direction might not be necessary. But, he cannot expect spontaneous confidence. They wish to know his designs and it is best they should be informed of them by himself. Many a parent, upon the first announcement of a measure in school, has stoutly opposed it, who, upon a little explanatory conversation would entertain a very different opinion, and ever after would be most ready to countenance and support it. Parents frequently entertain a suspicious spirit. Would not this be done away, if there was no *mystery* about the school.

3. *Encourage parents to visit frequently.* The teacher should early invite them to come in. Not in general terms — fix the time. As often as they come they will be benefited. When such visits are made, the teacher should not depart from his usual course on their account. Let praises and reproofs, rewards and punishments be as faithfully and punctually dispensed as if no visitor were present. Faithfully exhibit the school *just as it is,* its lights and its shadows, so that they may see all its workings, its trials as well as its encouragements. But if the teacher makes a false appearance and unusual airs, they will, sooner or later, discover his hypocrisy, and very likely despise him for an attempt to deceive them.

4. *Be frank in all representations concerning their children.* Let a particular answer, *and a true one,* always be given to the inquiry — "How does my child get along?" The parent has a right to know and the teacher has no right to conceal the truth. Tell the whole story plainly and frankly. While the teacher should make his conversation instructive, he should assume no airs of superior learning or infallible authority. He should remember the truth in human nature, that men are best pleased to learn without being reminded that they are learners.

Many professionals who enjoy working with troubled children are much less enthusiastic about working with parents of these children. McKinnon (1980) found that teachers frequently listed parent contact among major job dissatisfiers. Kroth and Scholl (1978) identified a number of dynamics that interfere with successful collaboration with parents in school programs. They include:

1. *Teachers who feel intimidated.* Many professionals fear involvement of the parents because they do not know how to work with them, although they may recognize the value of parent participation.

2. *Parents who feel alienated.* Parents feel uncomfortable with professionals who use strange jargon in describing their work with children, and they may view schools as large bureaucratic hierarchies that are unresponsive to their involvement or influence.

3. *Structures that block communication.* Lines of communication between school and parents are often unclear and parents are unsure of where to go for help, particularly in larger schools. Working hours of parents and school professionals are the same, which further impedes ready contact.

When parents join together in formal or informal associations, they can acquire a real or perceived base of power that can be highly intimidating to professionals. As Morse (1979) notes, parent groups have been known for their tendency to adopt adversarial stances, such as threats of lawsuit, rather than cooperative approaches; this impulse is born of negative experiences with and mistrust of professionals. When parents and professionals become entangled in a disagreement, they are likely to hold different opinions about who is to blame. Vernberg and Medway (1981) indicate that the parents are likely to view responsibility for the problem as resting first of all with the school, second with the child, and only third with the home. On the other hand, school personnel are more likely to blame the problem first on the home, second on the child, and only third on the school. Such contradictory notions of problem ownership do not facilitate problem resolution.

Parents and professionals both can display styles of behavior that impede effective communication (Losen & Diament, 1978). *Professional defensiveness* can take the following forms:

1. *Hostility.* Professionals may display a host of angry responses when threatened by parents, ranging from overt antagonism to covert signs of annoyance such as bored expressions and tone of voice.

2. *Passive avoidance.* Professionals may avoid responding assertively by delaying, avoiding, placating, or doing nothing.

3. *Authoritarian dogmatism.* Wrapping themselves in a mantle of expertise, professionals may inhibit discussion by implying that if one disagrees, one is wrong.

4. *Interrogation and interpretation.* Particularly common among psychological counselors and social workers, the professional pins the parent into the role of patient. This is a variation of what Eric Berne in *Games People Play* (1964) calls "psychology."

Parent difficulties that hinder communication have a variety of manifestations:

1. *Parents who are critical.* School personnel may be highly threatened by parents who are outspoken and politically active. This is
   particularly true when a parent is articulate and publicly vocal,
   using such forums as the press, board meetings or direct appeals
   to the administration.
2. *Passive-resistant parents.* For reasons that usually are unclear to
   the professional, the parent may seek to undermine or undo all
   the initiatives of staff. Typically such parents are highly mistrust-
   ful of the professional's intentions.
3. *Parents who seem unable to be coequals.* Some parents may seem
   to the professional to be incapable of collaborative partnership
   because of apparent inadequacies. Likewise, such parents may
   feel unable to communicate with professionals on an equal
   footing.
4. *Neglectful or abusive parents.* Although there are usually statutory
   procedures to follow in cases of child abuse, professionals feel
   uncertain about whether or how to confront parents with their
   concerns in these areas.
5. *Parents who seek panaceas.* Parents who have difficulty accepting
   the limitations of their youngster or the limitations of the professional's knowledge often seek quick remedies or make the
   rounds in search of some professional who will tell them what
   they want to hear.

Parents of children with special needs frequently express the feeling
that professionals lack empathy and understanding about the problems
they face with their children. The reactions of some parents are so
strong that conferences with professionals become major traumatic
events to be dreaded and avoided (Fox, 1979). Turnbull and Turnbull
(1978), who have both made major professional contributions to the
field of special education, write tellingly of the catastrophic interactions that they encountered when, as parents of a retarded child, they
found themselves in need of professional help. They report feeling as
though they had been demoted from the role of professional to that of
parent and were treated as if they had caused the child's condition.
Their experience led them to conclude that genuine collaboration
between parents and professionals is almost nonexistent: "The disease
of professionals is that we believe that we are too good for the illnesses
and problems with which we are required to deal" (Turnbull & Turnbull, 1978, p. 6). On one rare occasion the Turnbulls encountered a
professional who didn't fit this pattern. While sharing some very personal concerns about their child's future with a psychologist, tears
came to the cheeks of the professional listener. With the realization
that someone finally understood, the respect of the parents for that
professional grew 100-fold.

Staff in residential treatment programs for troubled youth have been no more effective in building strong relationships with parents than have teachers. There are still programs that arbitrarily refuse to admit a child unless parents also enter therapy; staff may see this requirement as evidence of a sophisticated family orientation; more likely, professionals are communicating their belief that parents are inadequate, confused, mentally ill, and obviously at fault for the problems the young person presents.

Traditionally, residential group care programs have served as family substitutes rather than as a family support system. Those who have worked in such settings know how easy it has been to assume the role of "good parent," a stand-in for the child's presumably inadequate parents. Swept into the role of being the child's rescuer, the professional tended to assume that the parents must be the enemy. Almost inevitably, staff attempted to control the contact between the child and the family. Social workers read the mail — until the courts said that this violated the child's rights. Regular topics of concern were how often and how long parents would be allowed to visit and when they would be allowed to telephone. The semantics told the story. Those empowered to *allow* parent–child contact must, of course, own the child. Only in recent years has the field of residential group care begun to reach out in new ways to parents, treating them as full partners rather than as enemies or patients.

Still, many parents of troubled children do have significant personal or family problems. For this reason many professionals question whether it is practical to involve parents meaningfully in re-education. It has been very convenient to use the cop-out that parents won't participate. Perhaps the person who most challenged the authors to expand their thinking on the role of parents is Brian Richardson from western Australia. Dr. Richardson directs the Chidley Education Centre in Perth. This residential school serves exceptional children who come from an area approximately the size of the western United States. In spite of the seemingly insurmountable logistical problems in relating to parents, some of whom are native to the primitive, underdeveloped areas of Australia, he reports that over 90% of the parents spend one or more weeks per year on the campus working directly with the school's staff.

Educational and treatment programs are now experimenting with an exciting array of ways to increase the quantity and quality of parent involvement (Kroth & Scholl, 1978; Whittaker, 1979). These strategies include: parent education, parent support groups, parents as volunteers in schools or residential milieus, parent advisory groups, home visitation programs, parent advocacy, and conjoint family therapy.

Among other representative approaches for involving parents are *school site councils* (Rosaler, 1979) as developed in the State of California. These advisory bodies in individual schools are composed half of school personnel and half of parents and students. They are charged with the responsibility to develop educational programs matched to the needs of children in a particular setting. Bronfenbrenner (1979) describes a program of parent–teacher cooperation that involved parents in *supervising home assignments* for their own elementary-aged children. Pioneering the concept of *learning vacations,* Gallaudet College placed parents and professionals together in a natural setting, such as a camp, where they could interact and learn from one another (Lebuffe & Lebuffe, 1982). These are but a sampling of the virtually limitless possibilities for enhancing parent–professional cooperation.

There is a rapidly expanding literature of work with parents in special education and treatment settings. Contributions directed toward school and community settings include those of Graubard (1977), Cooper and Edge (1978), Selisman (1979), and Jones (1980). Works that discuss the involvement of parents in residential group care settings include Trieschman and Whittaker (1972); Mayer, Richman, and Balcerzak (1977); Keith-Lucas and Sanford (1977); and Whittaker (1979).

In addition to work with the family, Whittaker (1975, 1979) emphasizes that successful treatment programs must also build linkages with other major community systems in which the child participates. These systems may include juvenile justice or mental health agencies, churches, recreational programs, and the world of work. For a comprehensive discussion of ways in which the transactions between the child and his ecology can be assessed and modified, the reader is referred to Apter's work, *Troubled Child/Troubled System* (1982).

It is almost certain that no single program or set of procedures offers "the answer" for working with parents. Perhaps the greatest need is for professionals to abandon their traditional authoritarian role of imposing a process on parents, and instead learn to work with them in a consultation format (Hobbs, 1975). The greatest gains will not come by some new invention for treating parents, but by a radical change of orientation in which parents become full partners with professionals. Only with parent participation will the team be able to generate the most creative ideas for the optimum development of children.

New participatory roles for parents will revolutionize the re-educational process in many ways (Simches, 1975). By working side by side with professionals, parents will learn skills that enable them to help their children more effectively. Through participation in decision-making, parents will help professionals find appropriate programs and placements for children. As advocates of children, parents will protect children's rights and will work to extend and expand the educational opportunities available to all children. By replacing token involvement with full parent participation, we will have released a potent force capable of changing the entire system (Simches, 1975).

After a century of expansion in the size and complexity of people-processing bureaucracies, there is renewed interest in developing ways to restore to these organizations a sense of community and shared values (Burkholder, Ryan, & Blanke, 1981). Creating this ethos requires that professionals, parents, and children work together in a climate of mutual caring and respect. Depersonalized systems must give way to structures uniquely fitted to the goal of shared, cooperative teamwork. In Etzioni's (1961) terms, this new organization will not be motivated by coercion but by referent-group relationships and by a sense of moral commitment to a common mission.

REFERENCES

Apter, S. J. *Troubled children/troubled systems*. New York: Pergamon, 1982.

Argyris, C. *Management and organization development: The path from XA to YB*. New York: McGraw Hill, 1971.

Barth, R. S. *Open education and the American school*. New York: Agathon Press, 1972.

Berne, E. *Games people play*. New York: Grove Press, 1964.

Bronfenbrenner, U. *The ecology of human development*. Cambridge, MA: Harvard University Press, 1979.

Brookover, W. B. *Measuring and attaining the goals of education*, Association for Supervision and Curriculum Development, 1980.

Buckholdt, D., & Gubrium, J. Doing staffings. *Human Organization*, 1979, *33*, 255–264.

Burkholder, S., Ryan, K., & Blanke, V. Values, the key to community. *Phi Delta Kappan*, 1981, *62*(7), 483–485.

Carney, M. *Country life and the country school*. Chicago: Row Peterson, 1912.

Cooley, C. *Social process*. New York: Charles Scribner's Sons, (1918), (Reprinted 1927).

Cooper, J., & Edge, D. *Parenting: Strategies and educational methods*. Columbus, OH: Charles E. Merrill, 1978.

Cox, H. *The secular city*. New York: MacMillan, 1965.

Duke, D. S. *The retransformation of the school: The emergence of contemporary alternative schools in the United States*. Chicago: Nelson Hall, 1978.

Dunathan, A. Teacher shortage: Big problems for small schools. *Phi Delta Kappan*, 1980, *63*(3), 205–206.

Eisikovits, R. A., & Eisikovits, Z. C. Detotalizing the institutional experience: The role of school in residential treatment of juveniles. *Residential and Community Child Care Administration*, 1980, *1*(4), 365–374.

Eisner, E. W. *The educational imagination: On the design and evaluation of school programs*. New York: MacMillan, 1979.

Etzioni, A. *A comparative analysis of complex organizations*. New York: Free Press, 1961.

Fox, D. Shoe on the other foot: Parents teach professionals. *Education Unlimited*, 1979, *1*(5), 36–37.

Gardner, J. W. *Self-renewal: The individual and the innovative society*. New York: Harper & Row, 1965.

Garner, H. *Teamwork in programs for children and youth: A handbook for administrators.* Springfield, IL: Charles C. Thomas, 1982.

Goffman, E. *Asylums: Essays on the social situation of mental patients and other inmates.* New York: Anchor Books, 1961.

Graubard, P. *Positive parenthood: Solving parent-child conflicts through behavior modification.* New York: Bobbs-Merrill, 1977.

Gula, M. *Child-caring institutions: Their new role in community development of services.* U.S. Children's Bureau Pub. No. 368. Washington, DC: U.S. Government Printing Office, 1958.

Hersey, P., & Blanchard, K. H. *Management of organizational behavior: Utilizing human resources.* Englewood Cliffs, NJ: Prentice-Hall, 1977.

Herzberg, F. *The motivation to work.* New York: John Wiley and Sons, 1959.

Herzberg, F. Piecing together generations of values. *Industry Week,* October 1, 1979, 58–63.

Hobbs, N. *The futures of children.* San Francisco: Jossey-Bass, 1975.

Illich, I. *Deschooling society.* New York: Harper & Row, 1970.

Jones, V. *Adolescents with behavior problems: Strategies for teaching, counseling, and parent involvement.* Boston: Allyn & Bacon, 1980.

Kahn, A. J. Agenda for change. In D. M. Pappenfort, D. M. Kilpatrick, & R. W. Roberts (Eds.), *Child caring: Social policy and the institution.* Chicago: Aldine, 1973.

Katz, M. B. *Class, bureaucracy, and schools: The illusion of educational change in America.* New York: Praeger, 1971.

Keith-Lucas, A., & Sanford, C. *Group child care as a family service.* Chapel Hill, NC: University of North Carolina Press, 1977.

Koontz, H., & O'Donnell, C. *Essentials of management.* New York: McGraw-Hill, 1978.

Kroth, R., & Scholl, G. *Getting schools involved with parents.* Reston, VA: Council for Exceptional Children, 1978.

Lacks, P., Landsbaum, J., & Stern, M. Workshop in communication for members of the psychiatric teams. *Psychological Reports,* 1970, *26,* 423–430.

Lebuffe, L., & Lebuffe, J. The learning vacation: A formula for parent education. *Teaching Exceptional Children,* 1982, *14*(5), 182–185.

Lerner, M. *Values in education: Notes toward a values philosophy.* Phi Delta Kappa: Bloomington, Indiana, 1976, p. 84.

Likert, R., & Likert, J. *New ways of managing conflict.* New York: McGraw-Hill, 1976.

Lippit, G. L. *Organizational renewal.* New York: Appleton-Century-Crofts, 1969.

Losen, S., & Diament, B. *Parent conferences in the schools: Procedures for developing effective partnership.* Boston: Allyn & Bacon, 1978.

McGregor, D. *The human side of enterprise.* New York: McGraw-Hill, 1960.

McKinnon, A. Attrition, burnout and job satisfaction of teachers of the emotionally disturbed. Presented to Council for Children with Behavioral Disorders Conference, Minneapolis, August 13, 1980.

Maslow, A. *Motivation and personality.* New York: Harper & Row, 1954.

Mayer, M., Richman, L., & Balcerzak, E. *Group care of children: Crossroads and transitions.* New York: Child Welfare League of America, 1977.

Miller, W. B. Two concepts of authority. *The American Anthropologist, 1955, 57* (April), 271–289.

Morse, W. (Ed.). *Humanistic teaching for exceptional children—An introduction to special education.* Syracuse: Syracuse University Press, 1979.

Mumford, L. *The culture of cities.* New York: Harcourt, Brace, 1938.

Nesbit, R. A. *The quest for community.* New York: Oxford University Press, 1953.

Newman, F. Reducing student alienation in high schools: Implications in theory. *Harvard Education Review,* 1981, *51*(4), 546–564.

Ouchi, W. *Theory Z: How American business can meet the Japanese challenge*. New York: Avon, 1981.

Page, D. *Theory and practice of teaching*. New York: A. S. Barnes, 1847 (rev. 1885).

Parsons, C. School then work/work then school/school then. . . . *The Christian Science Monitor*, April 21, 1980, p. B-3.

Payne, W. H. *Chapters on school supervision*. Cincinnati: Wilson, Hinkle, 1875.

Ponder, G. Schooling and control: Some interpretations of the changing social function of curriculum. In O. L. Davis (Ed.), *Perspectives on curriculum development 1776-1976*. Washington, DC: Association for Supervision and Curriculum Development, 1976.

Rosaler, J. *How to make the best school council in the world: A guidebook for school improvement councils and other school-community groups*. Sacramento, CA: California State Department of Education, 1979.

Sarason, S. S., & Doris, J. *Educational handicap, public policy, and social history: A broadened perspective on mental retardation*. New York: The Free Press, 1979.

Sarri, R. C., & Maple, F. F. (Eds.). *The school in the community*. Washington, DC: National Association of Social Workers, Inc., 1972.

Schalock, D. Research on teacher selection. In D. C. Berliner (Ed.), *Review of research in education*. Tuscon University of Arizona: American Educational Research Association, 1979.

Selisman, M. *Strategies for helping parents with exceptional children: A guide for teachers*. New York: MacMillan, 1979.

Simches, R. F. The parent professional partnership. *Exceptional Children*, 1975, *41*, 565-566.

Smucker, G. A. *Organizational factors associated with conflict between child care workers and clinical workers in residential institutions for emotionally disturbed children*. Ph.D. Dissertation, University of Chicago, Chicago, IL, June 1975.

Sonnenschein, P. Parents and professionals: An uneasy relationship. *Teaching Exceptional Children*, 1981, *14*(2), 62-65.

Stone, N. D. Effecting interdisciplinary consideration in clinical services to the mentally retarded. *American Journal of Orthopsychiatry*, 1970, *40*, 835-840.

Thomas, D. C. An assessment of the patterns of the quality of care in central/south Texas child care institutions and the implications of the patterns in quality of care. Centennial Lecture, Incarnate Word College, San Antonio, TX: March 1981.

Trieschman, A., & Whittaker, J. (Eds.). *Children away from home: A sourcebook of residential treatment*. Chicago: Aldine, 1972.

Turnbull, A., & Turnbull, H. *Parents speak out: Views from the other side of the two way mirror*. Columbus, OH: Charles A. Merrill, 1978.

Veblen, T. *The higher learning in America*. New York: Century Press, 1918. (Reprinted, 1965.)

Vernberg, E., & Medway, F. Teacher and parent causal perceptions of school problems. *American Educational Research Journal*, 1981, *18*(1), 29-37.

Vorrath, H., & Brendtro, L. *Positive peer culture*. Chicago: Aldine, 1974.

Wagner, R. J. Rehabilitation team practice. *Rehabilitation Counseling Bulletin*, 1977, *21*, 206-217.

Whittaker, J. The ecology of child treatment: A developmental education approach to the therapeutic milieu. *Journal of autism and child schizophrenia*, 1975, *5*(3), 223-237.

Whittaker, J. *Caring for troubled children: Residential treatment in a community context*. San Francisco: Jossey-Bass, 1979.

Whittaker, J. K., & Trieschman, A. E. (Eds.). *Children away from home: A source book of residential treatment*. Chicago: Aldine, 1972.

PART II

Formats for Teaching and Treatment

In the preceding chapters we have identified individual, group, and organizational variables that provide the foundations of the powerful environment. In the following five chapters we shall discuss a range of intervention strategies that can be built on these foundations. Chapter 5 presents a psychoeducational approach to differential diagnosis and outlines various treatment interventions including (1) managing immediate behavior, (2) systematic behavior modification, (3) crisis management, and (4) affective re-education. In Chapter 6 we re-examine one of the classic early concepts in counseling aggressive children, the life-space interview, in light of contemporary practice. Chapter 7 discusses the increasing use of peer group approaches and provides specific guidelines for appropriate applications of this methodology and the generalization of caring behavior. Chapter 8 discusses the contributions that therapeutic recreation activities can make to education and treatment approaches with disturbed and delinquent children. Finally, Chapter 9 highlights the role of the creative arts in the various theories for re-educating troubled children.

The strategies considered in this section are only representative and do not include many other useful approaches. For example, treatment formats such as Glasser's (1969, *Schools Without Failure*, New York: Harper & Row) reality therapy and instructional formats such as Hewett's engineered classroom (Hewett and Taylor, 1980, *The Emotionally Disturbed Child in the Classroom*, Boston: Allyn and Bacon) have found wide acceptance. Although limitations of space preclude discussion of such worthwhile approaches, literature on these methods is readily available elsewhere. The seriousness of children's problems and the complexity of their needs should challenge the concerned practitioner to consider carefully a variety of possible formats for teaching and treatment.

Psychoeducational Management: Individualizing Treatment

5

LARRY K. BRENDTRO, ARLIN E. NESS, AND JOANNE F. MILBURN

> To be judged fairly, this
> young man must only be
> compared with himself.
> — Itard in *The Wild
> Boy of Aveyron*

Because behavior is the result of unique personal and situational factors, appropriate treatment requires an understanding of the individual child in relation to the environment. This chapter proposes a holistic model for the differential diagnosis and treatment of troubled children that combines Redl's classic contributions on treatment with current concepts of learning and behavior. We believe that the most powerful approach to re-education results from the synthesis of methods that have long been seen as contradictory rather than complementary.

THE DEVELOPMENT OF THE PSYCHOEDUCATIONAL MODEL

In the 1950's Fritz Redl formulated what was perhaps the first truly comprehensive strategy for managing children in conflict (Redl & Wineman, 1951, 1952). In contrast to certain psychiatric approaches then in vogue, Redl saw behavior as more than "just a symptom." He recognized that those who worked directly with children — teachers, group workers, and recreation and child care workers — needed immediate and viable intervention techniques. They could not afford to wait until the therapist arrived to place the child in the pressure chamber of individual psychotherapy where a child's long repressed early memories would be probed by the analyst. Rather, these front-line workers needed techniques that would work in the here and now.

Redl developed a strategy for treating troubled children that was remarkably thorough and pragmatic. In *Controls from Within* (Redl & Wineman, 1952) the major components of this approach were outlined. They included the physical setting, routines, relationships, and activities as well as methods for managing behavior and emotions. Perhaps Redl's most well-known contribution was his concept of the life-space interview. Redl identified two kinds of interviews. *Emotional first-aid* involved supporting children in time of crisis and *clinical exploitation of life events* made use of behavioral incidents for the purposes of re-education.

The foundations of Redl's methodology were eclectic; concepts were drawn from psychodynamic, ecological, and crisis intervention theory, and the approach was characterized by a strong practice orientation. It is important to remember that most of Redl's writing occurred at a time when behavioral approaches with troubled children had not yet achieved prominence. His intended audience included psychotherapists who often espoused permissive psychoanalytic philosophies. Redl himself was an educator and psychologist without medical training; however, he did possess impeccable credentials in psychoanalysis, having studied with two of Sigmund Freud's most outstanding colleagues — the pioneering delinquency expert August Aichorn, and Freud's own daughter, Anna. With this background, Redl was something of a renegade to the classic therapist who had little knowledge of or involvement in managing troublesome behavior.

Redl's ideas are as relevant and poignant now as when they were first penned. Nevertheless, his creative style of writing can confuse those accustomed to a literature of tightly reasoned empirical studies. Furthermore, because he was addressing himself to psychoanalytically trained colleagues, it is unfair to evaluate these works against the criteria of contemporary behavioral literature. When Redl talks of "antiseptic bouncing" or of "hypodermic affection" he is speaking of what others today might call "nonpunitive time out" or "social reinforcement." Only by recalling the psychiatrically dominated context in which he was trying to communicate can one understand clearly the metaphor and imagery.

DIFFERENTIAL DIAGNOSIS AND TREATMENT

Practitioners have for a number of years been confronted by two fundamentally opposed views of disordered behavior. (1) The classic *psychodynamic position* held that disturbed behavior was only a symptom and that the real problem was an underlying personality conflict that had to be resolved. (2) The classic *behaviorist view* was that behavior itself was the problem, and changing the behavior eliminated the problem. Redl's writings seem to acknowledge the value in each of these seemingly polarized views.

Redl challenged his psychoanalytic colleagues with the argument that "surface behavior" was itself worthy of observation and manipulation and that many problems would yield to influence at the behavioral level without employing complex psychotherapeutic procedures. On the other hand, he did not routinely ignore the perceptual and affective processes; his clinical research showed clearly that the child's inner life often served to elicit or perpetuate problem behavior. Thus he believed that it was necessary to make an informed judgment about whether a given problem could best be handled at the level of behavior or at the level of emotions. This required a differential diagnosis, that is, an assessment of the child and his life space in order to understand the meaning and significance of the behavior.

Assessing the Problem

As we have seen, a central tenet of the psychoeducational approach is to understand the situational and personal variables that give rise to a specific problem and then to select the appropriate intervention. When confronted with the complexity of a unique individual in his or her unique environment, one can easily feel at a loss for where to begin. Given an immediate behavioral problem, how can we assess its meaning and significance? Only when we know what the behavior means can we make an intelligent decision about the appropriate intervention. Morse (1980) suggests that we can understand behavior by testing for depth and spread. Table 5-1 summarizes this process. As we can see from the vertical dimension (depth), the problem can be viewed at one of two levels, namely, as *behavioral* or *emotional*. The horizontal dimension (spread) separates problems that are tied to an immediate situation from those that are part of a recurring and persistent pattern of behavior. Notice that the four cells of the grid are labeled as behav-

Table 5-1. Assessing the Problem: Testing for Depth and Spread

	Situational	← SPREAD →	Pervasive
Behavioral level ↑ D E P T H ↓ Emotional level	Behavioral incident		Pattern of disordered behavior
	Crisis reaction		Pattern of distorted values, attitudes or feelings

ioral incident, pattern of disordered behavior, crisis reaction, and pattern of distorted values, attitudes, or feelings. Perhaps some specific examples will clarify these categories.

1. *Behavioral incident.* Two boys jostle over the front seat of the school bus. If this is all we know about the situation, we might assume that this is an isolated problem not heavily connected with emotions or feelings.

2. *Pattern of disordered behavior.* Ralph almost never completes chores assigned to him. Here we are dealing with a problem that apparently is recurrent and suggests a persistent or pervasive pattern of behaving. We may not, however, have any reason to believe that this problem is related to underlying feelings.

3. *Crisis reaction.* Two girls who were the best of friends are now both very upset because of something that happened between them. Here we have reason to believe that some specific event or stress produced the behavior. Because strong feelings are evident, we interpret this behavior as an emotional response to a specific situation.

4. *Patterns of distorted values, attitudes, or feelings.* When not chosen in a game, John mutters quietly, as if to himself, "See, everybody hates me." Here there are indications of a strong emotional component to the problem and the suggestion that John's reaction is part of a pervasive pattern of seeing the world as against him.

Table 5-2 provides other possible examples of behavior as they might be assigned to various quadrants in the grid. It should be noted, of course, that, depending on other information available, any of these behaviors might be placed in another category.

Table 5-2. Examples of Behavioral Problems Classified

	Situational ← SPREAD → Pervasive	
Behavioral level ↑ D E P T H ↓ Emotional level	*Behavioral incident* Susan uses inappropriate language. Don becomes noisy and restless just before the bell is to ring.	*Pattern of disordered behavior* Mary pokes any child who walks near her. Billy always shouts out without raising his hand.
	Crisis reaction Angela is upset when her parents are the only ones not to visit. Billy is disturbed because his dog was killed by a car this morning.	*Pattern of distorted values, attitudes, feelings* Karl shakes down weaker peers for money with no sign of guilt. When praised, Tony says it is a lie and we are being paid to say nice things.

Selecting the Intervention

Assuming that we have properly assigned the problem to the appropriate quadrant, we are now able to select an intervention that matches the particular problem. Table 5-3 identifies the four basic strategies for intervention based on differential diagnosis for depth and spread. If behavior is seen only as a disruption in the immediate situation, then the intervention would be to manage the immediate behavior and no more. If, however, we are looking at a pattern of disordered behavior,

Table 5-3. Selecting the Intervention Strategy

	Situational ← SPREAD → Pervasive	
Behavioral level ↑ D E P T H ↓ Emotional level	Managing immediate behavior	Systematic behavior modification
	Crisis management	Affective re-education

then the likely intervention would be some program of systematic behavior modification. At the emotional level, if the problem seems to be a response to a specific situation of stress or crisis, the appropriate intervention would be crisis management. Finally, if the problem suggests a generalized pattern of distorted values, attitudes, or feelings, the appropriate intervention strategy to create long-range change would be effective re-education.

The flow chart in Figure 5-1 summarizes the process of differential diagnosis. By taking into consideration all the available information about the person in the life-space, these two basic assessments are made:

1. *Test for depth.* Does the problem appear to be clear-cut, limited to behavior itself? Or does the behavior appear to be influenced by some inner affective state? On the basis of this test, the problem can be assigned to the behavioral or emotional level.
2. *Test for spread.* Does the problem seem to be tied to a specific immediate situation? Or does it represent an example of a recurring and persistent pattern? With this assessment, the problem can be assigned to one of the four major intervention strategies.

Although it would be ideal if each behavioral episode or emotional problem could be managed with a carefully selected strategy, reality is never so tidy as this. The demands of the immediate situation sometimes force the youth worker to use a technique that is available rather than one that is desirable. It is important, however, that whatever methods are used facilitate insofar as possible both the short- and long-term behavioral adjustment of children.

Various professional groups working with troubled youth have tended to concentrate on one of these four broad strategies of intervention. Thus, front-line youth workers, teachers, and child care personnel spend most of their efforts managing immediate behavior and may not feel that they have either the time or the training to become involved in other more complex strategies. In contrast, behavioral psychologists have generally concentrated on systematic behavior modification. Their major interest has been identifying patterns of persistent disordered behavior, assessing these target behaviors, and applying reinforcement strategies to modify behavior. A different strategy is followed by professionals (and paraprofessionals) who are involved in crisis intervention counseling, such as with suicide prevention hot-lines or in runaway centers. Here the focus is on managing the precipitating crisis that is creating a situational emotional disturbance. Finally, psychotherapists have traditionally concentrated on what we have termed affective re-education. In fact, the classic therapist tended to avoid involvement in more immediate problems of the client in

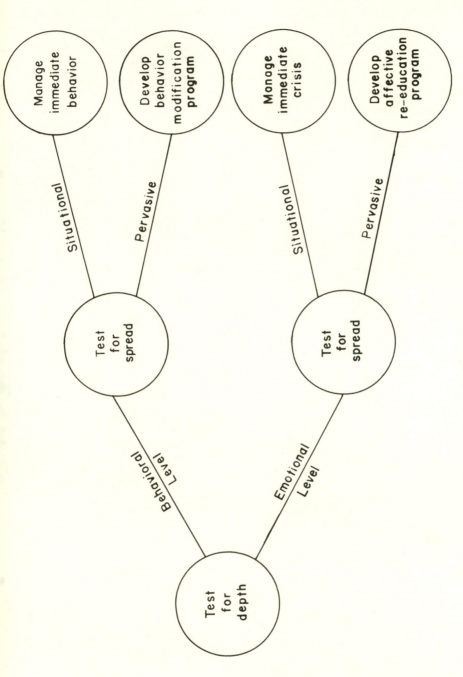

FIG. 5-1. Process of differential diagnosis and treatment.

order to concentrate on changing long-standing patterns of personality.

Table 5-4 suggests the wide range of intervention techniques that would be subsumed within the four broad strategies. It is our contention that the most effective practitioners in child and youth services will be those who are competent with multiple intervention strategies. In the following sections we shall consider these major strategies in greater detail.

MANAGING IMMEDIATE BEHAVIOR

The most common intervention strategy is to respond to the immediate behavior in the immediate situation. Perhaps the greatest bulk of behavior encountered by the practitioner is most easily understood as a product of a specific situation. When a child becomes restless shortly before recess, it would be a most unusual teacher who would assume this to be part of a long-term pattern or a deep-seated emotional problem. Probably the best test of whether a problem should be handled *in situ* is whether the intervention works. If a problem is resolved by a simple intervention (*"Please take your seat"*), there is probably no

Table 5-4. Examples of Intervention Techniques

	Situational	← SPREAD →	Pervasive
Behavioral level	*Managing immediate behavior* Redl's influence techniques Peer group control techniques Other behavioral techniques		*Systematic behavior modification* Token economies Behavioral contracting Other behavior modification techniques Social skills training
↑ D E P T H ↓	*Crisis management* LSI—Emotional first-aid Assertiveness training Other crisis intervention or stress management techniques		*Affective re-education* LSI—Exploitation of life events Individual or group counseling Values clarification Teaching self-control Other affective–cognitive techniques
Emotional level			

need to pursue it further. Most problems can in fact be handled in this manner, but if they recur another strategy may be elected. Frequently, a teacher or youth worker will sense that there is more to the visible problem than meets the eye but will still choose to handle it as immediate short-run behavior. Practical considerations may preclude a more sophisticated intervention, and one may just have to wait for another time. For example, one's options are rather limited when driving down a crowded freeway in a station wagon full of noisy youngsters, one of whom is giving objectionable hand signs to passengers in adjacent vehicles. Whatever the depth or spread of such behavior, sometimes you just do what you have to do.

Fritz Redl identified a full range of possible interventions that are employed to manage immediate behavior. He noted that sometimes one chooses strategically not to intervene, either because one accepts the behavior (e.g., "This is what we should expect from youngsters at this age") or because one tolerates the behavior ("I don't like it but I think they are going to have to learn to handle this themselves"). If the teacher or group worker decides to intervene, the following are the major methods available based on Redl's clinical research (Redl & Wineman, 1952).

1. *Planned ignoring.* If the adult assumes that a given behavior will run its course and have minimal impact, the decision might be to ignore the behavior. Sometimes a behavior is ignored because the child seems to be seeking attention for his naughtiness, and to respond even with a punishment would be reinforcing.

—Two boys are shadow boxing and seem to be taunting the adult to intervene and make them stop. The adult, concluding that they are not intent on harming one another, pretends it is not happening and the youngsters discontinue their activity.

Naturally, there are many situations in which ignoring behavior is the wrong thing to do. Ignoring a serious infraction may actually signal acceptance. Thus a teacher who ignores a racial insult directed at a minority youth would be giving tacit approval to such name-calling. Likewise, some incidents are highly likely to become contagious, and, if the teacher does not stop the behavior, several other behavioral problems will probably result.

2. *Signaling.* Sometimes a youngster is unaware of his or her behavior or is unable to control it but will respond to some nonverbal signal from the adult. This signal may be as simple as eye contact, perhaps while shaking one's head no, or it could be a more personalized signal understood to the parties involved. The advantage of signals is that the

adult can intervene quickly and quietly, and most signals do not elicit a negative response from the youth.

—Tony is standing on a piece of furniture. The adult catches his eye and simply points to the ground, whereupon Tony dismounts from his perch.

Signaling cannot be used in highly explosive situations and may be an insufficient response to a serious behavioral infraction. Signaling can be highly personalized; for example, an adult and youth can agree that whenever the youth is about to be drawn into negative behavior by a peer, the adult will signal a warning. Thus, signaling is an efficient intervention if applied to the proper behavior.

3. *Proximity and touch control.* Sometimes excitement, anxiety, and restlessness can be minimized by physical proximity between the child and adult. By walking to an area around or near the child, or by calling the child to an area near the adult, one may effectively alter the dynamics of the problem. Children respond in different ways to proximity, particularly if it involves very close contact, such as touching, and an adult must be aware of a given child's response.

—Two boys working on a craft project in a corner of the room are becoming unruly. The adult walks over toward that corner, not with the attitude of policing the area, but to inquire about how their project is coming. The youngsters resume task-oriented behavior.

One caution about the use of proximity is that certain children may learn to lure the adult closer to them through acting-out behavior. Other children find close proximity with an adult, particularly touching, to be highly aversive. The unique meaning that closeness and physical contact has to a child must be understood if the adult is to use this technique skillfully.

4. *Interest-boosting.* Many of the problems of troubled youngsters can be either ameliorated or prevented by increasing the interest level in the curriculum or activity at hand. However, if the adult cannot become excited about the topic or activity, it should not be surprising if the youngsters act bored. One can raise the interest level of any activity in various ways. One possibility is to promote those aspects of a given topic or activity that might attract the youngsters' attention.

—Youngsters who do not know much about soccer or show little interest in it become very involved by viewing an action-packed movie of a championship soccer game.

Another approach to interest-boosting involves tying the activity to an existing interest of the youngster.

— Knowing that a given child is interested in diesel trucks, one could tap this interest and tie it to a science experiment showing that air under high pressure becomes heated.

Many troubled youth seem to have an almost insatiable appetite for adventure, and thus it will be a considerable challenge to the adult to keep these children interested and involved. Of course, it is neither necessary nor desirable for the adult to keep a group in a constant state of "hype." Sometimes youngsters need the opportunity to learn to complete tasks or activities that are in fact unexciting and mundane. Nevertheless, the planful use of interest-boosting can be a powerful technique in the repertoire of the behavioral manager.

5. *Hypodermic affection.* Redl acknowledges that this was a rather contrived term, meant simply to convey that sometimes by giving a dose of warm attention, one can manage a particular problem.

— Redl tells of a situation in which a sobbing, violently upset child who felt that nobody liked him was making an attempt to jump out the second story window of the group home. Redl wrapped his arms around the youngster, told him everything was okay, and assured him he was loved. The youngster stopped sobbing and in a few minutes was back to normal.

Like the other management techniques, hypodermic affection has its contraindications. Redl himself noted that special doses of love should not be seen as cures for temper tantrums or negativistic behavior. Its strategic use is to help enable a youngster whose own self-control is deteriorating to regain his composure. If doses of attention followed most negative behavior, the obvious result would be that one would reinforce destructive and aggressive acts.

6. *Humor.* This technique probably has been used since humans first learned to laugh as a means of emotional release. The adult who can spontaneously but skillfully invoke humor into an otherwise difficult situation has learned to use an important tool. Not only does humor serve to reduce immediate tension, but it allows participants in a power struggle to save face and it legitimizes a complete reversal of the affective climate from negative to positive.

— Eddie was a bright 10-year-old youth with spinabifida enrolled in a residential hospital–school for crippled children. Because of his handicap he had to wear diapers and it was his responsibility to change them as needed. One day when it was obvious to every other youngster in the group and the adult that it was time for him to change, he refused. "You're not gonna make me change my diaper; the nurses aren't gonna make me change my diaper; the director isn't gonna make me change my diaper; nobody's gonna make me change my diaper!" he exclaimed. Just as the adult was about to become locked into a power struggle, the image of trying to forcibly change a 10-year-old's diaper flashed through his mind, and the teacher looked at the youth out of the corner of his eye and began to laugh uproariously. After a few seconds of puzzled expression, the boy himself began to giggle and then joined in peals of laughter, whereupon he left the room to take care of his chore.

Caution is also necessary with the use of humor. If humor is hostile, i.e., sarcasm, barbs, or making the child the butt of jokes, then the technique should be expected to backfire. There is a big difference between laughing *with* and laughing *at* an individual. Some disturbed children are so sensitive about others making fun of them that they are likely to misinterpret even well-meaning humor. In general, however, humor is one of the most useful and human of the intervention techniques.

7. *Lowering hurdles.* Many behavioral problems result from frustration at not being able to complete a task successfully. By lessening the difficulty, breaking the task into smaller steps, or helping the youngster approach the task from another direction, the adult can avoid the frustration of failure.

— The craft shop at the University of Michigan Fresh Air Camp always had an abundance of instant-success projects. They were designed so that a youngster with an extremely short attention span or a low frustration tolerance would have only to "blow" upon them and a beautiful, completed project would spring to life.

This technique too has its flaws, for there are benefits to frustration, and excessive use of hurdle help will serve only to keep youngsters incompetent and overprotected. Children should not be deprived of the opportunity of struggling with a difficult challenge and knowing the reality of both success and failure.

8. *Interpretation.* Redl did not mean by this term that one would go about the group offering amateur psychoanalytic insights as to why children were behaving as they do. Instead, this technique involves providing youngsters with concrete, reality-based explanations of what is happening to them in a given behavioral situation, under the assumption that this information might help them organize their experience.

—Everyone in the room was sweltering from spending too much time together in a place that desperately needed air conditioning. People were getting on one another's nerves and irritability was rampant. "I know we are all getting a little restless and short-tempered because of the heat," said the adult, "so we'll have to try extra hard not to make things worse for one another."

Interpretation can, of course, be easily overused. If it is to be effective, the people involved must be quite capable of interrupting their own behavior. We know that much behavior is not under such simple verbal control. Furthermore, a worker who goes about offering uninvited interpretations of everybody's actions can easily become more of an annoyance than a help.

9. *Regrouping.* Sometimes the simple device of changing the group's psychological constellation will eradicate a problem that otherwise would require considerable management effort. Regrouping at the extreme may involve removing a youngster from a given group and assigning him elsewhere, such as transferring a youth to a different school. More commonly, regrouping will occur within the immediate setting, perhaps by assigning the youngster to another subgroup.

—Although most of the class was working on the assignment, two boys were distracting peers in their respective corners of the room. Tony, as usual, had completed the exercise ahead of everyone else, was now bored, and was seeking to communicate with those around him. Bill, on the other hand, had scarcely begun, looked completely puzzled, and found it more fun to giggle with those around him than to face the task. The teacher resolved both problems simultaneously by calling Tony and Bill over to another corner of the room and asking Tony to help Bill understand the project and complete it. Soon these two boys were busily involved in the task at hand and those they had been distracting resumed their work.

Sometimes regrouping only avoids dealing with an issue that merits our attention. Thus although we might use regrouping to separate two youngsters who cannot get along, it might be preferable if we could figure out why they are having trouble and teach them to relate with one another.

10. *Restructuring.* Many behavioral problems can be prevented or resolved by altering the structure of a particular activity. When activities are completely unstructured, troubled youngsters frequently find it very hard to organize themselves and keep out of difficulty. Most young people require some sort of routine or ritual that can provide a sense of order and flow to their behavior. Transition times (moving from one structure to another) frequently are fraught with complications and

thus it even may be necessary with some children to structure these interludes.

> —Because the children always seem to have trouble choosing up sides, today I handed each a card with the numbers 1, 2, or 3 printed on it as they entered the room. I then began the activity by saying, "Everybody with the card number 1 please stand in this corner; everybody with the card number 2, over there; and everybody with card number 3, over here." It took half the time and there were none of the fights associated with choosing up sides.

Another important type of structure pertains to expectations. If youngsters know or can be told what is to happen in a certain situation, the behavior will most likely be more organized.

> —Knowing of the pandemonium that could result in our trip to the hockey stadium, I laid down this structure for the youth: "When we arrive, we are going to go to the rest room if we need to, buy our popcorn, and then we will all sit together in a group." Without setting these expectations, I have found that I cannot keep my group assembled.

The only obvious limitation of the use of structure would be using it excessively. All children need free time when their activity is not programmed for them. The purpose of structure is to help youngsters learn to organize themselves in the hope that they will eventually be able to organize their own behavior through internal structure rather than having it imposed externally.

11. *Direct appeal.* Frequently a drastic intervention is not at all necessary; youngsters may respond to a simple appeal. Redl authored a large list of potential examples of the use of this technique, including the following:

> —*Appealing to relationship:* "Listen, you don't have to act like this. I've been fair to you."
> —*Appealing to reality:* "You can't do that; it's dangerous. You might fall."
> —*Appealing to values:* "You wouldn't really want to do that, would you?"
> —*Appealing to group code:* "Do you think others in your group would think that is fair?"
> —*Appealing to authority:* "What do you think the principal (your parents, etc.) would think?"
> —*Appealing to pride:* "You don't have to act that way any more. You're much more mature now."

Youngsters vary greatly in their receptiveness to appeals. Because an appeal is an easy technique to use, it is also easy to overuse. The adult who is constantly asking youngsters to change their behavior can become very ineffective.

12. *Limiting space and tools.* The physical space itself, and the presence of seductive objects, can affect a youngster's behavior.

> —Six special education students were crammed in a classroom not much larger than an office. They were all within reach of one another, and could fiddle with props such as Venetian blinds, the thermostat, and pictures on the wall without even leaving their desks.

Many objects almost invite youngsters to handle and perhaps misuse them. Bats are for hitting; balls are for bouncing; knives are for cutting; flashlights are for shining; and if we are not interested in any of these activities, we should not have the objects near at hand. The manner in which concrete materials are distributed can also serve to create or eliminate problems.

> —The teacher who says, "You can each go up to the table and get your copy of the exercise" may be inviting a shoving match, whereas if the same objects were dealt out to children at their desks, problems could be prevented.

A number of years ago it was fashionable in classrooms of hyperactive and disturbed children to remove any kind of potentially distracting stimuli. Certainly this became excessive as teachers purged the classroom of guppies, posters, and brightly colored globes or maps, and even avoided wearing jewelry and attractive clothing. The hope was that if only a pencil, a worksheet, and a cubicle remained, the youngster would not be distracted. Although few now advocate such thoroughgoing stimulus deprivation, the effective youth worker or teacher needs to be very cognizant of the ability of the physical environment to elicit appropriate or inappropriate behavior.

13. *Physical removal.* Redl used the term "antiseptic bouncing" to refer to the nonpunitive removal of a youngster from the group situation. The purpose of this removal was not banishment, or even to deprive the youngster of positive reinforcement, but to allow him or her an opportunity to gain behavioral composure in the absence of an audience.

> —Marie became so uncontrolled while watching "Peter Pan" on television that she began "flying" across the room, jumping from couch to couch, much to the delight of her peers. When she was unable to stop after verbal appeals, the staff member led her from the room and had her sit quietly until she was more composed and could return to the room.

There has been a great deal of concern about the misuse of techniques for removal in a number of treatment programs. In most settings, workers find it necessary at some point to remove youngsters from the group, but the manner in which this is done varies greatly from setting to setting. The process may be given names such as "time out," "seclusion," "solitary," or "going to your room." Of particular concern with emotionally disturbed children is the kind of supervision they receive during this time when they are removed. Many quality treatment programs have clearly defined procedures governing the use of exclusion that specify the kind of monitoring required for the youth during such time. Since it is known that the risk of suicide among disturbed youth is much higher when they are in seclusion because of behavioral problems, staff have a very profound responsibility to ensure the physical (and psychological) safety of the youth. A youth who has been excluded at a time of emotional upset and aggressive behavior can readily turn that aggression on himself, as seen in the following example taken from a psychiatric residential treatment center.

—Todd had been having difficulty with peers all evening and finally ended up brandishing a pool cue as a weapon in some disagreement with peers. The psychiatric resident on call was summoned and Todd was confined to his room. In a few minutes Todd began destroying his room and throwing drawers out the door, whereupon he was removed to a more secure isolation room, which was locked and furnished with only a mattress on the floor. The procedures then in effect called for staff to visually check on him through a small window in the doorway at least every 15 minutes. At the first check, staff noticed that the mattress had been torn to shreds but Todd was not visible. Upon unlocking the door, it was discovered that Todd had taken strips of cloth, wrapped them around his neck, tied them to the inside doorknob and attempted to hang himself in a seated position. Fortunately, Todd was still conscious; the staff removed Todd's homemade noose. While moments before Todd had been attacking everyone in sight, all he could do now was to sob, "Why did you stop me? Let me die. I'm no good; let me die."

Although this incident ended fortunately, the residential treatment program now requires continuous visual observation of youngsters who are in locked isolation.

14. *Physical restraint.* However skillful staff are in using less extreme measures, there is always the possibility that a particular youngster will be so upset and out of control that his behavior presents a serious risk to himself and to others. It may not be possible or advisable to use an isolation room for restraint. (Where would one isolate a youngster while on a camping expedition?) Physical restraint becomes an extreme but sometimes necessary intervention technique.

If the adult is considerably larger and stronger than the child, then physical restraint can usually be executed with little danger of hurting either the child or the adult. A useful technique is for the adult to stand behind the child and wrap the child's arms across the child's stomach. The child cannot hurt himself in this position, and if the adult is cautious about the possibility of being kicked or butted with the head, the adult can also avoid injury. A particularly strong youngster may need to be held on the floor in a prone position. Although a youth so restrained will probably accuse the adult of hurting him, in reality the child is not being hurt when properly held.

If the child's physical size, strength, or agility closely matches or exceeds that of the adult, then it is inadvisable to use physical restraint since restraint itself is likely to cause injury to one or both parties. In that stituation it may be necessary to call for assistance. In a school setting this might involve summoning the principal, coach, or custodian. With young people who are virtually adults in size and strength, it may even be necessary in isolated situations to call on school security or law enforcement personnel.

Another approach that has worked effectively in peer group treatment programs is to involve other youth strategically in the process of containing a youth who is otherwise going to hurt someone. The fact that difficult youth can undertake this task responsibly is a surprise to many people who are accustomed to seeing peer groups cheer on youth who are in combat with one another or with authority figures. However, a generally concerned and well-trained group can assist in restraining a youngster who otherwise would hurt himself or others. Needless to say, the adult present in such a situation bears the ultimate responsibility for taking whatever precautions are necessary to minimize the likelihood that anyone will be hurt in the process.

Observations of many instances in which physical restraint has been used suggest that most youngsters behave in a predictable fashion when restrained (Long & Duffner, 1980):

> *The struggle.* Initially the youngster will fight violently to break loose, will make every manner of verbal threat or appeal he can think of. He may threaten to kill everybody; he may scream that the adult or group restraining him is breaking his arm; he may shout, plead, spit, bite, or butt. It is important that the person or persons doing the restraining carry it out with a quiet, gentle strength. Any counter-aggressive hostility, verbal or nonverbal, will serve only to support the youth's distorted perception that he is being attacked and will interfere with subsequent attempts to communicate about the episode. Thus in a quiet, steady, concerned manner, the person or persons restraining should communicate to the youth that he needs to settle down and relax, that no one will hurt him, that everybody is concerned about helping him, and that he is able to get control of himself.

Emotional release. Unable to prevail through aggression, the child loses emotional control, defenses collapse, and toughness is stripped away. As he realizes that he cannot extricate himself and that he is, in fact, being controlled, his aggression turns to tears. As the tenor of the crying changes from anger to child-like dependency, the adult is usually able to relax the restraint slightly.

Regaining self-control. The youth next may enter a period of silence in order to regain control of emotions and behavior. If the physical restraint has not been removed already, it can usually be discontinued at this time. The youngster may now be ready to communicate in a more coherent and logical fashion. Some children may need to sulk for awhile, but a skillful adult can determine the time and manner for reopening communication.

Few individuals have learned through normal life experiences how to handle physical restraint in a therapeutic manner. Everything about such an episode tends to call forth responses of either fear or aggression from the adult. Thus a crucial factor in using physical restraint is that the adult be able to monitor and control his own feelings of anxiety or aggression. As the adult is able to communicate genuine concern even in this kind of crisis, he has the opportunity of making a significant impact on the way the child views the adult and himself.

On rare occasions, one can encounter a youngster who seems to seek out physical restraint and obtain some sort of gratification from being held by the adult. Of course in this situation one does not want to use physical restraint in such a reinforcing fashion. It may be better with such a youngster to (1) try to avoid physical restraint, (2) use physical isolation as an alternative to restraint, or (3) physically restrain the child in a manner that minimizes physical contact between the child and adult. In this regard, a variation with smaller youngsters is to place the child in a chair and restrain him in the usual fashion with the adult holding the child's arms but kneeling behind the chair. This avoids the "cradled in the arms of adults" position, which is probably reinforcing to a small number of children. Finally, physical restraint is among the most extreme interventions and should be used only when absolutely necessary, when all other possibilities have been ruled out, and when it can be applied in a safe and therapeutic manner.

15. *Authoritarian interference.* Some behavior is so unacceptable and even outrageous that it requires a sharp and clear statement by the adult that it is completely forbidden. In such a situation we are not appealing to a youngster to stop his behavior; rather, we simply say *NO* in such a way that children understand that we mean it, that there is no choice in the matter, and that we will not yield to arguments, explanations, or anything else. Some adults are much more comfortable (and effective) using this technique than others. Certainly if the adult used this style all of the time, he or she would be considered tyrannical. But

all people who work with youngsters need to know how to lay down the law in a way that conveys effectively "this is it." Needless to say, when the adult acts that strongly, he or she is going to have to back it up if young people do not respond. Thus it is important that this technique be used only when such a strong statement is necessary and when the adult is willing to follow through with some appropriate action. It has been said that working with troubled youth is a situation of saying no, meaning no, and then learning how to save face. Although that may be true in some situations, it is not the case with this technique.

16. *Promises and rewards.* All teachers and youth workers seem to use positive reinforcement or the promise of positive reinforcement in the attempt to mold behavior. Certainly this is one of the most powerful techniques available and, perhaps because of this, Redl is careful to caution the behavior manager about the problems with this approach. He notes that some children live only in the present and are not able to respond to possible future rewards. Also, many troubled youngsters cannot handle the deprivation of a reward without experiencing it as a personal attack. The unequal disposition of rewards can give rise to high levels of sibling rivalry between youngsters. Finally, rewards can communicate to a youngster that we like him only when he is good. Redl's views on rewards may seem dissonant to contemporary practitioners cognizant of the huge literature supporting the value of positive reinforcement. Nevertheless, he is not suggesting that rewards cannot be useful in the teaching process, but only that we need to be attuned to the inner processes that may accompany our dispensing of rewards or the promise of rewards. In fact, the phenomenon of "counter-control," which has frequently been noted in behavior modification programs, gives support to Redl's notion that how youngsters see rewards can be most important. We observed an example of counter-control in a particularly sophisticated 12-year-old boy who enjoyed leading his peers in wild activities carefully calculated to lose all of the 200 possible points that each of them could earn in the token system for a particular day. Such activity would not have surprised Redl at all, for he always made it clear that every intervention must be considered not only in light of its effect on observable behavior but also for its impact on the inner life of the child.

17. *Threats and punishments.* As Redl suggested, the issue of punishment is probably one of the most befuddled topics in educational practice and thought. Professionals cannot even communicate intelligently about punishment because there are so many definitions of punishment. Redl saw threat as related to punishment in the same way that promise was related to reward, and just as he raised concerns about how young people would interpret the process of "rewarding" so also he raised troubling questions about how youngsters might inter-

pret the process of punishing. According to Redl, punishment can be effective only if certain conditions are met:

— The punishment must be experienced as unpleasant or aversive.
— The negative feelings resulting from punishment must be tied to the behavior being punished and not to the person inflicting the punishment.
— The punishment must be internalized in such a way as to control the behavior in question effectively, rather than to produce defensiveness, anxiety, aggression, self-recrimination, or withdrawal.

Redl went on to show how troubled youngsters frequently distort the punishment experience. Some youngsters with very poor self-concepts or self-abusive tendencies may in fact draw punishment to themselves. Others may seem to enjoy the punishment experience, perhaps because that is the way in which they have received attention in the past. Troubled youth may distort the intention of the punishing adult, thus becoming preoccupied with the adult as an enemy rather than as one trying to help them change their behavior. For many youngsters punishment is not the end of the chain of causation but the beginning of one; the punishment allows an excuse or reason for all manner of subsequent maladaptive behavior, such as vengeance, aggression, withdrawal, and lowered self-esteem.

In spite of these cautions it should be noted that Redl himself provides numerous examples of situations in which punishment was used effectively in his Pioneer House program. Usually these applications had the quality of natural or logical consequences. For instance, dangerous behavior in the station wagon would be met by the withdrawal of the station wagon from use in activities. In addition to natural consequences, which Redl seems to support, he also notes that restitution is not the same as punishment. Thus, when a youngster messes up the bunks of other children, there can be value in requiring him to correct the problem he created. Such restitutional arrangements can help youngsters reduce guilt feelings and re-establish their positive relationships with individuals whom they have hurt. Redl also notes that some of the verbal interventions used in life-space interviews may seem to an outsider to be punishing. For example, a reality rub-in may involve a strong challenge to a youngster's behavior and being confronted can in fact be painful. The distinction that Redl makes is that of intent: the purpose of the confrontation is not to create pain but to help the youngster look at himself.

Redl also makes the distinction between threats and warnings. If a specific reality response will ensue from a particular line of behavior, the adult should feel free to warn the youngsters. Children can, for example, be told that if they cannot handle a certain activity without getting wild, they will have to return to some less exciting pastime.

Many of the 17 techniques described by Redl are not as separate from each other as their labels might imply. Most workers influence children's behavior by using a variety of these methods. Redl's goal in identifying these techniques was to highlight the wide range of interventions possible and to stimulate a careful analysis of the strengths and limitations associated with various procedures. Redl emphasized that he had no interest in substituting a bagful of interference tricks for a complete program of therapeutic processes. It is crucial, however, that adults know what they are doing when they have to interfere with behavior in the daily life of troubled children.

Alternative Views of Punishment

The punitiveness that has frequently marked the education and treatment of youth has been the subject of great debate for centuries. Over the years philosophers, educators, and social scientists of many orientations have decried punishment. Jeremy Benthem (1748–1832) said that "all punishment is mischief: all punishment is itself evil." Believing that schools should be ruled by kindness rather than fear, Pestalozzi abolished flogging to the amazement of his contemporaries. In more recent times both psychodynamic and behavioral approaches question the indiscriminate use of punishment because of its unpredictability, volatility, and tendency to suppress rather than change behavior.

Among those who advocate totally eliminating corporal punishment as a means of dealing with youth is Valusek (1980). He categorizes corporal punishment of children with other forms of human violence such as rape, riots, wife-battering, child abuse, attacks on teachers, and the use of fists, knives, and physical assault. His thesis is that if we could teach all people never to hit anyone under any circumstances, violence and its impact on mental health would cease to be a major problem. Drawing on research that suggests that most violent adults and juvenile delinquents have themselves been brutalized, Valusek notes that our society almost universally forbids physical violence, even in prisons, and yet permits hitting any and all of our children in homes, schools, and in many youth programs. To those who consider his ideals fanciful, he points out that we have already eliminated all legal uses of physical pain as a form of punishment of adults, and now have remaining only one segment of the population to which such protection has not been extended—namely, children who are dependent on us.

Cautioning that vengeful, capricious, and ill-timed punishment of aggressive children will only provide a vicious model for the child, Kauffman (1981) offers guidelines for the humane use of punishment including:

—Use only when positive approaches fail and when continuation of the behavior would be more harmful than the punishment.
—Administer without hostility, threats, or moralization and only by persons who have a warm, loving relationship with children.
—Apply consistently and promptly for specific behavior that the child knew was punishable, and apply early in the chain of undesired behavior.
—Avoid excessive intensity and relate the punishment to the misdeed (e.g., repair a broken item); withdrawal of privileges is preferable to aversive procedures such as spanking.
—Use in conjunction with other techniques that enhance the child's self-control.

The use of punishment with troubled children raises numerous philosophical, practical, and legal issues (Wood & Lakin, 1978). The emerging view appears to be that although there are appropriate roles for limited use of punishment, great care needs to be taken that procedures are properly scrutinized and controlled.

SYSTEMATIC BEHAVIOR MODIFICATION

Not all behavior yields to immediate manipulation; certain patterns of behavior persist over time and across different situations. Behaviors that tend to recur in spite of management intervention may require a systematic plan of behavior modification if they are to be changed.

A wide variety of approaches all bear the designation "behavioral," and they differ in important ways. Criswell (1981) has identified the following four categories:

1. *Radical behaviorism.* Radical means *fundamental*, that is, following rigorous empirical procedures modeled on the natural sciences. Radical behaviorists use the system of applied behavior analysis developed by Skinner to determine what environmental stimuli evoke or maintain behavior. Treatment is seen as shaping new behavior, increasing or decreasing existing behavior, and generalizing behavior beyond the treatment setting.

2. *Cognitive behavior modification.* This approach emphasizes the role of thoughts, such as counterproductive self-perceptions and self-talk, in behavior. By modifying these cognitions, it is assumed that behavior can be changed. Typical approaches are rational-emotive therapy as advanced by Ellis (1977) and the self-control

strategies of Meichenbaum (1977), described in more detail later in this chapter.

3. *Social learning theory.* This is an eclectic behavioral position extending traditional learning theories to include social modeling, and affective and cognitive dimensions. This approach is seen primarily in the work of Bandura (1977).

4. *Behavior modification.* This term has taken on a nonspecific meaning different from that put forth by Skinner (1953). Its popular usage currently refers to a wide range of techniques for changing behavior, particularly those involving the manipulation of reinforcers.

The use of behavioral methods of treatment is appropriate when behavior is free-standing, that is, when it is not entangled with distorted perceptions, attitudes, feelings, or values. When problem behavior seems to be under the direct control of specific reinforcers, then the most efficient intervention is to modify those reinforcers. Frequently children behave in ways designed to get a reward from the environment; a youngster may be naughty and then look to see if peers are noticing, or the child may whine to attract attention rather than as a genuine expression of hurt. At other times the problem is not what a child *does*, but what he is unable to do; if a child never looks other children or adults in the eye, one may decide to increase that behavior or to teach the child a specific social skill. Specific habits or styles of behavior that are most amenable to behavioral intervention are usually rather clear-cut, easily measurable, and limited in scope. If a youngster displays a potpourri of seemingly unconnected behavioral problems, behavior modification strategies may not be efficient or sufficient and it may be advisable to look for some underlying emotional factors that produce or maintain these behaviors.

Just because a child does not show overt connection between behavior and feelings does not mean, in all cases, that one would intervene at the behavioral level. For good reasons, one may still elect to intervene on a cognitive or affective level. For example, a youngster may behave callously and apparently show no guilt; if one wished to create an emotional connection with that behavior, intervention at the affective level would be indicated. Another child may act in a thoughtless manner and seem surprised at the outcome, apparently unable to predict consequences; a cognitive intervention may be indicated to help the youngster learn to think in a causal–sequential manner.

Historically behavioral psychologists have focused on behaviors that can be directly observed and manipulated. However, Skinner (1953) acknowledged that other behaviors, such as thinking or loving, are private events known only to the individual. A growing literature on cognitive-behavior modification (CBM) seeks to extend traditional behaviorism to encompass this inner life of thoughts. Fundamentalists view this as "soft behaviorism" and an abdication of the basic science of behavior. Approaches that entail self-monitoring are by definition subjective and fail to meet the basic scientific criteria for precise independent measurement. Ledwidge (1978) questions whether cognitive-behavior modification is a "step in the wrong direction" and Johnston and Pennypacker (1980) believe that behaviorists should confine their work to behaviors that are directly accessible. Nevertheless, CBM holds promise for the development of new management and teaching techniques and perhaps will narrow the gulf between behavioral and psychoeducational approaches.

Although advocates of the psychoeducational position would question treating cognitions as isolated from attitudes, feelings, and values, the similarities at the level of practice may be considerable. Many CBM strategies appear actually to be long-understood methods of pedagogy and problem-solving. Lloyd (1980) identifies a common approach used by many studies in CBM, including: identifying a problem, developing a plan, following the plan, and evaluating the outcome. A comparison with the steps in the life-space interview (see Chapter 6) shows striking similarities. In fact, the crucial difference is probably the emphasis on affective relationship underlying the technique of the life-space interview. Morse makes this distinction unequivocally: "The empathic relationship is more imposing in its impact than is method per se" (1980, p. 267).

Recent behavioral literature has sought to come to grips with patterns of behavior that do not seem readily explicable using traditional assumptions of reinforcement. For example, many aggressive children sometimes engage in *counter-control* of those who are attempting to modify their behavior (Kaufman, 1981).

> It seems as if some children take great delight in frustrating adults by being "oppositional" — often much more delight, in fact, than they take in the "rewards" and "reinforcers" being offered to them by well-meaning teachers or parents. Such children frequently endure punishment that they could easily avoid, behaving in a most "obstinate" and "self-defeating" way (but perhaps in a way *they* perceive as self-enhancing in the face of a pig-headed adult) (Kaufman, 1981, p. 207).

Such power struggles would cause most practitioners to reassess whether another approach that better incorporates the feelings of the young people might be more productive.

Appropriately employed, behavioral techniques are an important component of a holistic re-education. As behavioral approaches have broadened (e.g., social-learning theory encompassing cognitive and affective dimensions), they have become more eclectic and share many commonalities with psychoeducational approaches. Social-learning theory procedures for modifying behavior and teaching social skills will be considered in greater detail in a subsequent section of this chapter.

CRISIS MANAGEMENT

Many behavioral problems occur because a child's equilibrium is significantly disrupted by stressful situations. According to Kaplan and Lindemann, a series of complicated interchanges between the individual and his environment is necessary to keep a person in balance, "on an even keel" (Waldfogel & Gardner, 1961). To a considerable degree, this balance depends on stable interpersonal transactions that meet the person's emotional needs. If a period of stress temporarily renders a person incapable of adaptive responses, then a state of emotional upset or *crisis* exists. Crisis can produce disorganized behavior as well as inner tension and unpleasant feelings.

The manner in which crises are resolved (or continue unresolved) has a profound effect on a person's character development. Waldfogel and Gardner (1961) report data that suggest that emotional problems are more reversible if handled at early stages; if a crisis is allowed to persist it can, in time, evolve into chronic emotional maladjustment. Unresolved previous conflicts can cause a pattern of distorted perceptions and a compulsive tendency to recapitulate the nonadaptive behavior of the past. Thus the goal of crisis management is to resolve conflicts so that they do not have long-term negative effects on the person's emotional state.

Certainly, stress itself is not an abnormality, and a manageable degree of stress, frustration, and challenge facilitates the development of emotional maturity. It is not a sign of deep-seated, long-range pathology for children to act in emotionally disturbed ways when they are under stress. Even otherwise well-adjusted youth can manifest disturbed behavior during times of unusual strain. Redl (1965) makes a distinction between an emotionally disturbed *child* and *behavior* which reflects a state of emotional disturbance. Developmental, psychological, and material stress are among the conditions that can lead to an emotional crisis.

Developmental Stress. McFarland, Allen, and Honzik (1955), studying normal children, found certain behavioral problems to be very common at each age level from infancy to adolescence. Each of Erikson's (1950) stages of development present potentially stressful situations to an individual. Other developmental stresses can include leaving home for school, confusion over sexuality, gaining peer group acceptance, bodily changes, and career choice (Long & Duffner, 1980).

Psychological Stress. The moods of normal children can be highly variable, swinging from elation to depression and marked by anger, fear, shame, inadequacy, embarrassment, or frustration (Newman, 1967). These feelings can be evoked by discrimination, social isolation, being treated as stupid or worthless, and failing to meet unrealistic expectations. Family conflict, overprotection, inconsistency, sibling rivalry, and negative peer pressure are all important sources of stress in the lives of many children. At the extreme, some children have been subjected to emotional, physical, or sexual abuse at the hands of adults who are disturbed, alcoholic, or drug-abusing—usually the child's own parents. Any of these factors can produce profound psychological stress in the life of the child (Long & Duffner, 1980).

Material Stress. Concrete sources of stress (which may combine with developmental or psychological stress) include economic deprivation and inadequate survival resources, such as food, clothing, shelter, safety, or rest. Other tangible stressors can include being physically restrained, attacked, or punished, or such mundane frustrations as losing an assignment, tearing an article of clothing, colliding with another person during a game, or being deprived of a possession.

One of the more subtle varieties of stress particularly common with adolescents is a pervasive feeling of isolation (Lipsitz, 1977). These young people can feel isolated within themselves, within their age group, and cut off from society. Such feelings of isolation have been widely assumed to be related to the high incidence of self-destructive behavior in this age range, including drug abuse, life-threatening recklessness, and suicide. Another common source of stress in children arises from conflicts with significant others such as peers, parents, or other adult authorities.

Long has developed the concept of a stress cycle to demonstrate how the transactions between a person and significant others in his or her environment can serve to enhance stress and create a major crisis (Long & Duffner, 1980). According to Long's model, the cycle begins with a *stressful incident,* which could be precipitated by any of the wide range of stressors mentioned above. Next, the stress *produces feelings* such as frustration, anger, and anxiety. These feelings then manifest themselves in *observable behavior:* the youngster may attack others, run away, steal, tease, lie, fight, use drugs, withdraw, or engage in conflict with authority figures, peers, or family members. This negative behavior produces a corresponding *negative reaction* in other individuals (e.g., a teacher or parent). Thus, an aggressive pupil can produce an aggressive adult. Therefore, the manner in which the adult responds *creates more stress* in the life of the child. The stress cycle can lead to an intense power struggle between the child and the adult with each party in the controversy bringing out the worst in the other. Long's model of the stress cycle makes sense to anyone who has experienced the frustration of attempting to manage aggressive behavior in a therapeutic manner. In fact, the basic skill of avoiding such power struggles may be among the most important techniques for crisis management. It is crucial that the adult behave in such a way as to help the young person disengage from a conflict cycle rather than to continue being swept up in it.

A key psychoeducational strategy for managing children during periods of crisis is the life-space interview (Merritt, 1981; Redl & Wineman, 1952). Redl identified five goals for the life-space interview when used for emotional first-aid on the spot. These include:

1. *Ventilating feelings.* Redl called this "draining off frustration acidity," referring to the catharsis that we all have felt when someone simply allows us to "get it off our chest."
2. *Supporting during emotional upset.* Children may have strong feelings of panic, fury, or guilt, and the supportive adult will help them manage these feelings by staying with them and communicating during this period of turbulence.
3. *Maintaining turbulent relationships.* In times of conflict, troubled children can withdraw from relationships or push away adults who might otherwise have a significant impact on their lives. A life-space interview can keep communication going during these difficult times.
4. *Regulating social conduct.* Children may need assistance in understanding appropriate social roles and consequences to their behavior during times of high impulsivity and emotional upset. In such situations, the life-space interview can support the regulation of behavior.
5. *Arbitrating conflict.* Redl referred to this function as "umpire services," and it consists of helping youngsters work out conflicts that they have with significant others or within themselves.

These categories are not exhaustive but only suggest the kinds of support that can be given during times of emotional upset.

Many of the problems experienced by youth are the direct result of specific conflict situations between the child and some significant peer or adult in the child's life. Often such conflicts can be readily resolved through a life-space interview. In such situations, the adult may well find that he or she is in the role of mediator between the youngster and some other person or persons. One who accepts the responsibility of peacemaker must be careful lest the various parties to the conflict draw the helper into taking sides. The proper role for a mediator has been discussed by Bandler, Grinder, and Satir (1976) in their account of the activities of a family therapist. The basic process of successful mediation involves making contact with each of the parties in order to gain an understanding of their respective views; serving as a translator between the parties so that the concerns of each can be known to the other; and, finally, engaging the parties to the conflict in direct communication with one another.

Certainly the life-space interview is not the only way of reducing or managing crisis situations. A number of other useful strategies have been identified by Long and Duffner (1980) and Fagen (1980). These approaches, summarized in Table 5-5, include both environmental manipulations and strategies for personal development.

In summarizing the major techniques for crisis management, Waldfogel and Gardner (1961) suggest that most of them are relatively simple and straightforward. They involve providing emotional support, ventilation of feelings, relief from guilt or anxiety, clarifying conflict, developing plans for managing conflict, and altering environmental stressors. A caution is in order, however. Some youngsters may be so seriously overwhelmed by a crisis that they are not responsive to any of

Table 5-5. Approaches to Managing Stress

Environmental manipulation	Personal development
Lowering environmental pressure (e.g., reducing unrealistic expectations from parents or teachers)	Establishing positive relationship (e.g., with a supportive teacher)
Encountering the source of frustration (e.g., learning to be assertive)	Rechanneling feelings (e.g., expressing feelings through physical activities, creativity)
Seeking help from others (e.g., learning to ask for and accept assistance)	Learning to accept disappointment (e.g., increasing tolerance for frustration and failure)
Separation from setting (e.g., temporary or long-term change of milieu)	Enhancing problem-solving skills (e.g., learning to identify problems; working on one problem at a time; modifying the goal or the strategy)
Referral (e.g., assignment to a remedial or a therapeutic program)	Helping others less fortunate (e.g., involvement in community services for the handicapped)

Warning Signs of Potential Suicide[a]

Previous suicide attempts or gestures
Purchase of pills, weapons, ropes
Talking or writing about the desire to end one's life
A recent loss of a loved one, particularly someone in the family
Loss of a pet
Giving away personal possessions
Clear diminution in fear of death
Sense of failure
Abrupt (and subtle) changes in behavior, such as cutting off friendships
Violent or abusive behavior
Change in eating and sleeping patterns, e.g., insomnia, increased sleeping, loss of appetite, or overeating
Declining school performance, coupled with expressions of helplessness and apathy
Pervasive sadness, especially among young children who cannot articulate what is disturbing them
Family disruptions, such as a divorce or other changes within the home; or
A sudden lifting of sadness, depression, or withdrawal, which may indicate that the decision to commit suicide has been made.

This list is not exhaustive, although it does contain most of the major warning signs. The presence of these signs does not invariably mean that the youth is contemplating suicide, but the signs can sensitize the people around the youth to explore more carefully his or her state of mind.

[a] Adapted from *Suicide Among Children and Youth: A Guide for People Around Them,* U. S. Department of Health and Human Services Publication No. (OHDS) 80-30292.

the techniques immediately available to us, or we may be limited by our role in the extent of help that we can give.

No skilled youth worker should be reluctant to ask for assistance. No matter how expert our professional skills, some serious problems are best handled by sharing them with another professional. An example would be indications of suicide. Any of us who has worked with troubled children and youth over an extended period of time have come face-to-face with this most frightening of all troubled behavior. Suicide is not confined to adolescents, and the authors have encountered children as young as five who have made serious attempts to end their lives. It is disquieting to notice how little attention is given to techniques for managing children at risk for suicide. Although a thorough discussion of this topic exceeds the bounds of this volume, we would feel amiss if we did not share the warning signs for suicide among children and youth and some basic concepts of management for these problems. The tabulations on pp. 155 and 156 are adapted from publications of the Department of Health and Human Services.

Managing Suicidal Children[a]

Step 1: *Listen.* A person in mental crisis needs someone who will listen to what s/he is saying. Every effort should be made to understand the problems behind the statements.

Step 2: *Evaluate the seriousness of the youngster's thoughts and feelings.* If the child has made clear suicide plans, the problem is more acute than when his/her thinking was less definite.

Step 3: *Evaluate the intensity or severity of the emotional disturbance.* It is possible that the youngster may be extremely upset but not suicidal. Often, if a person has been depressed, and then becomes agitated and moves about restlessly, it can be cause for alarm.

Step 4: *Take seriously every complaint and feeling the child expresses.* Do not dismiss or undervalue what the child is saying. In some instances, the child may minimize his/her difficulty, but beneath an apparent calm may be profoundly distressed feelings.

Step 5: *Do not be afraid to ask directly if the child has entertained thoughts of suicide.* Suicide may be suggested but not openly mentioned during the crisis period. Experience shows that harm is rarely done by inquiring directly about suicide at an appropriate time. As a matter of fact, the child frequently is glad to have the opportunity to open up and discuss it.

Step 6: *Do not be misled by the youngster's comments that s/he is past the emotional crisis.* Often the youth will feel initial relief after talking about suicide, but the same thinking may recur later. Follow-up is crucial.

Step 7: *Be affirmative, but supportive.* Strong, stable guideposts are essential in the life of a distressed child. Provide emotional strength by giving the impression that you know what you are doing, and that everything possible will be done to assist the young person.

Step 8: *Evaluate available resources.* The child may have inner resources, including various mechanisms for rationalization and intellectualization, which can be strengthened and supported, and other resources such as ministers, relatives, and friends who can be contacted. If these are absent, the problem may be more serious.

Step 9: *Act specifically.* Do something tangible; that is, give the youngster something definite to hang onto, such as arranging to see him/her later or subsequently contacting another helping person. Nothing is more frustrating to a child than to feel as though s/he has gained nothing from the discussion.

Step 10: *Obtain appropriate assistance and consultation.* Do not try to handle the problem alone. Seek the advice of physicians, school specialists, mental health professionals, or other knowledgeable persons.

[a]This listing of guidelines was prepared by Dr. Calvin Frederick, National Institute of Mental Health, and appears in *Trends in Mental Health: Self-Destructive Behavior Among Younger Age Groups*, Department of Health, Education and Welfare, Publication No. (ADM) 76-365.

AFFECTIVE RE-EDUCATION

As we have seen, unresolved crises can eventually lead to established patterns of distorted values, attitudes, or feelings. It will not always be apparent where efforts at crisis management blend into affective re-education. In this section we shall highlight representative methods for dealing with long-standing affective problems. We shall limit our discussion to approaches that can be employed by teachers and group workers and shall exclude formal systems of psychotherapy.

Table 5-6 suggests ways of identifying affective behavioral problems that reflect long-standing patterns of distorted attitudes, values, or feelings.

Clinical Exploitation Life-Space Interview

A major portion of Redl and Wineman's pioneering work on the aggressive child (1952) focuses on the use of the life-space interview (LSI) for clinical exploitation of life events. Here the goal is to make basic changes in a child's interpersonal style or life theme. Redl identi-

Table 5-6. Indications for Crisis Management or Affective Re-education

Crisis management may be indicated when:	Affective re-education may be indicated when:
Onset is marked and tied to certain life experiences (e.g., a public humiliation, a family tragedy, or other stressful situation)	*Onset is unclear,* as problem is a continuation of usual style of distorted behavior, feelings, or attitudes in the absence of any known cause of stress
Unpredictable, unpatterned potpourri of seemingly unrelated examples of behavior disorganization and emotional upset (e.g., when one is short-tempered, hyperactive, laughs inappropriately, swears more than usual, is explosive, sulks, is overly sensitive. Adult's reaction might be "Now what is bothering him?")	*Predictable pattern* of behavior is seen, which has come to be known as characteristic of a person's response style (e.g., a person is characteristically distrustful, values negative behavior, expects failure in all situations, etc. Adult's reaction might be "There he goes again.")
Intensity of expression is out of character ("That's not like her.")	*Intensity* of behavior is characteristic of past style
Variability of mood is noted; person is unsettled, overreacts, isolates, acts out, etc., all in a short period of time	*Constancy* of behavior and affect suggests that the person has adapted to this unique personal style

fied five goals of life-space interviews designed for affective re-education. Each of these is briefly considered below.

1. _Clarifying reality_. Redl referred to this process as "reality rub-in."
   The common element underlying this type of LSI is the student's
   inability to connect cause and effect in a recent series of events in
   which he or she has been involved (Bloom, 1981). The youngsters
   may have no idea why they or others acted in certain ways and
   may fail to see the connection between behavior and consequences. However, neither children nor adults seem to like being
   confronted by others with their behavior, and confronting a
   youth can demonstrate very quickly the fragility of our relationship with the youngster. This technique is not likely to succeed
   unless the young person likes, respects, and trusts the adult, and
   that, of course, must be based on some prior history of caring
   relationship. Bloom (1981) notes that the interviewer must be
   free from hostility. If the adult cannot confront empathically,
   only antagonism will result. Regardless of the sensitivity of the
   adult, if this technique seems to create more agitation in the
   youngster, it may be advisable to try a more passive approach.
   Effectively utilized, the reality rub-in helps a young person to see
   his or her behavior as others see it.
2. _Devaluing negative behavior_. Redl's label was "symptom estrangement," which can be a bit puzzling to the contemporary
   reader. What Redl meant was simple, however: Children often
   behave in cruel or hostile ways (the "symptom") and are perfectly
   comfortable with this hurting behavior (Tompkins, 1981). The
   goal is to _estrange_ them from this behavior, to make hurting
   behavior alien. Thus, even if the child has derived considerable
   secondary gain from the problem behavior, the goal is to teach
   him or her that the price is too high. For example, negative
   behavior should not be seen as cool. For some children, this
   means that we will teach a basic value. A child who hurts others
   without any sense of remorse must learn to become uncomfortable with such hurting behavior. The idea of making children
   uncomfortable with their behavior or teaching them to feel guilt
   in certain cases can run counter to a long tradition in which
   mental health was equated with the reduction of guilt.

   > Conscience has had a rather bad time of it in the past half century or
   > so. The severe and excessive inhibitions and guilts found in many
   > neurotic personalities were felt to be the causes of their restrictions
   > and anxieties, and releasing people from their inner guilts became
   > one of the dominant goals of therapeutic treatment. Today, for many

reasons more powerful than therapy, there is evidence that there is some scarcity of guilt, that too great permissiveness if not just confined to parent–child relationships but society as a whole has created a conscienceless race (Perlman, 1979, p. 206).

Redl coined the term "guilt squeeze" to refer to this process of eliciting guilt feelings that should be appropriate to the particular piece of unacceptable behavior.

3. *Enhancing positive values.* Redl referred to this type of interview as "massaging numb value areas." Some children already have the underlying values that should preclude negative behavior but these values are inoperative. Such a person might rationalize that a certain behavior is "not too bad because . . . ." A street-wise boy may protect his own grandmother but go along with peers to steal a purse from someone else's grandmother. The goal of this interview is to help the person use his existing but latent positive values in controlling his behavior—so to speak, making his conscience holler louder. Werner (1981) stresses that in massaging numb value areas it is crucial that the interviewer not take a moralistic approach lest he make matters worse. If the youth feels he has "paid the price," he may disavow any further responsibility. If the child has been made to feel excessively guilty, he may act out more intensely. In the successful interview, the adult must carefully blend confrontation with support and empathy, thereby helping the youngster find the middle ground between denying a problem or being overwhelmed by it. With some youth it is not even necessary for the adult to point out their failures. These children may feel intensely guilty for not living up to what they know is right, and our goal is only to help them make the conscience-connection before rather than after they act.

4. *Teaching interpersonal skills.* Redl coined the phrase "new tool salesmanship" to denote this type of interview. Here the goal is to teach more effective styles of interpersonal behavior. Many troubled children have difficulty expressing their true feelings in ways that are socially acceptable. Sanders (1981) provides an example of a boy who purposely "bumped" a girl he liked on the bus; she got mad, called him a name; he swore at her, and in the end ruined a potential friendship. Through a skillful interview, this incident was carefully reconstructed so that the boy could see the contradiction between his real feeling and his behavior. After discussion and role play of the incident and of possible alternative behaviors, the youngster concluded, "It's much easier to be

tough than to be nice to others. It takes more to be nice!" (Sanders, 1981, p. 33).

5. *Enhancing self-autonomy.* Redl used the terminology "manipulation of body boundaries" to describe the process of teaching children a positive autonomy and independence of group control. Many rejected students, because of their feelings of isolation and desire for acceptance, are vulnerable to the social influence of others. Such youngsters can easily be exploited and misled by peers (Long, 1981). The goal with such children would be to teach them to recognize how they can be drawn in by peer influence or group contagion. We would want to help them develop the confidence in themselves to avoid being controlled in this manner and to seek out friends who will respect them rather than misuse or mislead them.

The above goals for the life-space interview do not constitute totally discrete categories but simply represent some of the key ways in which the LSI can be used to create long-term change in a child's attitudes, values, or feelings. Redl cautioned that these five goals "were meant to be illustrative rather than system-binding" (1959, p. 10). He also saw the LSI as only one approach to affective re-education and he recognized that some children would require other forms of counseling or psychotherapy.

Teaching Values

Verbal counseling procedures including the life-space interview are relatively recent additions to approaches that have long been used to teach values. Traditionally, religious and moral training by the family and church constituted the major avenue for imparting values that would shape the behavior of youth. Although the family continues to have the major influence on values of children, the effect of religious values on behavior of many youngsters is less direct now than in the past. Whereas earlier research showed that young people did not begin to question their religious teachings and express doubts until age 17 or 18, recent studies show that this conflict now appears for many adolescents at age 13 or 14 (Potvin, Hoge, & Nelson, 1976). Nevertheless, religious training undoubtedly has a profound effect on the lives of many young people in spite of the scant attention this topic typically receives in professional youth work literature. In addition to the previously cited work by Potvin and colleagues, the relationship of religious training to the values and conflicts of youth is discussed by Strommen (1974) in *Five Cries of Youth*.

Without the historical perspective, we can easily lose sight of how far educational institutions have distanced themselves from value education. *The McGuffey Readers*, which dominated the American educational scene for much of the nineteenth century, proudly embraced the dual goals of academic and moral training. Likewise, the first official textbooks in Canada, *The Irish Readers*, which were introduced in 1896, admonished pupils with texts such as this:

> Then let me always watch my lips,
> Lest I be struck to death in Hell,
> Since God a book of reckoning keeps
> For every lie that children tell.

Although few would argue for a return to such a curriculum for today's pluralistic society, opinion is growing that schools may have traversed too far in the quest for neutrality. Carried to its extreme, this tendency has given rise to a new overarching value of "anything goes" or "one belief is as good as another."

After many years of avoidance by schools of teaching values, interest in this area has revived widely as a result of the development of methods for *values clarification* (Raths, Harmin, & Simon, 1966; Simon, Howe, & Kirschenbaum, 1972). Raths and his colleagues differentiate their approach from traditional methods of teaching values, which are summarized below: *modeling*—setting examples; *persuasion*—using reasoning or arguments; *limiting choice*—structuring options to those acceptable to the authority; *inspiring*—appealing to the emotions; *rules and regulations*—using rewards and punishments to mold behavior; *invoking a principle*—appealing to cultural or religious heritage; and *invoking guilt*—appealing to conscience.

These authors conclude that such approaches often fail to achieve deep commitments and may run counter to the principle of free choice. They propose a process of values clarification for the adult who desires to help children face alien value issues in their lives. This process involves the following steps:

1. Encourage children to make choices and to make them freely.
2. Help them discover and examine available alternatives.
3. Help children weigh alternatives thoughtfully, reflecting on the consequences of each.
4. Encourage children to consider what it is that they prize and cherish.

5. Give them opportunities to make public affirmations of their choices.
6. Encourage them to act, behave, and live in accordance with their choices.
7. Help them to examine repeated behaviors or patterns in their life (Raths, Harmin, & Simon, 1966, pp. 38–39).

Another approach to values education is *moral development* following the work of Kohlberg and colleagues (Kohlberg, 1964). Here the intent is not so much to *clarify* values but to teach a higher level of moral reasoning. Research on the effect of various values clarification and moral development on children is reviewed by Lockwood (1978).

Teaching Self-Control

Another curricular approach to affective re-education is the model for teaching self-control in the psychoeducational program developed by Fagen, Long, and Stevens (1975). They identify eight clusters of skills which they believe to be essential to developing self-control. They propose teaching these skills as a prerequisite to successful academic functioning since "a child cannot be expected to fulfill educational task requirements unless he has acquired an indentifiable set of skills which promote self-control" (p. 261). They reason that a child must be able to (1) attend to the teacher's directions (selection), (2) remember instructions (storage), (3) organize self to perform assignments (sequencing and ordering), (4) predict the outcome of one's behavior (anticipate consequences), (5) cope with obstacles (managing frustrations), (6) delay actions even when excited (inhibition), (7) express feelings through appropriate words and actions (appreciation of feelings), and (8) think positively about the self (appreciate feelings). Specific curriculum tasks are suggested for each of these skill areas.

The development of self-control has been a major focus of both affective (Morse, Ardizzone, & Macdonald, 1980) and social learning theory approaches (Cartledge & Milburn, 1978).

Curriculum and Activities

A number of contributors have stressed the important role of activity programming in affective re-education. VanderVen (1972) notes that activities can enhance self-esteem, socialization skills, expressing and recognizing feelings, and processing information from the environment. Curriculum and activity issues will be considered more fully in subsequent chapters. Further treatment of this topic is found in Treischman, Whittaker, and Brendtro, 1969; Whittaker, 1979; and Wood, 1975.

SOCIAL SKILLS TRAINING

A recently developed and increasingly popular approach to teaching and treating children with problems is that of social skills training. Although social skills approaches originated initially from behavior modification research, social skills training has expanded to include a combination of behavioral, affective, and cognitive skill development through the use of educational methods. Along with the psychoeducational approaches described earlier in this chapter, the term "psychoeducational therapy" has also been suggested as an alternative name for social skills training (Goldstein et al., 1981).

The major assumption underlying the social skills approach is that many emotional and behavioral problems of children are a result of faulty learning or inadequate socialization opportunities. It is assumed that many problems of children, both those that are situational and those that are more pervasive and chronic, exist because children lack the skills to build relationships, handle interpersonal conflicts, and manage their own emotions in constructive ways. It follows, then, that one answer to remediation of such problems is through teaching of more acceptable ways to behave, to express feelings, to respond to others, and to meet the demands and expectations placed by the surrounding world. It is assumed further that the skills needed for improved social adjustment can be taught with many of the same methods used to teach any kind of academic or behavioral skill. Goldstein et al. (1981) point out that not only can social skills training serve to remediate problems, but in addition it can be regarded as preventive, training children in advance to meet the problems of living, with the hope of lessening the future need for remedial treatment.

Social skills training encompasses many of the kinds of interventions mentioned previously in this chapter. In the prescriptive model for intervention outlined in Table 5-4, elements related to social competence can be found both in interventions oriented toward situational problems and in those aimed at remediating more pervasive problems. Training in specific behavioral responses, as in assertiveness training, self-control training, and affective-cognitive techniques, are all considered aspects of teaching social skills.

One approach frequently applied to the teaching of social behaviors is an instructional model that involves defining the skill to be taught, assessing the learner's competence in the skills, devising and carrying out specific strategies to teach the skills, assessing the results of teaching, and developing means to maintain the skill over time and generalize it into other environments.

Assessment of Social Skills

The need for instruction in social skills is usually identified through a recognition that a child continually exhibits too much of a problem behavior or not enough of behaviors considered desirable. In most approaches to teaching social skills, assessment is considered essential to pinpoint the child's specific social skills and defects, and the conditions under which they occur, as well as to measure the effectiveness of training. Increasing numbers of books and articles are being devoted to the subject of social skills assessment (Eisler, 1976; Foster & Ritchey, 1979; Hersen & Bellack, 1977; Hops & Greenwood, 1981; Michelsen & Wood, 1980). Techniques for assessing social skills include observation of the child in natural or contrived settings, interviews, questionnaires, rating scales, self-report measures, sociometric procedures, and assessment in analogous situations using role-playing scenarios.

Procedures for social skills assessment that have been developed in connection with research are concerned with the reliability and validity of data, and thus often involve such elements as complicated or expensive equipment, highly trained observers, informed confederates, and role-playing scripts requiring practice. For people working with children in applied settings, however, the kinds of procedures used by researchers to produce reliable and valid data may not be practical or even necessary. The principal question to be asked in the classroom, clinic, or residential setting is whether the child needs to be taught the social behavior he seems to lack or whether he needs more opportunities and incentives to do something already in his repertoire.

Selection of Social Skills

Research in the field of social skills has identified specific social behaviors that contribute to adjustment of children in various settings. For example, large numbers of studies have been devoted to the relationship between social behaviors and school achievement (Cartledge & Milburn, 1978). Behaviors considered prerequisite to success in school include paying attention, persistence to task, self-control, compliance with teacher demands, and the ability to follow directions and to work independently. A variety of studies have demonstrated that student behaviors are an important determinant of teacher responses and the nature of teacher interaction with the student. Teachers, for example, direct more questions to students who volunteer more, and they respond more positively to students who smile and nod, make positive comments, take notes, answer questions, and make correct responses.

Interpersonal relationships with adults and peers are important not only for school adjustment but also for long-term adjustment and adult mental health. A literature review by LaGreca and Mesibov (1979) identified a group of nine specific skill areas that were related to a child's acceptance by peers. These areas included: smiling, greeting others, joining ongoing peer activities, extending invitations to others, conversing, sharing and cooperating, complimenting others, physical appearance and grooming, and play skills, all of which lend themselves to a social skills teaching approach.

A number of taxonomies or inventories of social skills have been developed, some of which have been expanded into teaching curricula. One aimed at the young emotionally handicapped child is the Developmental Therapy program (Wood, 1975). Stephens (1978) developed an inventory and curriculum with 136 social behaviors for elementary-age children. A similar inventory of social competence skills is that of Turnbull, Strickland, and Brantley (1978) in which skills are identified according to primary, intermediate, junior high, and senior high levels. An inventory of social skills for adolescents has been developed by Goldstein et al. (1980) as part of the Structured Learning Curriculum. Typical of items in taxonomies of social skills are those in Rinn and Markle (1979, pp. 110–111):

1. Self-Expressive Skills
   a. Expression of feeling (sadness and happiness)
   b. Expression of opinion
   c. Accepting compliments
   d. Stating positives about oneself
2. Other-Enhancing Skills
   a. Stating positives about a best friend
   b. Stating genuine agreement with another's opinion
   c. Praising others
3. Assertive Skills
   a. Making simple requests
   b. Disagreeing with another's opinion
   c. Denying unreasonable requests
4. Communications Skills
   a. Conversing
   b. Interpersonal problem solving

Instruction in Social Skills

Most programs for social skills instruction contain the same basic elements, which are inherent in some form in any teaching program. Included are (1) the presentation to the learner of a model to observe and imitate; (2) opportunities for the learner to make imitative responses; (3) feedback to the learner about his responses; and (4) practice and refinement of the imitated behavior, which may include activities to generalize the new behavior into different situations. This instructional sequence can be applied to a wide variety of social behaviors and, depending on the pacing and mode of presentation, to both younger and older children. A curriculum based on this model is that of Stephens (1978).

In this model for teaching social skills, after the behaviors to be taught have been defined and the child's competence assessed, the instructional process is as follows:

1. *Set the stage for instruction.* The need for learning the target behavior must be established for the child. This can be accomplished through individual or group discussion, possibly using such materials as books, films, or film strips, that deal with the subject. (A useful tool is *The Book Finder* by Dreyer, 1977, a reference guide to children's literature.) Actual problem situations occurring in the environment can serve also to stimulate discussion. The discussion might include an examination of alternative behaviors in problem situations, reasons for engaging in positive alternatives to problem behavior, and the emotions present in the situation. As an example, the social skill of good sportsmanship when losing a game could be discussed in relation to the advantages of being a good sport; how one feels when losing, or winning, or when playing with a poor sport; how well-known sports figures handle winning and losing, and what happens to them as a result.

2. *Define the social skill in operational terms.* The trainer needs to describe the behavior to be learned in terms that are easily understandable to the child. Being a good sport about losing a game, for example, might be operationalized into: smiling; walking up to the winner; extending your hand to shake his/her hand; congratulating the winner or making a compliment about how he or she played the game. The specified behaviors can be written on a chalk board to serve as prompts. In this example, a list of good sportsmanlike comments might be generated. Two very useful skills for the teacher of social skills are those of generating behavioral objectives and task analysis. The former makes it possible to identify the positive behaviors that are opposite to or incompatible with problem behaviors and to develop them into

social skill teaching objectives. For example, "being a poor sport" can be turned into such social skills objectives as: the child follows the rules when playing a game; the child accepts losing in a competitive game; the child is considerate of opponents when winning a game. Task analysis involves breaking globally stated behaviors down into component parts, which can then be taught in sequence. Most social behaviors are actually a complex set of subskills, some of which are prerequisites for others. The essential steps in task analysis for instruction include: (1) specifying the desired behavior; (2) identifying the subskills of the composite behavior; (3) stating the subskills in terms of observable behaviors; (4) sequencing the subskills according to order of instruction.

3. *Set up a role-playing situation.* The behaviors described in the previous step are demonstrated by the adult or peers or a combination of both, followed by a discussion reviewing what was observed. Opportunities are then provided for the learners to role-play the behaviors in a number of practice sessions. Using the good sportsmanship example, after the trainer demonstrates examples of the behaviors previously identified as components of being a good sport, children might be given brief scenarios such as "you have just lost a game of checkers" or "your team has just lost the volleyball game" and asked to act out being a good sport. Inappropriate losing behaviors might also be demonstrated, and the trainer might ask children to identify which behaviors were preferable and why.

Although children may learn a great deal by imitating the people around them and the models they encounter through media, books, and other means, Bandura (1977) suggests that modeling that involves guided participation is more successful and yields a higher expectation of mastery and competence than vicarious experiences alone. Thus, the importance of role-playing in social skills instruction is underscored. Role playing can be conducted in a group or individually, in a clinical interview, in a structured teaching sequence such as that described earlier, or spontaneously in the context of a life-space interview in which a child and adult may replay a problem situation, role-playing alternatives to what actually occurred.

4. *Provide feedback for role-playing performance.* Repeated practice accompanied by feedback is highly important, since by receiving information about his performance, the child is able to make corrections to improve his skills. The typical role-play situation incorporates a discussion or evaluation phase for purposes of offering feedback. Feedback not only provides the child with information about his performance and what should be improved, but also provides opportunities to reinforce desirable aspects of the performance. Eisler and Frederiksen (1980) suggest that feedback should be (1) objective and accurate;

(2) specific; (3) corrective, with alternatives suggested; and (4) either positive or neutral, ignoring inappropriate aspects. They suggest also that positive comments should outnumber neutral and corrective statements by a margin of one to three.

5. *Provide opportunities for generalization and maintenance over time.* It is not unusual in behavior change programs to find that behaviors do not occur beyond the setting where they are taught. In a review of literature related to generalization of behavior, Stokes and Baer (1977) conclude that generalization does not automatically occur but must be programmed and should be built into the training process. Several elements appear to influence whether behaviors will occur in new settings, will occur with people other than the trainer, and will persist over time. Research on generalization of social behaviors suggests that varying the situations where training occurs, varying the people involved in training, and introducing verbal and cognitive "mediators" such as self-reports, self-instruction, and imagery are all ways to help the process of generalization. During social skills training, after sufficient practice sessions have been allotted for the behavior to be learned, conditions need to be set up for the behavior to be demonstrated in a variety of real-life situations, with incentives to encourage the behavior to occur. In the case of good sportsmanship, for example, it would be a simple matter to set up a variety of competitive game situations in which desirable winning and losing behavior would be noted and reinforced. If the behavior previously taught were not occurring, it might be necessary to institute more practice sessions or increase the level of incentives to motivate the child to use the behaviors previously rehearsed. Additionally, further individual or group discussion followed by role-playing that emphasizes cognitive and affective aspects of winning or losing might be indicated.

Cognitive and Affective Dimensions of Social Skills

In addition to instruction in the physical performance of a social behavior, cognitive and affective aspects of social behavior are increasingly being included in social skills training programs. It is recognized that how a person feels and thinks influences in a major way how effective and how appropriate he or she will be in social interactions. In addition, the process of socialization involves learning to express inner events in acceptable public ways.

The social skills approach to teaching about thoughts and feelings focuses on the observable manifestations of these inner events and makes use of the kinds of teaching procedures outlined above. Social skills training dealing with emotions begins with identifying and labeling one's own emotions, followed by recognizing and labeling the expression of feelings in others, abilities that many children do not have. The ultimate goal involves learning acceptable ways to express a variety of feelings in varying situations. Social perception, the ability to interpret a social situation accurately, has been identified as an important aspect of social skill (Morrison & Bellack, 1981). Training in social perception focuses on nonverbal communication, emphasizing understanding what is being communicated through facial expressions, body language, and physical and environmental cues (Minskoff, 1980). A number of programs have been developed for teaching about emotions and social perception, including: DUSO (Developing Understanding of Self and Others) program (Dinkmeyer, 1973), Project AWARE (Elardo & Cooper, 1977), and the TAD (Toward Affective Development) program (Dupont, Gardner & Brody, 1974).

Along with social perception, cognitive approaches in social skills training with children have focused on problem-solving techniques, self-instruction training, cognitive restructuring, and self-monitoring. The work of Spivack, Platt, and Shure (Spivack & Shure, 1974; Spivack, Platt, & Shure, 1976; Shure & Spivack, 1978) has made a major contribution to the area of teaching problem-solving skills to children. Oriented first to preschool children, their Interpersonal Cognitive Problem Solving program (ICPS) begins with the teaching of language and conceptual skills that are assumed to be prerequisite to the child's being able to go through a problem-solving process. The specific skills addressed in ICPS training, as outlined by Goldstein et al. (1981, pp. 226–228) include:

1. Alternative solution thinking, ability to generate different solutions;
2. Consequential thinking, ability to predict the possible outcomes of various courses of action;
3. Causal thinking, ability to see cause and effect relationships;
4. Interpersonal sensitivity, awareness that interpersonal problems exist;
5. Means–end thinking, identification of the steps necessary to achieve a goal; and
6. Perspective-taking, recognition of differences in motives and viewpoints, similar to empathy or role-taking.

Variations of problem-solving training have been developed by others into programs for use with different age levels. For example, The Rochester Social Problem Solving (SPS) Program (Weissberg et al., 1980) similarly involves teaching children to identify feelings, think of alternative solutions, and anticipate consequences of behavior. It incorporates role-playing as an important aspect of the training.

Self-instruction and related skills having to do with self-control constitute another major area relevant to building social skills. Most self-instruction programs are built on an adaptation of a model originated by Vygotsky (1962) and Luria (1961) and developed further by Meichenbaum (1977). One assumption of this approach is that much behavior is guided by internalized self-statements, and that behavior can be changed by altering the child's self-statements.

Self-instruction with children generally involves teaching children a series of problem-solving steps along with self-controlling verbal statements presented by a coach or model, which the child is to repeat while completing a task or engaging in social problem-solving.

The *Think Aloud* program (Bash & Camp, 1981; Camp, 1977; Camp & Bash, 1981) makes use of both Meichenbaum's procedures to teach self-instruction and the Spivack and Shure approach to problem-solving. Teaching materials include scripts for use by the teacher who completes a demonstration task, modeling the self-instruction steps. These tasks include coping with errors and making self-evaluative statements. After observing the teacher, the child attempts a similar task, using the same self-instruction sequence. To teach problem-solving skills, the program uses pictures and scripts to guide discussion around problem situations.

A curriculum for teaching self-control through verbal self-instruction (VSI), also built on the Meichenbaum model, has been developed by Kendall (1981). Self-instruction training is a relatively new approach to teaching self-control to children. Like other problem-solving approaches, one of the strengths of self-instruction training is that it teaches children "a general coping skill rather than a situation-specific response" (Cole & Kazdin, 1980).

A further aspect of cognitive training relevant to social skills is the alteration of dysfunctional self-statements. A major example of this approach is the Rational Emotive Therapy (RET) model of Albert Ellis (1962). Ellis proposes that maladaptive behavior results from irrational belief systems based on a set of imperatives about what one should do or must have happen. Cognition, emotion, and behavior are interrelated; irrational beliefs are responsible for disturbing emotions, which then result in dysfunctional behavior.

Gambrill (1977, pp. 498–499) provided a listing of irrational beliefs according to the principles of rational emotive therapy. They are given below:

1. The idea that it is a dire necessity for an adult human being to be loved or approved by virtually every significant other person in his community;
2. The idea that one should be thoroughly competent, adequate, and achieving in all possible respects, if one is to consider oneself worthwhile;

3. The idea that certain people are bad, wicked, or villainous and that they should be severely blamed or punished for their villainy;
4. The idea that it is awful and catastrophic when things are not the way one would very much like them to be;
5. The idea that human unhappiness is externally caused and that people have little or no ability to control their sorrows and disturbances;
6. The idea that if something is or may be dangerous or fearsome, one should be terribly concerned about it and should keep dwelling on the possibility of its occurring;
7. The idea that it is easier to avoid than to face certain life difficulties and self-responsibilities;
8. The idea that one should be dependent on others and needs someone stronger than oneself on whom to rely;
9. The idea that one's past history is an all-important determinant of one's present behavior, and that because something once strongly affected one's life, it should indefinitely have a similar effect;
10. The idea that one should become quite upset over other people's problems and disturbances; and
11. The idea that there is invariably a right, precise, and perfect solution to human problems, and that it is catastrophic if this correct solution is not found.

Rational emotive therapy principles have been developed by Knaus (1974) into the Rational Emotive Education (REE) program for children. Based on the philosophical tenets of RET, REE is presented through experiential learning strategies including simulation, tasks, and group problem-solving exercises.

A set of related cognitive self-control procedures that have proved useful in changing behavior and show promise for maintaining changed behavior over time are those of self-monitoring, self-evaluation, and self-reinforcement. Self-monitoring involves the ability to observe and report one's own behavior. One aspect of self-monitoring is "correspondence training," teaching the child to make accurate reports about his behavior. Correspondence training procedures include teaching the child to monitor his own behavior, comparing the child's report with data from an independent observer, and providing reinforcement to the child for accuracy of his data or his verbal reports. There is some evidence to suggest that the act of self-recording alone, regardless of accuracy, can significantly change behavior (Nelson & Hayes, 1981).

Another aspect of self-monitoring is self-evaluation or making comparisons between self-observed behavior and the criteria or performance standards set for the behavior. The kinds of criteria established for evaluation clearly affect whether the criteria can realistically be met and the evaluation can be positive. Many children seldom make positive self-evaluations, possibly because of excessively high standards for their own performance. Research on the effect of goal-setting on behavior suggests that training children to set realistic performance goals can help to increase motivation and hence performance (Sagotsky, Patterson, & Lepper, 1978). An explanation for the effect of self-evaluation on behavior change is that the process of attending to one's own behavior and comparing it to a criterion triggers self-reinforcing or self-punishing thoughts, which may in turn serve to increase or decrease the behavior (Nelson & Hayes, 1981).

Self-reinforcement is the process of rewarding oneself contingent on the performance of specific behaviors according to some criterion. It is also seen as a skill to be taught. For example, a social skills training goal might be to teach the child a repertoire of positive statements to make about his own attributes and accomplishments, along with fostering the ability to discriminate when to use them. In most self-reinforcement programs it is assumed that if the child monitors his behavior, evaluates it positively, and can deliver a tangible self-reward or make an overt positive statement about the behavior, the process of internalized self-reinforcement will also be present.

Self-reinforcement is considered an important means by which new behaviors can be perpetuated. It is assumed that improved social behaviors should be maintained in part by the positive social responses they evoke. Along with praise, smiles, and positive attention from others, another goal of social skills training is to develop in the child an ability to assess and reward his or her own appropriate social behavior.

The approaches outlined in this chapter are not exhaustive but only represent the interventions possible in a holistic approach to management. As Paul suggests,

> Human behavior is complex and there are several different definitive scientific and quasi scientific ways to understand it. It is a mistake to argue that one perspective is correct and the others are incorrect, or that one is necessarily more correct than others. The various theories or perspectives are not mutually exclusive (1982, p. 29).

In the following chapter we shall examine in greater detail the concept and application of the life-space interview as it is used for crisis management and affective re-education.

REFERENCES

Bandler, R., Grinder, J., & Satir, V. *Changing with families.* Palo Alto, CA: Science and Behavior Books, 1976.

Bandura, A. *Social learning theory.* Englewood Cliffs, NJ: Prentice-Hall, 1977.

Bash, M. A. S., & Camp, B. W. Teacher training in the Think Aloud classroom program. In G. Cartledge & J. F. Milburn (Eds.), *Teaching social skills to children.* Elmsford, NY: Pergamon Press, 1981.

Bloom, R. The reality rub-in interview with emotionally disturbed adolescents. *Pointer*, 1981, *25*(2), 22–25.

Camp, B. W. Verbal mediation in young aggressive boys. *Journal of Abnormal Psychology*, 1977, *86*, 145–153.

Camp, B. W., & Bash, M. A. *Think Aloud*. Champaign, IL: Research Press, 1981.

Cartledge, G., & Milburn, J. F. The case for teaching social skills in the classroom: A review. *Review of Educational Research*, 1978, *1*, 133–156.

Cole, P. M., & Kazdin, A. E. Critical issues in self-instruction training with children. *Child Behavior Therapy*, 1980, *2*, 1–21.

Criswell, E. The behavioral perspective of emotional disturbance. R. Algozzinne, R. Schmid, & C. D. Mercer (Eds.), *Childhood behavior disorders*. Rockville, MD: Aspen Systems, 1981.

Dinkmeyer, D. *Developing understanding of self and others (DUSO Program)*. Circle Pines, MN: American Guidance Service, 1973.

Dreyer, S. S. *The book finder*. Circle Pines, MN: American Guidance Service, Inc., 1977.

Dupont, H., Gardner, O. S., & Brody, D. S. *Toward affective development*. Circle Pines, MN: American Guidance Service, Inc., 1974.

Eisler, R. M. Behavioral assessment of social skills. In M. Hersen & A. A. Bellack (Eds.), *Behavioral assessment: A practical handbook*. Elmsford, NY: Pergamon Press, 1976.

Eisler, R. M., & Frederiksen, L. W. *Perfecting social skills*. New York: Plenum Press, 1980.

Elardo, P. T., & Cooper, M. *Project AWARE: A handbook for teachers*. Reading, MA: Addison-Wesley, 1977.

Ellis, A. *Reason and emotion in psychotherapy*. New York: Lyle Stuart Press, 1962.

Ellis, A. The basic clinical theory of rational-emotive therapy. In A. Ellis & R. Grieger (Eds.), *Handbook of rational-emotive therapy*. New York: Springer, 1977.

Erikson, E. *Childhood and society*. New York: W. W. Norton, 1950.

Fagen, S. Adaptive frustration management. In N. Long, W. Morse, & R. Newman (Eds.), *Conflict in the classroom*. Belmont, CA: Wadsworth Pub. Co., 1980.

Fagen, S., Long, N., & Stevens, D. *Teaching children self control*. Columbus, OH: Charles Merrill, 1975.

Foster, S. L., & Ritchey, W. L. Issues in the assessment of social competence in children. *Journal of Applied Behavior Analysis*, 1979, *12*, 625–638.

Gambrill, E. *Behavioral modification*. San Francisco: Jossey-Bass, 1977.

Goldstein, A. P., Carr, E.G., Davidson, W. S., & Wehr, P. *In response to aggression*. Elmsford, NY: Pergamon Press, 1981.

Goldstein, A. P., Sprafkin, R. P., Gershaw, N. J., & Klein, P. Social skills training through Structured Learning. In G. Cartledge & J. F. Milburn (Eds.), *Teaching social skills to children*. Elmsford, NY: Pergamon Press, 1980.

Hersen, M., & Bellack, A. S. Assessment of social skills. In A. R. Ciminero, K. S. Calhoun, & H. D. Adams (Eds.), *Handbook for behavior assessment*. New York: Wiley, 1977.

Hops, H., & Greenwood, C. R. Social skill deficits. In E. J. Mash & L. G. Terdal (Eds.), *Behavioral assessment of childhood disorders*. New York: The Guilford Press, 1981.

Itard, J. *The wild boy of Aveyron*. New York: Appleton-Century-Crofts, 1962.

Johnston, J., & Pennypacker, H. *Strategies and tactics of human behavioral research*. Hillsdale, NJ: Lawrence Earlbaum Associates, 1980.

Kauffman, J. *Characteristics of children's behavior disorders*. Columbus, OH: Charles E. Merrill, 1981.

Kendall, P. C. Cognitive-behavioral interventions with children. In B. B. Lahey & A. E. Kazdin (Eds.), *Advances in clinical child psychology* (Vol. 4). New York: Plenum Press, 1981.

Knaus, W. J. *Rational emotive education*. New York: Institute for Rational Living, 1974.

Kohlberg, L. Development of moral character and ideology. In M. Hoffman &

L. Hoffman (Eds.), *Review of child development research* (Vol. 1). New York: Russell Sage Foundation, 1964.

LaGreca, A. M., & Mesibov, G. B. Social skills intervention with learning disabled children: Selecting skills and implementing training. *Journal of Clinical Child Psychology*, 1979, *8*, 234–241.

Ledwidge, B. Cognitive-behavior modification: A step in the wrong direction? *Psychological Bulletin*, 1978, *85*, 353–375.

Lipsitz, J. *Growing up forgotten*. Lexington, MA: D. C. Heath & Co., 1977.

Lloyd, J. Academic instruction and cognitive-behavior modification: The need for attack strategy training. *Exceptional Education Quarterly*, 1980, *1*(1), 53–63.

Lockwood, A. The effects of values clarification and moral development curricula on school-age subjects: A critical review of research. *Review of Educational Research*, 1978, *48*(3), 325–364.

Long, N. Manipulation of body boundaries, *Pointer*, 1981, *25*(2), 34–36.

Long, N., & Duffner, B. The stress cycle or the coping cycle? The impact of home and school stresses on pupils' classroom behavior. In J. Long, W. Morse, & R. Newman (Eds.), *Conflict in the classroom*. Belmont, CA: Wadsworth Pub. Co., 1980.

Luria, A. *The role of speech in the regulation of normal and abnormal behaviors*. New York: Liveright, 1961.

Mcfarland, J., Allen, L., & Honzik, M. *A developmental study of behavior problems of normal children between 21 months and 14 years*. Berkley, CA: University of California Press, 1955.

Meichenbaum, D. *Cognitive-behavior modification: An integrative approach*. New York: Plenum Press, 1977.

Merritt, C. Bandaids for the bumps. *Pointer*, 1981, *25*(2), 16–19.

Michelson, L., & Wood, R. Behavioral assessment and training of children's social skills. In *Progress in behavior modification* (Vol. 9). New York: Academic Press, 1980.

Minskoff, E. Teaching approach for developing nonverbal communication skills in students with social perception deficits. *Journal of Learning Disabilities*, 1980, *13*, 118–124, 203–208.

Morrison, R., & Bellack, A. The role of social perception in social skills. *Behavior Therapy*, 1981, *12*, 69–79.

Morse, W. Worksheet on life-space interviewing for teachers. In N. Long, W. Morse, & R. Newman (Eds.), *Conflict in the classroom*. Belmont, CA: Wadsworth Pub. Co., 1980.

Morse, W., Ardizzone, J., Macdonald, C., & Pasick, P. *Affective education for special children and youth*. Reston, VA: Council for Exceptional Children, 1980.

Nelson, R. O., & Hayes, S. C. Theoretical explanations for reactivity in self-monitoring. *Behavior Modification*, 1981, *5*, 3–14.

Newman, R. *Psychological consultation in the schools: A catalyst for learning*. New York: Basic Books, 1967.

Paul, J. Emotional disturbance in children. In J. Paul and B. Epanchin (Eds.), *Emotional disturbance in children: Theories and methods for teachers*. Columbus, OH: Charles E. Merrill, 1982.

Perlman, H. *Relationship: The heart of helping people*. Chicago: The University of Chicago Press, 1979.

Potvin, R., Hoge, D., & Nelson, H. *Religion and American youth*. Washington, DC: United States Catholic Conference, 1976.

Raths, L., Harmin, M., & Simon, S. *Values and teaching*. Columbus, OH: Charles E. Merrill, 1966.

Redl, F. Strategy and techniques of the life-space interview. *American Journal of Orthopsychiatry*, 1959, *29*, 1–18.

Redl, F. Foreword. In N. J. Long, W. C. Morse, & R. G. Newman, (Eds.), *Conflict in the classroom* (1st ed). Belmont, CA: Wadsworth Pub. Co., 1965.

Redl, F., & Wineman, D. *Children who hate*. New York: Free Press, 1951.

Redl, F., & Wineman, D. *Controls from within*. New York: Free Press, 1952.

Rinn, R. C., & Markle, A. Modification of social skill deficits in children. In A. S. Bellack & M. Hersen (Eds.), *Research and practice in social skills training*. New York: Plenum Press, 1979.

Sagotsky, G., Patterson, C. J., & Lepper, M. R. Training children's self control: A field experiment in self monitoring and goal setting in the classroom. *Journal of Experimental Child Psychology*, 1978, *25*, 242–253.

Sanders, L. The new tool salesmanship interview. *Pointer*, 1981, *25*(2), 32–33.

Shure, M. B., & Spivack, G. *Problem-solving techniques in child-rearing*. San Francisco: Jossey-Bass, 1978.

Simon, S., Howe, L., & Kirschenbaum, H. *Values clarification*. New York: Hart Pub. Co., 1972.

Skinner, B. *Science and human behavior*. New York: McMillan, 1953.

Spivack, G., Platt, J. J., & Shure, M. *The problem-solving approach to adjustment*. San Francisco: Jossey-Bass, 1976.

Spivack, G., & Shure, M. B. *Social adjustment of young children: A cognitive approach to solving real-life problems*. San Francisco: Jossey-Bass, 1974.

Stephens, T. *Social skills in the classroom*. Columbus, OH: Cedars Press, 1978.

Stokes, T. F., & Baer, D. M. An implicit technology of generalization. *Journal of Applied Behavior Analysis*, 1977, *10*, 349–367.

Strommen, M. *Five cries of youth*. San Francisco: Harper & Row, 1974.

Tompkins, J. The symptom estrangement interview. *Pointer*, 1981, *25*(2), 26–28

Trieschman, A., Whittaker, J., & Brendtro, L. *The other 23 hours*. Chicago: Aldine, 1969.

Turnbull, A., Strickland, B., & Brantley, J. *Developing and implementing individualized education programs*. Columbus, OH: Charles E. Merrill, 1978.

Valusek, S. People are not for hitting; a new social maxim for reducing violence. *Residential Group Care*, 1980, *6*(3), 6–7.

VanderVen, K. Activity programming. In G. W. Foster and others (Eds.), *Child care work with emotionally disturbed children*. Pittsburgh: University of Pittsburgh Press, 1972.

Vygotsky, L. *Thought and language*. New York: Wiley, 1962.

Waldfogel, S. & Gardner, G. E. Intervention in crises as a method of primary prevention. In G. Kaplan (Ed.), *Prevention of mental disorders in children*. New York: Basic Books, 1961.

Weissberg, R. P., Gesten, E. L., Liebenstein, N. L., Schmid, K. D., & Hutton, H. *The Rochester social problem solving (SPS) program*. Rochester, NY: Primary Mental Health Project, Center for Community Study, 1980.

Werner, A. Massaging numb values interview. *Pointer*, 1981, *25*(2), 29–31.

Whittaker, J. *Caring for troubled children*. San Francisco: Jossey-Bass, 1979.

Wood, F., & Lakin, D. (Eds.). *Punishment and adversive stimulation in special education: Legal, theoretical, and practical issues in their use with emotionally disturbed children and youth*. Minneapolis, MN: University of Minnesota, Department of Psychoeducational Studies, 1978.

Wood, M. (Ed.). *Developmental therapy: A textbook for teachers as therapists for emotionally disturbed young children*. Baltimore: University Park Press, 1975.

The Life-Space Interview: A Re-examination

6

LARRY K. BRENDTRO AND
ARLIN E. NESS

> So it is more useful to watch
> a man in times of peril and in
> adversity to discern what kind
> of man he is; for then at last
> words of truth are drawn from
> the depths of his heart, and the
> mask is torn off, and reality remains.
> — Titus Lucretius Carus (99–55 B.C),
> *On the Nature of Things*

One of the earliest approaches specifically designed for communicating with troubled children was the life-space interview (Redl & Wineman, 1952). In the previous chapter we discussed the life-space interview as a major intervention in the psychoeducational strategy of management. As we have noted, the LSI is a *here and now* intervention that uses a child's *direct life experiences* for purposes of *problem-solving*. These interviews are conducted by a *person with influence* in the child's daily life and are used for the two broad goals of *crisis management* ("emotional first-aid") and *affective re-education* ("clinical exploitation of life events").

Although there has been relatively little formal research on the LSI, accumulating clinical experience has increasingly validated the importance of this kind of approach to communicating with troubled children. The LSI is not a simple technique that lends itself to easy measurement. However, formal research will be imperative if the LSI is to compete in a heavily empirical literature, and we presume such will be forthcoming. This problem is even more a challenge to re-

177

searchers than to practitioners: how can one design studies that do justice to the richness of the methodology? Perhaps for the short term we shall have to settle for studies that merely verify what the practitioner already knows from experience, namely, that the intervention can have a powerful impact on behavior.

A RESURGENCE OF INTEREST

There has been a renewal of interest in recent years in discovering more effective ways of talking with children. This interest is seen among practitioners of various philosophical orientations. Meichenbaum (1980) suggests that a major reason for the growth of cognitive approaches among behaviorists has been the accumulating evidence of the lack of long-term carry-over of changes made by traditional behavior modification techniques. Within the psychoeducational tradition, Long and Fagen broke a decade-long lull in the literature on the life-space interview by publishing 18 original articles on the methodology (Fagen & Long, 1981).

Those who work with children have long recognized the value of verbal "counseling" to shape attitudes of behavior. There is little doubt that teachers have systematically used variations of these approaches for hundreds of years (Hall, 1829). Although the degree of teacher directiveness, the type of contact, the formality of structure, and the nature of the relationship vary, the intent always seems to be the same: changing behavior by talking about it.

Among the various "talking" strategies proposed in recent years are the following:

The *teaching interaction*, a highly structured format for communicating with troubled children about specific problem behavior and its consequences that was developed within the Teaching-Family model (Phillips et al., 1972).

The *psychosituational interview*, another behavioral technique designed to assess how environmental variables and attitudes reinforce and maintain behavior through direct questions and answers (Bersoff & Grieger, 1971; Walker & Shea, 1976).

Rational-emotive therapy, a directive and confrontational technique for changing behavior by eliminating irrational thoughts (Ellis & Grieger, 1977).

Teacher effectiveness training, a nondirective format for communicating with youth without adopting a judgmental or authoritarian manner (Gordon, 1974).

Reality therapy, a common-sense procedure for teaching responsibility and providing supportive relationships (Glasser, 1965). More directive than Gordon's approach and more empathic than Ellis' method, reality therapy has found a sympathetic audience among educators and therapists.

Noting the renewed attention being given the life-space interview, Morse says:

> There has been a resurgence of interest in the LSI recently which suggests an active future. The interest is pragmatic. The fact is one cannot deal with or talk to kids in the manner previously used. It is now illegal to treat youngsters in the arbitrary ways of the past. There is due process which includes interaction. At the same time, authorities are still responsible. Hence, the search is for humane ways to interact (1981, p. 68).

The emphasis on deinstitutionalization and mainstreaming has fostered a growing utilization of part-time interventions for people in crisis. A whole new generation of social agencies has arisen to provide brief therapy, including suicide hot-lines, the crisis drop-in center, and the runaway shelter. Schools are making increased use of resource rooms or helping teacher programs and involving counselors and administrators in short-range intervention as an alternative to kicking out and suspending students. All of these developments give impetus to the search for more effective methods of verbal communication with troubled youth.

APPLICATIONS OF THE LIFE-SPACE INTERVIEW

Much of the literature on the life-space interview was produced before 1970. Although contributions have continued, many of them have been a restatement of Redl's key concepts in a variety of forms for the purpose of staff training (e.g., Gardner, 1979). Applications of the life-space interview have been directed to professionals in a wide variety of settings including the following:

Therapeutic camping. Morse and Wineman (1957), Morse and Small (1959), and Morgan (1981) discuss applications to camping programs with disturbed children.

Residential treatment. Redl (1959), Long and colleagues (1961), Kitchener (1963), Wineman (1972), and Small (1976) describe applications of the LSI in various residential group care settings.

Medical facilities. Vernick (1963) describes the use of the LSI in a medical hospital with an adolescent who verbally harasses staff and with a young child anxious about impending surgery.

School settings. A variety of applications in classrooms or resource rooms is reported by Redl (1963), Long (1963), Newman (1967), and Morse (1971, 1980).

Counseling and administration. Special issues related to the use of the LSI by school counselors (Beck & McConnell, 1980) and principals (Bernstein, 1963; Poore, 1981) are discussed. Newman (1981) outlines the use of the LSI in counseling school *staff* in moments of crisis.

Poore (1981) identifies a number of goals for the LSI in the school setting including:

—To salvage as much time and energy as possible for school work. Emotional conflict wastes vast amounts of time that could be spent productively in learning.
—To help students to understand their feelings and learn to act in appropriate ways.
—To help them learn to "own" behavioral problems.

Poore also notes that teachers frequently are reluctant to ask for help from a principal trained in a life-space interview because they may see this as a sign of weakness or may feel that their classroom secrets will be revealed. He suggests that principals must come to grips with the need for reality consequences if they are to gain the support of parents or staff. He does, however, see the LSI as a useful tool for the principal.

Heuchert (1981) gives examples of the use of the LSI to support students in the classroom where the primary control strategy is behavior modification and suggests that the adults must know when to stay on the level of observable behavior and when to move to the level of feelings. He gives an account of a youth who got into regular confrontations when he did not earn the tokens. Through an LSI, staff learned that the real issue was not the stars but the boy's pervasive feeling of rejection, feeling weird, being required to take daily shots and urine tests for diabetes, and feeling that God was punishing him. As he came to feel the acceptance of the teacher, he was able to abandon negative behavior.

Long (1963) describes some of the problems of trying to train teachers in the use of the LSI technique. Initially teachers were enthusiastic and the children responded. As they became more involved in problem-solving activities, teachers encountered a lack of support from other school staff. Rather than face resistance, teachers stopped talking to their peers about their activities and, in time, many abandoned the use of the technique. This research suggests that if the LSI is to work in a school setting, teachers must be part of some support system. Lay and Duffner (1981) outline a procedure for developing support teams, preferably with several people who can work flexibly to assist one another in mutual support. They note that it is possible to teach interviewing skills to staff in four weekly sessions of 2 hours each.

Lay and Duffner (1981) present a data-based system of studying the schools' behavior management climate before implementing an in-service training model for the LSI. They gather information from the faculty on three forms pertaining to: (1) pupil behavioral needs, (2) teacher support from co-workers, and (3) teacher support from administration. If these instruments indicate a need, an LSI system is implemented. Specific checklists are completed on each referral for an LSI as well on each completed interview. This provides a systematic record of the intervention and is a major step toward answering the valid criticism often leveled against the LSI, namely, that data on outcome are lacking.

Two attempts at applying behavioral research methods to the LSI are reported by DeMagistris and Imber (1980). In the first study (Reilly, Imber, & Kremmens, 1978), the use of the LSI in a resource room setting led to reduction in inappropriate target behaviors. The second study dealt with disturbed junior high school students in a special class in a residential treatment center. Eight boys with a variety of targeted maladaptive behaviors were assessed through behavioral observation and academic testing. These data also clearly supported the efficacy of the LSI procedure in improving academic and social performance (DeMagistris & Imber, 1980).

Finally, Newman (1981) outlines ways in which LSI's can be used in an informal and relaxed way to *help staff members* who get caught in distressing situations with their students or colleagues. Adults in youth work often can feel helpless, inept, ridiculous, cruel, or embarrassed; without resolution, such feelings can lead one to have increased problems in child management and ultimately to leave the job.

THE PROBLEM-SOLVING PROCESS

The life-space interview is by its very design a highly spontaneous and exploratory communication. Thus the danger exists that by specifying a concrete series of steps for conducting an LSI, one may oversimplify a complex process or ritualize what would be creative and individualized communication. Yet practitioners require some framework for proceeding, not as a rigid sequence, but as a set of guidelines.

In this section we shall outline the principles and procedures for effective LSI's. This material has been gathered from a rather extensive if scattered literature of the LSI as well as from the authors' experience training professionals in this approach over a period of 20 years.

The LSI is a specific style of communication between two or more persons involved in shared problem-solving activity. In order for participants in the LSI to be able to work cooperatively in the problem-solving task, certain preconditions must be met. Borrowing concepts that have emerged from small group research (H. Maier, cited by Whittaker, 1980), we might label these necessary conditions as: (1) locating commonness, (2) creating exchange, and (3) developing mutual identification.

1. *Locating commonness.* To work effectively, individuals must believe that they have something in common. If the interviewer begins with a moralistic approach, this serves only to exaggerate the difference between the adult and child. The tone becomes, "You are wrong; I am right; I don't see how you could ever do such a thing," etc. By contrast, an empathic approach puts participants in a shared existence: "I can see how you must have felt."

2. *Creating exchange.* The empathic approach encourages the young person to express his viewpoint. As the youngster comes to feel accepted and understood, he will be more receptive to the views of the adult (or peers) who have been willing to listen to him. However, in a moralistic interview, the communication is one-sided: "I will talk, you listen; I don't want to hear your excuses." Such an approach extinguishes genuine exchange.

3. *Developing mutual identification.* Adults whose main orientation to youth is to seek to control them are more likely to see young people as adversaries than as co-participants in problem-solving. Those who strive to control troubled youth can easily come to either despise those whom they cannot dominate or be despised by those whom they can. But one who truly seeks to understand another cannot as easily hate or be hated. When teachers learn to see problems through the eyes of the child, they develop a supportive relationship that fosters trust and identification (Fagen & Long, 1981).

The process of problem-solving in the LSI has been outlined by Morse and Wingo (1962), Morse (1971), and Fagen (1981). Figure 6-1 represents this process schematically. A specific incident or situation forms the basis for an LSI. The content of a typical interview consists of identifying the problem as perceived by the child, clarifying distortions to establish what really happened, and developing an appropriate plan for future action.

Note that although these elements are critical to the LSI, children do not always allow us to deal in sequence as the diagram might suggest.

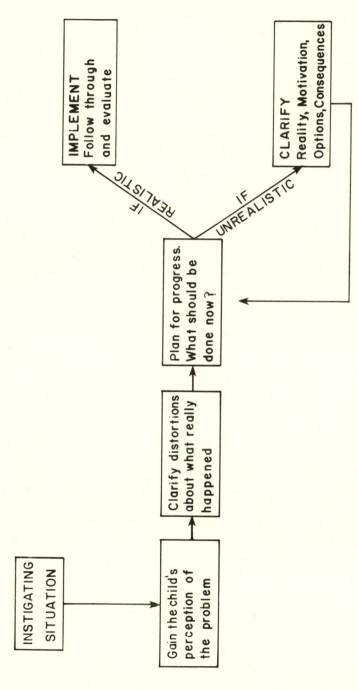

FIG. 6-1. Problem-solving in the life-space interview.

For example, a wildly upset youth who has been in a fight may begin with a ready-made plan: "You'd better let me out of here because I'm going to go and kill him." In another situation a child may be so overwrought with feelings that he or she is temporarily too angry, too withdrawn, or too disoriented to communicate in a reasonable manner about what really happened.

Gaining the Child's Perception of the Problem

In the initial stages of the interview, the adult is more concerned with establishing truth as it is seen through the eyes of the child than truth in the legalistic sense. If the adult is too quick to attack the distortions of the youngster, this may serve only to close off communication. The adult must initially enhance a feeling of understanding and acceptance so that a youth feels free to express honestly and fully how he feels in a situation. This may be facilitated by comments such as: "That must have really made you angry;" "I can see you are really sad;" "You probably don't feel like talking."

A highly upset child may need an opportunity to ventilate feelings before being able to attend to content in a more rational manner. The essential nonjudgmental stance with which the adult opens the interview presumes that the adult is in fact in control of his own emotions. If the adult feels that he has strong negative feelings, he should probably not begin the interview (Brenner, 1969). Essentially, the initial portion of an interview involves making contact with a youngster; any of the relationship-building techniques discussed in Chapter 2 may be useful in this process.

The youngster may use any of a wide range of defensive maneuvers to avoid dealing with the topic at hand. The defenses used by the child should not be seen merely as an obstruction to problem-solving. In fact, these behaviors may be one of our best sources of data about the child. Often the defense is not an isolated response but is part of a broader pattern (Roberts & Jurin, 1968):

— The defensive behavior may reflect the *modus operandi* that has worked in the past.
— The defensive behavior may give us clues about how adults have responded to the child in the past.

With a highly agitated, out-of-touch child, it may be necessary to establish communication by skillfully shifting attention to some more concrete, neutral, or positive topic. For example, youngsters have been distracted from a tirade by talking about some prized possession, a slogan on a sweatshirt, the comic book in their pocket, or an upcoming activity. When such a child is closer to reality and interacting more rationally, one can return to the incident at hand. Another useful means of making contact with some upset children is to give attention to a physical hurt (be it real or exaggerated): "My, that must have hurt. Do you want me to get something for it?" Sometimes such a direct expression of physical concern may help establish a trusting communication with an otherwise guarded and self-protected child. A child who has to be physically restrained sometimes will allow such attention as a means of reopening a communication before he will be willing to start talking.

Several specialized methods have been developed to improve communication with the verbally reluctant child. Rather than abdicate the interview or become angry at the child for his or her silence, the adult can use the technique of a monologue or dialogue. The adult fills the silence by carrying on a conversation with himself, so to speak, or with another adult who is in the room. Of course, the content of this conversation is designed for the youth's consumption, such as,

> *Monologue:* "I know you don't want to talk; I suppose I'd feel that way, too. It must be disappointing when something like this has happened. . ." etc.
>
> *Dialogue:* Adult 1: "Why do you suppose she is hiding her face?" Adult 2: "I don't know. This is the same way she acted earlier this morning when some of the other kids teased her about something." Adult 1: "Perhaps she thinks nobody cares about her." Adult 2: "Or that if she pouts they will notice her. . . ."

Often the tone is more important than exactly what is said. Through the skillful use of such dialogue one can negate the child's "I won't talk, so there is nothing to talk about" strategy. Many children will soon join in the conversation as if they had participated all along, perhaps initially entering the dialogue to disagree about something, with a response such as "That's all you know about it!" and the way is then opened for direct communication.

Clarifying Distortions

Through the initial period in the interview it will usually be possible to gain an understanding of the psychological truth as seen through the eyes of the child. Often the child's perceptions are fragmented or distorted, so it then becomes the goal of the interviewer to help the child organize his recollections. Probably the most useful technique in this regard is to develop a *chronological sequence*. The adult guides the interactions so that the youngster recalls what happened in each step that led to the problem. This may be very difficult for some youngsters who become fixated on what someone has done to them but have difficulty looking back to see what earlier events may have precipitated the problem. Numerous other techniques for clarifying distortions are available, for example:

— Providing additional facts the child is unaware of or "forgot."
— Explaining how it "seemed" to the adult or other onlookers.
— Encouraging the child to analyze how other parties to the conflict must have felt.

A concrete technique for clarification is *re-enactment* of the incident (Roberts & Jurin, 1968). Some complex problems can best be untangled by an instant replay. Even if the adult has a pretty good notion of what has happened, by expressing some confusion one can tease out more information. ("Just who was standing where? Then show me what happened next.") Of course, the pitfall in this approach is that it can allow the youngster the opportunity to re-enact the situation in a distorted manner. Another technique of clarification suggested by Roberts and Jurin (1968) is *planful distortion or exaggeration*. For example, the adult might say, "So I am to understand you were not provoking anyone. You were just sitting there working and out of the blue the teacher came up to you and said, 'Excuse me, you are kicked out of the room. I'm sorry to interrupt your work.'" This strategy, which is familiar to most teachers, usually succeeds in challenging the youngster to offer more information.

The process of clarifying distortions can be complicated by the child's adoption of patterns of defensive or distracting behavior. The skillful interviewer can often learn more about the youngster by this behavior than if the child were to communicate politely about the topic at hand.

Dembinski (1981) and Roberts and Jurin (1968) have described a variety of defenses and distractors that students may use in attempting to avoid facing problems. These specific verbal or nonverbal behaviors are often characteristic of the interpersonal response style that the youth has found to be useful in the past. Some of the more common defenses encountered in interviews and the implications for decoding and managing them follow below.

1. *Movement.* By jumping around, pacing the floor, playing with props, spinning the chair, hitting or kicking objects (or persons), or trying to leave the room, the child may seek to distract the interviewer. Such action may be rewarding to the youth as it allows tension to be reduced and the hostility to be expressed. The interviewer may suggest that there are other ways to show anger or that it would be easier to talk about the problem than to try to run from it. If the child's actions can

damage property or people, then firmer intervention or even physical control may be temporarily needed. Minor movement can usually be ignored if it does not impair communication.

2. *Noisemaking.* This includes laughing, giggling, crying, banging objects, making animal sounds, singing, mimicking, or using other noise that competes with the interviewer's attempts to communicate. The child has learned that such behavior exasperates adults, who quickly come to feel that talking is hopeless or the child is "crazy." The goal is to get the adult to abandon efforts at communication. Generally a direct approach is indicated such as, "You're acting silly [or crazy] so that we will leave you alone and not talk about this."

3. *Profanity.* There appear to be three major types of profanity, each suggesting a different management strategy.

a. *Profanity as a response:* This is the result of a strong emotional state, such as a feeling of physical or psychological stress. Sometimes in the protected setting of the LSI, it may be best to ignore this kind of profanity. One might, of course, respond differently in another setting, such as when a student bumps his knee while taking a seat in the concert hall. Of course, the child who responds to every slight frustration with profanity may need to learn a better way of coping or may be reflecting another underlying problem.

b. *Profanity to create an effect:* Here the youth is trying to gain a certain response. He may be seeking to frighten or intimidate others, or this behavior may simply be a ploy to throw the adult off the track by substituting a minor problem (swearing) for a major one (Duffner, 1976). Ordinarily the adult will seek not to be distracted by this bluster but to keep the focus on the real problem. Sometimes this can be achieved by a question such as, "Do you think that by talking like that you can cover up the real problem?"

c. *Colloquial profanity:* Some children have been socialized in a family or peer group culture that regularly uses profanity to punctuate normal conversations. Such youth may very casually invoke what are highly emotionally charged words to most others. Although there is certainly long-term educational value in teaching youth the appropriate language for specific situations, this type of profanity does not ordinarily interfere with problem-solving communication unless it engenders feelings in the adult or other participants in the interview.

4. *Omnipotence.* The child may be bossy, controlling, or challenging to the adult. The defiance may be very aggressive and even irrational, such as, "Keep your hands off me or I'll kill you," "Shut up," "F---you," "I'll do what I please," and "You can't stop me." Such behavior suggests that the youngster has been successful in controlling adults through threats, intimidation, and defiance. This child needs a firm,

strong, secure adult who can show that the adult is in control, not the child's omnipotence. However, counter-aggressive behavior by a threatened adult must be scrupulously avoided.

5. *Manipulation.* Although most behavior is to some degree manipulative, we refer here to the young people who are masters at out-maneuvering adults. They may use a wide variety of techniques such as:

a. *Changing the subject:* By shifting to a neutral or less threatening topic or sometimes even inventing make-believe problems, they may keep the adult occupied.

b. *Seductive charm:* Some youth are highly skillful at making pals out of adults or gaining sympathy from adults. They may be very appealing youth who use their personalities to escape the consequences of their behavior or to draw the adult into a nurturant role.

c. *Penitence:* Some youngsters may express pseudo-remorse, overflowing with shallow promises for reform or insincere apologies. These youth may be able to generate "forgiving" adults by this act.

d. *Role-switching:* Some children turn the interview around and begin questioning the adult, focusing on what the adult could have done differently to improve matters.

e. *Projection:* By shifting attention to the real or supposed problems of others, the child can avoid dealing with the problems he has himself.

f. *Twenty questions:* Some children have learned to play a game that may also be called "You guess and then maybe I'll tell you." Before long the adult is doing all the work and they are just nodding or shrugging their shoulders.

g. *Flooding:* Here a youngster will dump so many problems and issues on the table that progress cannot possibly be made in solving any of them. The general response to such manipulation is to indicate an awareness of the manipulative maneuver as it develops and to interpret it as a way of avoiding discussion of the real problem.

6. *Fear, Withdrawal.* The child may curl up, or feign sleep, deafness, or muteness. Behavior may suggest genuine panic as when a child screams, or recoils, as if anticipating attack. Some of these children will threaten the adult, but their behavior signals a quality of fear rather than omnipotence. They may promote physical reprisal, even suggest, "Go ahead and hit me." Such children usually have experienced overly punitive or abusive treatment from adults in their lives. The appropriate approach in these cases usually is gentleness, reassurance, and support. The adult may verbalize the child's unexpressed fears of reprisal and assure him that they are unfounded.

7. *Embarrassment, Shame.* This demeanor usually reflects genuine affect. It may relate to a particular situation (such as bedwetting) or to a deeper, more widespread uncertainty such as a problem with sexual identity. Such behavior often indicates a child who has been teased, shamed, humiliated, or rejected by adults and made to feel stupid, evil, inadequate, or crazy. When such negative self-directed feelings become excessive, a child can even become self-destructive. These children require very careful handling. Adults must be supportive and reassure the child that he or she will not be scolded, punished, or rejected if these problems are expressed.

As the interview progresses, one usually encounters a change in the youngster. Roberts and Jurin (1968) call this the "moment of truth" when a child abandons defensive behavior. Examples would include:

—A physically restrained child abandons her defiance and seeks attention for some real or imagined bump or scratch.
—The thick-enough-to-cut-with-a-knife hostility between two youth is broken by some humorous interaction that leads to a feeling of camaraderie.
—The sarcastic pseudo-bravado style of a defiant youth gives way to a quivery voice, tearful eyes, and an attempt to share a deeply felt concern.

Planning for Progress

With defenses down, it is generally much easier to clarify any distortions in the child's perception of the problem. Once the problem and the child's perception of the problem have been clarified, it is usually time to plan a course of action. Typically, the adult will try to elicit from the young person what it is he or she plans to do about the problem. Sometimes the youngster will suggest a realistic and responsible plan and all that will remain will be to implement it. This plan, however, cannot be imposed on the young person by the adult, for the youth must have ownership in the plan if the solution is to be realistic.

One of the roles an adult can play in the planning process is to help the youngster clarify the range of options available. If an option is inappropriate, then the adult may need to help the youngster see this, or if necessary to communicate directly that a particular choice is not acceptable. The youngster should understand the consequences of his decision, which in certain instances could even involve a contract worked out in the life-space interview.

Insofar as possible, the plan should be highly specific. If others are to be involved, then their roles need to be clarified. It is important for the youngster to understand exactly what response is expected from him. Thus, for example, "What will you do when he tries to get you mad?" may require further discussion, demonstration, and role-playing. Sometimes a strategic change in the schedule or activity will be worked out, such as "You will eat alone today" or "Sit over there away from him." Perhaps the plan will involve arranging some signal system so that the adult can remind a youngster of the plan or mark a problem as it is developing (or a successful demonstration of a new social skill.)

Sometimes at the end of an interview we are still left with some problems unresolved. It may still be necessary to gain closure, perhaps by "cauterizing" emotions after a particularly stormy session so the problems do not spill over into subsequent activities. If the issue cannot be fully resolved, it may be useful to create an interim solution, such as two boys agreeing not to fight until the issue can be reopened at a later date. Sometimes the adult will decide to avoid closure. There may be value in emphasizing that the issue is not yet settled. Thus the youth who feels little guilt when he seriously injures others may be told "We're not yet finished with this. Tomorrow we will decide what is to be done." This technique relies on what psychologists call the "Ziegarnik effect," which relates to the tendency for incompleted tasks to keep foremost in our thinking.

Implementation: Follow-through and Evaluation

When the life-space interview has not involved those peers or adults who are party to the instigating conflict, then the return to the group must be carefully planned. Adults or other students who are nursing angry feelings are quite capable of setting off the conflict again. Newman (1967) notes that the teacher who still feels like beating the culprit may only be frustrated by seeing her troublemaker return all smiles in the company of a benign counselor or principal. She makes these concrete suggestions:

— If possible, accompany the child back to the class or group milieu to prevent a triumphant re-entry.
— A clear note written with the knowledge and perhaps participation of the child can be useful but should be followed up with a conference.
— If the adult still has strong feelings, he or she could perhaps benefit from an LSI if he or she has a trusting relationship with the counselor.

Other methods, which have been suggested by Roberts and Jurin (1968), include:

— Letting a child sit alone for a time until he is ready to rejoin the group
— Rewarding an appropriate return with positive, affectionate feelings, or high-interest activities
— Acting casual (neither effusive nor negative) with a child who still has a need to sulk for a time

The outcome plan should be specific with follow-up evaluation points; for example, it might include having a youth not react to another boy's teasing for 1 week, counting the number of times he tries to tease, and sharing this information with the teacher daily (Fagen, 1981). It is of utmost importance to arrange a follow-through. If something has been decided, who will see that it is carried out? Platitudes and good intentions are of less value than precise understandings of who is going to do what and when.

The various stages of a typical LSI are exemplified in "The Case of Philip" that follows. A qualification is in order. There is no "typical" LSI, for, as Heuchert and Long advise, "LSI is not a simple technique but an adventure in teaching and learning during a time of crisis (1981, p. 8). We can provide some guidelines, rationale, and cautions; the interviewer must supply humane sensitivity and sophisticated communication skills. This account was provided by Kristen Juul:

> *Instigating situation:* Philip has been in continual conflict with other students in the junior high school English class. During the week since he joined the class, he has not developed any friendships. With words and gestures, he teases and insults the other students. They in turn reject him and tease and insult him. When he walks into the classroom, the other students groan loudly. Philip is very much aware that he is not accepted. He comes to the teacher after class crying and complaining about the other students. On the basis of this pattern of behavior, the teacher decides to conduct a life-space interview.
>
> 1. *Obtaining the child's perception of the problem.* The teacher encourages Philip to talk about the event and other events leading up to it. The intent is to find out how Philip sees the cause and effect relationships and what his image of himself is. During this initial period, the teacher relates to Philip in a completely accepting and nonjudgmental way. It is important that Philip feel that the teacher understands and is on his side, even though the teacher does not side with him. The teacher sits beside Philip rather than directly facing him in order to create the feeling that both are looking at the problem shoulder-to-shoulder. Philip recounts at length examples of how other children pick on him and gang up on him. The teacher reflects back to Philip his feelings and remarks with a sympathetic and accepting voice. He says that all the students hate him, tease him; they don't want him in the class; he has no friends. The other students always start the trouble — he never does.

2. *Clarifying distortions.* After obtaining Philip's perception, the teacher concludes that further clarification of what really happens in Philip's interactions with others will be necessary. The teacher must have facts to rectify Philip's emotional distortions of the events. These facts are presented in a matter-of-fact way, not to make a liar of him, but rather to help him see that it is his misperceptions of the facts that get him into trouble.

Philip was presented with some observations from the class period. He was the one who whispered something objectionable to a boy the minute he entered the class. He had made an unfriendly grimace at a girl. He had pushed another student's book off the desk. Philip did admit to the teacher that in a great many of the incidents he was the instigator. At this point in the interview Philip had dropped his defensive demeanor and seemed genuinely interested in doing something about his problem. In order to appraise Philip's motivation to change, the teacher asked Philip if he wanted to go on like this or if he was interested in learning some ways of getting along. Philip said he was very unhappy with being disliked by everybody and not having friends, and he was willing to try anything to get along.

3. *Planning for progress.* The teacher and Philip discussed various ways in which the situation might be improved. After considering a number of options, they agreed on a specific plan, which included the following steps: (a) Philip would stop all acts that might antagonize the other students. (b) Philip would begin to say friendly things to the other children, offer them gum, smile, praise, and so forth when it was appropriate. (c) Philip would ignore any provocations. Both Philip and the teacher agreed that they would monitor the plan to see if it was being followed and if it worked, and it was understood that other alternatives might have to be considered if this plan was not sufficient.

4. *Implementation: follow-through and evaluation.* Philip proceeded to carry out the agreement that he had made and was able to follow the plan without reminders from the teacher. After a week Philip had no more problems in the class, he established a close friendship with another boy, his unhappiness with his classmates ended, and his crying stopped. The teacher praised him occasionally for the nice way he was getting along and for his courage and initiative in putting his own house in order. There was no further need for talks about his classroom adjustment.

MODIFYING THE LSI FOR DEVELOPMENTALLY IMMATURE CHILDREN

A significant contribution to the practice of life-space interviews is the developmental approach of Wood and Weller (1981). They emphasize that the LSI is not an intrinsically appropriate or effective technique but is useful in varying degrees with particular children. For some children, to attempt an LSI is to enter an exercise of futility and frustration.

Wood and Weller note that many troubled youngsters at upper

elementary or secondary levels have not yet mastered the social–emotional milestones characteristic of much younger children. Their work at the Rutland Center and the University of Georgia has shown that those children with socioemotional skills equivalent to a typical child beyond 8 years old are best able to benefit from this verbal approach. Presumably, other strategies such as behavioral approaches might be a better fit with some extremely developmentally delayed children. Still, immature youngsters can benefit from the LSI if modifications are made to adjust to the child's developmental level.

Children who are developmentally delayed may have the following difficulties that impede effective use of verbal intervention:

— They are totally impulsive and egocentric. They cannot postpone action to verbalize feelings.
— They have the ability to feel psychological pain but not to communicate about feelings. They tend to be motoric rather than verbal.
— They have difficulty in sequencing events and tend to fix on one piece of an incident (e.g., "He hit me"). Memory may be fragmented and they may need help fitting the pieces together to see a pattern.

Wood and Weller have identified a series of specific skills that are prerequisites for being able to benefit from a typical LSI (see Table 6-1). If the child does not yet possess these skills, then the usual LSI procedures should not be attempted without major modifications. Wood and Weller present a number of such modifications, including:

1. *Story completion:* The interviewer relates the incident in story

Table 6-1. Prerequisite Developmental Skills for Benefiting from Typical LSI Procedures

1. *Awareness* of self, events, and other people.
2. *Attention* to verbal interpersonal stimuli (the adult speaking) and sufficient self-conrol to sustain such attention for a reasonable period.
3. *Trust* that the adult really cares and a willingness to share minimal information with the adult.
4. *Conceptual ability* sufficient to recall a simple series of events (sequential thinking) and give simple reasons for why events occur (causal thinking).
5. *Verbal comprehension* sufficient to understand the words used by the adult (receptive vocabulary) and the meaning of the stream of thought being communicated.
6. *Verbal expression* sufficient to produce words or signs that describe the crisis event, personal experiences, and simple characteristics of self and others.

Adapted from Wood and Weller, 1981.

form and has the child fill in short missing pieces: "Then when they laughed at you, you _____?_____." The child may be asked simple questions and then the adult resumes the narrative.

2. *Role play by adult:* The adult takes the child's role and acts out the incident; usually the child will spontaneously add to the act or will watch intently.

3. *Story-telling:* If the real incident is too painful for the child to accept or cannot be easily understood, a parallel incident can be constructed with make-believe characters. When the fictitious problem is resolved, the adult gains closure by bringing the child back to the real situation.

4. *Directed discussion:* The adult uses simple, direct questions to elicit discussion about the incident. The session is short and leads to a simple resolution.

5. *Creative art media:* Puppets, drawings, tape recordings, etc., can facilitate verbal communication or provide alternative ways of communicating and lead to a resolution that may be essentially nonverbal.

Wood and Weller outline a series of socioemotional developmental levels through which children progress. Only at the upper levels is a child able to master the skills of participating constructively in a *group* LSI. This suggests that one of the reasons group LSIs have been often viewed as inherently unmanageable is that children lack the prerequisite social skills for participating in complex group problem-solving.

THE GROUP LIFE-SPACE INTERVIEW

The group life-space interview provides useful diagnostic information to the adult since it acts much like a microcosm of the group operations (Morse & Small, 1959). In addition, it helps the child develop a wide range of social skills that enhance his competence and self-concept. Among those skills identified by Wood and Weller (1981) are:

— Participating in group discussions, problem-solving, and other social interactions
— Asserting self, expressing feelings, and making contributions to the group
— Taking suggestions, responding to leadership, and respecting alternative viewpoints
— Developing a feeling of belonging and pride in group achievement

One of the most promising applications of the group LSI has been in resolving intergroup conflict, such as racial animosity. Morse's early research on the group LSI (Morse & Small, 1959; Morse & Wineman, 1957) showed positive improvement in many (but not all) groups as a result of this intervention. The most common target behavior was peer aggression such as fighting, scapegoating, name-calling, swearing, or bickering. Morse and Wineman (1957) noted that the effectiveness of group interviews depends on a number of factors:

— Group code: The group may condone anti-authority attitudes, secrecy, cooperation, etc.
— Group cohesiveness: The group may be tightly united or broken into cliques or subgroups, characterized by compatibility or incompatibility.
— Power structure: This may be hierarchical or shared; roles of leader vary; the group may tend to scapegoat, isolate, etc.

Although the group LSI shows promise, it is our impression that the group application has been anything but popular with many practitioners. If an individual LSI is complicated, then a group LSI is that much more difficult. Most group LSI's have been attempted in programs that frankly did not have a positive group culture in place. Thus if the group climate is seen as negative, there should be no doubt that the group LSI will be most difficult. This view of the group is expressed by Bloom: "It can be very difficult and overwhelming for the interviewer because of group contagion and anti-adult and anti-peer pressures and threats" (1981, p. 24). Many who are highly effective with individual LSI's have failed miserably in the group situation. While the unstructured nature of the individualized LSI allows full expression of a child's feelings, the same lack of structure can be the death of the group LSI. In reading much of the literature or listening to practitioners, one gets the feeling that leaders of group LSI's are sitting on a tinder box of potential contagion, with several adults sometimes being required to moderate the interactions and prevent chaos. What many have called group life-space interview sessions have really been only a series of individual interviews held in the presence of a reluctant audience. The resulting wild behavior was probably only useful for diagnosis, and it highlights the need for structure to help keep groups under control and on task.

Probably the biggest limitation in traditional group LSI approaches has been that this technique was something that adults did to a group; as our knowledge of group processes has expanded, we have come to see the importance of getting the youth involved in *conducting* the interviews, thereby replacing resistant group behavior with positive peer cultures.

It is noteworthy that Morse and Small (1959) found that three of 27 groups developed a strongly positive culture serendipitously; they called this *the spontaneous therapeutic interaction interview* and were clearly excited about the effect. They noted:

The whole atmosphere changes. Usually the focus on the problem is high, the involvement is intense, and all take an active part in the experience. Sometimes members participate by rapt attention rather than words . . . the revelations of their difficulties are given with feeling, occasionally approaching a specific abreaction with tremendous emotion. There is much mutual discussion, and real sympathetic concern for the plight of one another (1959, p. 38).

This is as fine a description of positive peer culture in action as exists. Morse and Small found that these three groups were all rated as "very positive" by independent observers not aware of the group interviews. Of course, rather than hope that a few such groups will arise "spontaneously," we now make it a major goal of re-education to create such a group climate, through specific strategies for guiding group interaction (Vorrath & Brendtro, 1974). We can conclude that life-space interviewing can be highly effective but requires significant modifications as compared to the individual interview. These modifications include the following:

— More structure
— Significant peer involvement in the process
— A genuine mutual care and concern by members
— Procedures for dealing with group negativism and problem avoidance
— Adults who see groups not as negative or threatening but as a positive potential

A model for group interviewing compatible with the psychoeducational tradition will be considered more fully in Chapter 7.

CAUTIONS AND LIMITATIONS

Any useful technique is subject to misuse. Fritz Redl (1959) was the first to identify various situations that can interfere with successful use of the LSI. These are worthy of note:

Improper incident. Interviews should be used strategically and not for problems that can be handled better in other ways. Further, some incidents are so ambiguous that we might better wait for a cleaner problem. For example, a specific behavior may be characteristic of a pattern with a given youngster, but in the case at hand other youth may have been equally culpable so that the youth would feel picked on if we singled him out for an LSI.

Improper role. Certain outrageous behavior may call for temporary authoritarian intervention incompatible with empathic problem-solving discussions. This does not, however, preclude conducting an LSI after things settle down a bit and the adult is able to relax his role.

Improper mood. If the child or the adult is particularly short-tempered, exhausted, and so forth, then it usually is not advisable to conduct an LSI under these circumstances.

Improper timing. If the child would be deprived of a high-interest activity (or allowed to escape responsibility for work or other assigned tasks), it may be counterproductive to conduct an LSI. Experience in residential treatment and camping settings suggests that the time shortly before bedtime is generally not a good time to schedule an LSI. Various other conflicts in the schedule for the adult or the child may dictate delaying the interview or waiting for another incident.

Improper setting. The terrain and props may support the child's resistance. A lack of privacy, interruptions, distracting objects, an uninviting room, lack of a comfortable place to sit—all of these may make it easy to escape the task. Even a counseling office may be an improper setting if it does not facilitate communication between a particular child and adult.

The life-space interview has been around long enough that its limitations as well as its strengths should now be readily apparent. Among the potential misuses of this approach, we have identified the following ten issues:

1. A frequently voiced concern is whether the LSI may in fact reinforce negative behavior by rewarding a child with attention from a friendly adult (Lay & Duffner, 1981). One answer to this comes with systematic record-keeping, which can pick up emerging problems. The LSI should not be used in situations where it serves to reinforce negative behavior. The adult must have a basic understanding of how attention can reinforce undesirable behavior and utilize this information accordingly in his or her interventions. In all fairness, it should be noted that LSI's are not the only interventions that could become rewarding. This even can be true of the blind use of time-out procedures, which practitioners ordinarily assume not to be reinforcing but which may well be reinforcing to some youngsters (e.g., a child who desires to escape the group). The perceptive adult can usually distinguish the child who is "acting up" for attention from one who is "acting out" a significant problem.

2. Some adults seem to get vicarious enjoyment from seeing negative acting-out behavior in young people. If the adult's motivation for using LSI's is tainted by this problem, then children are likely to suffer.

3. The LSI can meet the adult's need to communicate, which may not in fact be the child's need. Some adults derive great satisfaction out of talking about problems. The purpose of the LSI is not to give the adult satisfaction.

4. Time demands may interfere with the use of LSI techniques by those involved in direct teaching or management of a group of children. A natural response to this situation is to pass the LSI on to another staff who is either free or on call for such activities. However, having principals, counselors, or crisis teachers bail out front-line staff is not without its limitations. Morse's advice to crisis teachers is to be willing to take over the regular teacher's class on occasion so that the regular teacher could conduct his or her own LSI.

5. A life-space interview can become an end instead of a means ("We gave him an LSI"). Since something was done, it gives the illusion that something was accomplished.

6. The LSI can be seen as merely a technique instead of a philosophy of relating to troubled children. Morse cautions that the LSI is much more than a technique — in fact, it is a prototype of the kind of relationship between children and adults that must become the foundation of the program (Morse, 1981).

7. The LSI can become a ritual bound to Redl's structure and vocabulary. Redl himself was an explorer; he did not presume to present a summative synthesis. Although much of the literature on the LSI rather closely adheres to Redl's typology, it is important to know that Redl himself did not support such a doctrinaire position. In fact, he cautioned that the goals for the LSI were meant to be illustrative rather than system-binding (Redl, 1959). Thus it is important that any terminology employed should serve only the purpose of clarifying communication. Sometimes the jargon associated with the LSI has sounded strange to outsiders while it served as a badge of passage to insiders. We must remember that specialized vocabulary does not imply specialized treatment.

8. Nonaversiveness can be an illusion. Capturing a person and forcing communication can be a highly coercive activity, even if it is wrapped in sweet-talk such as, "Nobody is hurting you; we just have to talk about this." If we lose sight of an individual's role in controlling his or her destiny, we have violated one of the most basic assumptions of the psychoeducational method.

9. The LSI can become a synonym for almost any kind of communication. For example, some are inclined to use the term "new tool salesmanship" to apply to any situation in which they give a youngster advice on how to behave. Perhaps we need to differentiate more clearly between LSI's and other kinds of verbal intervention. Probably the LSI blends into more nonstructured communication of the type which James Newman (1979) calls "conversational counseling." A closely related error is to propose the LSI as a panacea that would supplant all other forms of counseling. Redl did not take this view but rather saw the LSI as an important "missing link" in a range of interventions that

went from environmental manipulation to detached psychotherapy (Redl, 1959).

10. In our preoccupation to solve affective problems, we can risk the danger of neglecting areas of cognitive functioning such as academics. There is nothing in the philosophy of LSIs that should necessarily conflict with academic achievement; however, if the program diverts significant amounts of class time to problem-solving activities, it is inevitable that academic learning will suffer. Involvement in individual or group interviews has on occasion become a contrived recess from academic work that is exploited by some students. On the other hand, if the LSI is used strategically, it can support academic productivity in the classroom. Furthermore, if the *individual* LSI interview is used exclusively, one may neglect the development of a *group climate* that supports academic work. The life-space interview must be carefully balanced with other approaches to create the holistic synergy of successful re-education.

REFERENCES

Beck, M., & McConnell, T. The theory of the psychoeducational model as applied to the school counsellor. *College Student Journal*, 1980, *4*(3), 307–311.

Bernstein, B. Life-space interviewing in the school setting. In R. Newman and M. Keith (Eds.), *The school-centered life-space interview*. Washington, DC: School Research Program, P.H.S. Project OM525, Washington School of Psychiatry, 1963, pp. 33–34.

Bersoff, D., & Grieger, R. An interview model for the psychosituational assessment of children's behavior. *American Journal of Orthopsychiatry*, 1971, *41*(3), 483–493.

Bloom, R. The reality rub-in interview with emotionally disturbed adolescents. *Pointer*, 1981, *25*(2), 22–25.

Brenner, M. Life-space interviews in the school setting. In H. Dupont (Ed.), *Educating emotionally disturbed children*. New York: Holt, Rinehart & Winston, 1969.

DeMagistris, R., & Imber, S. The effects of LSI on academic and social performance of behaviorally disordered children. *Behavioral Disorders*, 1980, *6*(1), 12–15.

Dembinski, R. The opening gambit: How students avoid the LSI. *Pointer*, 1981, *25*(2), 12–15.

Duffner, B. The management of profanity for classroom teachers. In N. Long, W. Morse, and R. Newman (Eds.), *Conflict in the classroom* (3rd ed.). Belmont, CA: Wadsworth, 1976.

Ellis, A., & Grieger, R. (Eds.). *Handbook of rational-emotive therapy*. New York: Springer, 1977.

Fagen, S. Conducting an LSI: A process model. *Pointer*, 1981, *25*(2), 9–11.

Fagen, S., & Long, J. Editorial. *Pointer*, 1981a, *25*(2), 4.

Fagen, S., & Long, J. (Eds.). Special issue on life-space interviewing. *Pointer*, 1981b, *25*(2).

Gardner, P. An overview of the life-space interview technique. Paper presented at the International Convention, Council for Exceptional Children, Dallas, TX, April 1979. (ERIC ed 171033 EC 115242).

Glasser, W. *Reality therapy.* New York: Harper & Row, 1965.

Gordon, T. *Teacher effectiveness training.* New York: Weiden, 1974.

Hall, S. *Lectures on schoolkeeping.* Boston: Richardson, Lord and Holbrook, 1829.

Heuchert, C. Gold stars to cover up dark fears. *Pointer,* 1981, *25*(2), 42–44.

Heuchert, C., & Long, N. A brief history of life-space interviewing. *Pointer,* 1981, *25*(2), 5–8.

Kitchener, H. The life-space interview in the differentiation of school in residential treatment. *American Journal of Orthopsychiatry,* 1963, *33*(4), 720–722.

Lay, C., & Duffner, E. LSI inservice training model for regular classroom teachers: procedures and issues. *Pointer,* 1981, *25*(2), 54–60.

Long, N. Some problems in teaching life-space interviewing techniques to graduate students in education in a large class at Indiana University. *American Journal of Orthopsychiatry,* 1963, *33*(4), 723–727.

Long, N., Stoeffer, V., Krause, K., & Jung, C. Life-space management of behavioral crisis. *Social Work,* 1961, *6*(1), 38–45.

Michenbaum, D. Cognitive behavior modification with exceptional children: A promise yet unfulfilled. *Exceptional Education Quarterly,* 1980, *1*(1), 83–88.

Morgan, R. Group life-space interviewing. *Pointer,* 1981, *25*(2), 37–41.

Morse, W. Worksheet on life-space interviewing. In N. Long, W. Morse, & R. Newman (Eds.), *Conflict in the classroom.* Belmont, CA: Wadsworth, 1971.

Morse, W. The crisis or helping teacher. In N. Long, W. Morse, & R. Newman (Eds.), *Conflict in the classroom.* Belmont, CA: Wadsworth, 1980.

Morse, W. LSI tomorrow. *Pointer,* 1981, *25*(2), 67–69.

Morse, W., & Small, E. Group life-space interviewing in a therapeutic camp. *American Journal of Orthopsychiatry,* 1959, *29,* 27–44.

Morse, W., & Wineman, D. Group interviewing in a camp for disturbed boys. *Journal of Social Issues,* 1957, *13*(1), 23–31.

Morse, W., & Wingo, G. *Psychology and teaching.* Chicago: Scott, Forseman, 1962.

Newman, J. The American educateur. Paper presented to the 5th Annual National Association of Homes for Children Conference, Dallas, TX, September 12, 1979.

Newman, R. *Psychological consultation in the schools.* New York: Basic Books, 1967.

Newman, R. The life-space interview for the school staff. *Pointer,* 1981, *25*(2), 50–53.

Phillips, E., Phillips, E., Fixsen, D., & Wolf, M. *The teaching-family handbook: Group living environments administered by professional teaching parents for youth in trouble.* Lawrence, KS: University Printing Service, 1972 (rev. 1974).

Poore, T. The LSI and the principal: A new dimension of skill. *Pointer,* 1981, *25*(2), 45–49.

Redl, F. Strategy and techniques of the life-space interview. *American Journal of Orthopsychiatry,* 1959, *29,* 1–18.

Redl, F. The life-space interview in the school setting. *American Journal of Orthopsychiatry,* 1963, *33,* 717–733.

Redl, F., & Wineman, D. *Controls from within.* New York: Free Press, 1952.

Reilly, M., Imber, S., & Kremmens, J. The effects of life-space interviews on social behaviors of jr. high school special needs children. Paper presented at the 56th International Council for Exceptional Children, Kansas City, MO, 1978.

Roberts, S., & Jurin, A. The life-space interview. University of Michigan Fresh Air Camp, 1968, Summer Institute: *Workshop in Learning and Behavior.* (Unpublished.)

Small, R. A summary of the Walker School program. *Child Care Quarterly,* 1976, *5*(2), 136–143.

Vernick, J. The use of the life-space interview on a medical ward. *Social Casework,* 1963, *44*(8), 465–469.

Vorrath, H., & Brendtro, L. *Positive peer culture.* Chicago: Aldine, 1974.

Walker, J., & Shea, T. *Behavior modification: A practical approach for educators.* St. Louis: C. V. Mosby, 1976.

Whittaker, J. Models of group development: Implications for social work group practice. In A. Alissi (Ed.), *Perspectives on social group work practice.* New York: Free Press, 1980.

Wineman, D. The life-space interview. In J. Whittaker & A. Trieschman (Eds.), *Children away from home: A sourcebook of residential treatment.* Chicago: Aldine, 1972.

Wood, M., & Weller, D. How come it's different with some children? A developmental approach to life-space interviewing. *Pointer,* 1981, *25*(2), 61–66.

Peer Group Treatment: Its Use and Misuse

7

LARRY K. BRENDTRO, ARLIN E. NESS, AND ABRAHAM W. NICOLAOU

> The very qualities of
> sagacity and daring, which
> formerly rendered them a
> terror to the community,
> will push them forward in their
> new career of virtue, honor
> and usefulness.
> —S. D. Brooks, Superintendent,
> New York State Training
> School (circa 1850)

During the last decade we have seen a renewal of interest in tapping the power of the peer group in the treatment of troubled youth. Group-oriented techniques have been used within a wide range of philosophical orientations including psychodynamic, behavioral, and psychoeducational. One of the most comprehensive systems of mobilizing peer group dynamics is the guided group interaction tradition as represented by McCorkle, Elias, and Bixby (1958), Keller and Alper (1970), Pilnick (1971), Empey and Lubeck (1972), Vorrath and Brendtro (1974), Weeks (1976), Petrock (1976), and others. The goal of these programs is to build a "positive peer culture" through a process of carefully guided group interaction. A positive culture is defined as a cohesive group process which promotes pro-social, responsible, caring behavior and improved self-esteem.

Helping a young person with problems requires that he develop feelings of self-worth, of significance, of importance to others, of dignity, of desire to

do good and be good. It includes examination of one's own behavior in
relation to the reactions of others in an atmosphere where the group intent
is to help and not to hurt. It includes intensive exposure to a subculture
permeated with the positive values of respecting and helping others as
well as self-respect (Vorrath, 1972, p. 5).

Peer group programs originated in residential treatment centers for
adolescent delinquents but have since been extended to varied populations in a wide range of settings, including public schools and community agencies. Known under a variety of labels, including guided group
interaction, positive peer culture, and peer group counseling, this
approach has become one of the most widely adopted techniques
applied to juvenile problems in the United States (Vinter, Kish, &
Newcomb, 1976). Although such programs represent a potentially
powerful means for going to the heart of negative youth subcultures
and reorienting them in a positive direction, there has been considerable controversy over their appropriate use (Whittaker, 1979).

Central to any consideration of peer group treatment is the ethical
issue of encouraging the use of group pressure to influence individuals.
There is little doubt that if such programs are allowed to become
excessively intrusive and coercive, they undermine the integrity of an
individual's psychological privacy. In an early exchange in the *American Sociological Review,* Gordon (1962) accused proponents of guided
group interaction of advocating techniques reminiscent of Communist
brainwashing in Korea by using the group leverage to demand public
confessions, total candor, and submersion of the individual to the
group. This issue is still very much alive as the media in recent years
have given much attention to programs that use excessively confrontive group processes to compel honesty and break down the defenses of
an individual member of the group.

We should like at the outset to clearly demark our position relative
to the issue of coercive confrontation. We share the concern of those
who criticize the manner in which some groups charge forth to collapse psychological defenses that have been constructed over a lifetime
without concern for the reasons (valid or not) that a person may wish
not to reveal himself fully to a group. Table 7-1 is an adaptation of an
earlier description (Vorrath & Brendtro, 1974) and differentiates a
peer group treatment process based on confrontive coercion from one
based on concern.

Below, we shall outline the components of a program geared to
develop positive, concerned peer group processes. Such peer groups
have been operating in a wide range of settings including public
schools, alternative day schools, group homes, and residential treatment centers.

Table 7-1. Comparison of Processes of Peer Group Coercion
and Peer Group Concern

Peer group coercion: Invasion and exposure	Peer group concern: Trust and openness
1. I am afraid of showing myself to the group.	1. I am afraid of showing myself to the group.
2. The group tells me that I must be totally honest with them. They try to find out about me.	2. The group tells me that in time I will feel free with them. They tell me about themselves.
3. I feel uneasy because they are trying to make me tell them things I don't wish to divulge.	3. I feel safe as the group shows me they will not hurt me or take advantage of me.
4. The others say I am being phony, but I can't see any reason why I should tell them anything. Why should I face my problems?	4. The others are bringing out their problems and seem to feel good about it. Why shouldn't I face my problems, too?
5. My defenses are not strong enough, so they break down my guard.	5. My defenses do not seem necessary, so I let down my guard.
6. I am exposed to the group.	6. I open up to the group.
7. They have been strong enough to uncover my problems.	7. I have been strong enough to bring out my problems.
8. I don't know how I feel after being exposed. I am concerned that they might use something I said against me.	8. I feel better after opening up. I don't believe they would use anything I said against me.
9. When a new member joins the group I will know he is a phony and dishonest.	9. When a new member joins the group I will know he is afraid and distrustful.
10. I will attack him just as they challenged me when I was new. If he won't be honest I will continue to apply more pressure until I discover what he is hiding.	10. I will help him get used to the group just as they did when I was new. If he finds it hard to trust I will continue to help him so that he does not have to be afraid.

Refusing to be caught up in a power struggle with a negative group, adults instead strive to mobilize the peer group in a positive direction. Even the most difficult and rebellious students are seen as having a potential for helping one another. Helping is seen as a process that goes beyond verbal problem-solving and extends into the total life milieu. Thus although formal group meetings are held on a regular basis to structure problem-solving, successful programs are those that teach ways of living together rather than ways of talking about problems. It is assumed that as young people become involved in the process of helping one another, they will discover new ways to meet their needs for significance and power, thus to a large extent obviating the need for negative acting-out behavior. Furthermore, as the total group process ceases to support negative behavior, much of this behavior will naturally extinguish. In its place will be a series of positive, helpful behaviors that will be supported by members of the group and hence reinforced.

VALUES FOR LIVING

We recognize that it is possible to use peer reinforcement to support a wide range of behaviors and to enforce rules laid down by either adults or the group. We are further convinced that effective programs must to a large degree concentrate on the behavior that can be observed or inferred by staff. Nevertheless, if peer group programs become only "enforcers" for some set of institutional rules, then there is little likelihood that change will generalize to the real-life situation of the young person. This is not to say that rules have no place in an organization or a society, but that, in and of themselves, rules are an insufficient road map for successful adjustment. Thus a systematic attempt must be made to relate rules to specific values.

Obedience to adult rules does not in itself prepare youth to live responsibly in the complexities and uncertainties of the real world. In fact our society provides an abundance of examples of individuals who have learned all the rules but fail miserably at the business of living. Rules frequently provide an easy way out of making solid independent judgments. Although systematic reinforcement of highly specific rules may be desirable with younger children, it can become legalistic and counterproductive with sophisticated adolescents. As Nicholas Hobbs noted in reflecting on his Re-ed experience, "Behavior modification works best with younger children. Almost inevitably adolescents, with their growing intelligence, make formal behavioral modification programs into a game of 'who's conning whom?'" (1979, p. 15)

Although our goal is to teach values, this certainly does not mean middle-class values or some specific political or religious ideology. Instead we are speaking of a value system that is not tied to social status, culture, or to a particular generation. This system is based on the value of the human being. We recognize that conflicts may arise between the best interests of the individual and the group. Suffice it to say that most problems do not pose these complexities, for young people are quite capable of seeing what specifically helps or hurts an individual human being. After a long period of debate as to whether education should be concerned with values, we seem, as Lerner suggests, to be putting this archaic question behind us:

> Every actor in the education drama — teacher, student, family, administrator, media, peer group — is up to his neck in values. Like it or not,

education is values-drenched. The real question is how well—with what awareness, with what skill and meaning, with what responsibility and restraint—it performs its functions as a value-carrier (1976, p. 13).

MAKING CARING FASHIONABLE

We now come to the crux of the matter. If it is our goal to take a group of young people and build them into a positive rather than a negative force, then the question must be: how can we make caring fashionable? It is immediately apparent that caring is not at all in style among many of these young people and perhaps among children in general.

— At this moment somewhere on the playground of some school there is a fight breaking out between two youth. Their peers are gathering around to cheer. Are they going to stop it? No, they're not. Oh, they might stop it if the principal approaches, but they don't seem to care if someone hurts someone else. They're more concerned in beating the system, keeping ahead of the authority figure.

— In another school there is a locker full of hard drugs and everybody, even the kids who go to Sunday School, knows from whom purchases can be made. Are they going to go to the school administrator and say, "Look, you've got to get this stuff out of our school"? Are they even going to go to the person and say, "Look man, I'm not going to the principal, but let's get that junk out of our school"? Obviously not. They would be labeled as a "narc" or something similar and ostracized. The peer culture serves to perpetuate negative behavior.

The structure of youth slang perpetuates, justifies, and rationalizes harmful behavior and intimidates those who would be caring or helpful. In other words, young people develop a terminology that serves to enhance the attractiveness of negative behavior while ridiculing positive behavior. Perhaps they learn this from adults. After all, it is the adults who write advertisements that promote cancer-causing chemicals with names like "Kool," "Fresh," "Lark," "True," or "Vantage." By pairing a destructive product with a positive image—like the Marlboro Man or the Virginia Slim—we help the viewer suppress those thoughts about the undesirability of the product. Can you think of a more asinine name for a cigarette than "True"? Now look at what our young people do with different names for drugs. Most of them have rather fresh, bright-sounding names—"Speed," "Smack," "Acapulco Gold," "Angel Dust"—they sound slick. None of them is called "brain injury," "seizures," "respiratory arrest," or even "intoxication." Instead they bear cool-sounding names to counter the fact that someone may be in trouble by ingesting, smoking, or shooting these products.

The process of value re-education will require reversing the valence of certain behaviors so that helping is seen as strong, mature, and powerful, while hurting and dishonesty is appropriately seen as inadequate and immature. A specific verbal strategy designed toward this end is *relabeling* (Vorrath & Brendtro, 1974):

> We have noted that the problem youth frequently has labeled his problem behavior as cool, sophisticated, and fashionable, and sees "good" behavior in a negative light. Whenever this distortion of values is reflected in the language of young people, staff must relabel the behavior so that hurting behavior will be made undesirable and helping behavior fashionable. Thus, for example, if the delinquent youth perceives criminal types as cool, mature, smart, and masculine, then we might counter this view by noting that many 50-year-old criminals are locked in cages because they act like babies and must be watched all the time.
>
> If "truancy" has an exciting quality to it we ought to give this problem a label that sounds less mature, perhaps "playing games of hide and seek." If delinquent youth feel that their mass rape of a girl is cool, then we should relabel this act as "messing over a helpless person." If stealing is seen as slick, then it should be relabeled as "sneaky and dumb." If a youth gets some rewards from his tendency to act in violent ways, then the attractiveness of such behavior can be diminished when it is relabeled as "having a childish temper tantrum" or "acting like a hothead."
>
> . . . Staff quickly become adept at describing all positive helping behavior with adjectives associated with strength and maturity, and relabeling all hurting behavior with adjectives associated with weakness and immaturity. Many labels are usable. Thus, reference to positive behavior as great, intelligent, independent, improving, winning will help to make such behavior more desirable for most students, while the description of negative behavior as childish, unintelligent, helpless, destructive, copping out, losing will help to establish such behavior as undesirable and unfashionable (pp. 30 – 31).

Great care must be taken that negative labels are applied only to the behavior, not to the person. One way to accomplish this is to pair a positive message with the negative (e.g., "That was an immature act for someone with your ability"). To be effective, relabeling must communicate a strong, consistent message that staff believe in the greatness of a person and expect him or her to act accordingly.

RECOGNIZING AND OWNING PROBLEMS

Most children and youth do not recognize or admit to their problems. Even supposedly "normal" youngsters fail to acknowledge and deal with problems in themselves and their peers, as is shown in the following example.

Some years ago an area high school asked the authors if an expert on delinquency could be arranged to talk to 100 seniors in social science courses. High school personnel were a bit taken aback at the suggestion that a group of delinquents be sent instead. Nevertheless they agreed, and so a group of teenagers from The Starr Commonwealth Schools, together with their teacher, accepted the engagement.

The regular students listened intently as the delinquents recounted how they helped one another work on problems. They explained that they met nearly every day for an hour or more in a formal group meeting. They outlined the group meeting process of reporting problems and helping members identify goals for positive change. The public school students were fascinated by all of this but seemed to be confused as to how someone could really help another person with a problem. One of the public school students said, "It seems to me that no one would admit to having any problems. What would you do then?"

Someone suggested role-playing, and a somewhat silly and attention-seeking youth from the public school volunteered to act as a new member to the group.

The student volunteer approached the visiting group, sat down, gave his name, and denied having any problems. The group quickly responded by asking, "Well, do you know what the problems are?" He looked puzzled. The group quickly began running down a list of problems including poor self-concept, authority problem, misleading others, easily misled, and so forth. One by one he denied having any of the problems they listed. When the group asked him about alcohol or drug problems, he nervously denied that, too. The group knew differently. "Wait a minute. When we were standing out in the hall before this meeting, you were the one that came up to us and said, 'Hey, if you guys want to get some stuff, I'm the man who deals around here.'"

A deathly silence fell over the room as the youth struggled to maintain his innocence, but he finally conceded, "Well, I just thought I'd be cool — I thought it would be cool with you guys to say that I deal." The group then suggested that he must have some kind of alcohol or drug problem because he thinks that's cool. Also, he has a lying problem or perhaps it might better be described as "fronting," that is, being afraid to be himself; he thinks he has to put on a front.

After the class was over, the public school students all gathered around the delinquents, showering them with questions like, "Could we get your address in case we have some problems?"

The foregoing example illustrates a number of aspects of peer group programs, including the use that groups can make of some sort of structured vocabulary for identifying and communicating about problems. One such vocabulary is that described by Vorrath and Brendtro (1974) and presented in Table 7-2. Although there is nothing definitive about this list, it has served in a wide range of settings to provide a useful, common-sense, jargon-free set of labels that allow young people to perceive and conceptualize patterns of problems.

Unless a person accepts responsibility for a problem, he or she has little reason to change. All of us seem to be naturally inclined to shift blame to others, and this tendency seems particularly pronounced with troubled youth. Frequently these youngsters refuse to acknowledge

Table 7-2. Goals for Problem-Solving

Problem description	Problem resolution
1. **Self-concept problem:** Has a low opinion of self, feels inferior.	Is self-confident and cannot easily be made to feel small or put down. Is able to solve his problems and make positive contributions to others. Doesn't feel sorry for self even though he may have short-comings. Believes he is good enough to be accepted by anybody.
2. **Inconsiderate of others:** Does things that are damaging to others.	Shows concern for others even if he does not like them or know them well. Tries to help people with problems rather than hurt them or put them down.
3. **Inconsiderate of self:** Does things that are damaging to self.	Shows concern for self, tries to correct mistakes and improve self. Understands his limitations and is willing to discuss problems. Doesn't hurt self or put self down.
4. **Authority problem:** Does not want to be managed by anybody.	Shows ability to get along with those in authority. Is able to accept advice and direction from others. Does not try to take advantage of authority figures even if they can be manipulated.
5. **Misleads others:** Draws others into negative behavior.	Shows responsibility for the effect of his behavior on others who follow him. Does not lead others into negative behavior. Shows concern and helps rather than taking advantage of them.
6. **Easily misled:** Is drawn into negative behavior by others.	Seeks out friends who care enough about him not to hurt him. Doesn't blindly follow others to buy friendship. Is strong enough to stand up for himself and makes his own decision. Doesn't let anyone misuse him.
7. **Aggravates others:** Treats people in negative, hostile ways.	Gets along well with others. Does not need to get attention by irritating or annoying others. Gets no enjoyment from hurting or harassing people. Respects others enough not to embarrass, provoke or bully them.

Table 7-2. Goals for Problem-Solving (*cont.*)

Problem description	Problem resolution
8. **Easily angered:** Often is irritated, provoked, or has tantrums.	Is not easily frustrated. Knows how to control and channel anger, not letting it control him. Understands the put-down process and has no need to respond to challenges. Can tolerate criticism or even negative behavior from others.
9. **Stealing:** Takes things that belong to others.	Sees stealing as hurting another person. Has no need to be sneaky or to prove himself by stealing. Knows appropriate ways of getting things he wants. Would not stoop to stealing even if he could get away with it.
10. **Alcohol or drug problem:** Misuses substances that could hurt self.	Feels good about self and wouldn't hurt self. Does not need to be high to have friends or enjoy life. Can face his problems without a crutch. Shows concern for others who are hurting themselves by abusing alcohol or drugs.
11. **Lying:** Cannot be trusted to tell the truth.	Is concerned that others trust him. Has strength to face mistakes and failures without trying to cover up. Does not need to lie or twist the truth to impress others. Tells it like it is.
12. **Fronting:** Puts on an act rather than being real.	Is comfortable with people and does not have to keep trying to prove himself. Has no need to act superior, con people, or play the show-off role. Is not afraid of showing his true feelings to others.

ownership of problems and in fact are very skillful at giving the problem to the adult. Brophy and Rohrkemper (1980) have noted that teachers are much more sympathetic in working with students who accept responsibility for problems or who share responsibility with the teacher. But it is not an easy matter to help young people to be open to criticism and to accept responsibility for problems. In fact, without careful handling, such interactions can deteriorate into hostile criticism.

Phillips and colleagues (1972) train teaching–parents to use specific procedures to teach youngsters how to accept criticism. Peer group programs have also developed a specific treatment intervention designed to assign responsibility for problems to young people. Basically, this is a verbal technique that takes the projection of a young person and turns it around 180 degrees so that he or she cannot escape responsibility for the problem. Teachers and youth workers become much more confident in their discussion of problems once they have mastered the relatively simple technique of *reversal of responsibility* (Vorrath & Brendtro, 1974). The following examples of this technique show how the strategic use of a question can refocus responsibility without drawing the adult into a big argument:

> *Child:* I got into trouble at school today because the teacher is so boring and can't teach.
> *Parent:* You mean that all kids with poor teachers get into trouble?
>
> *Child:* I hit her because she called me a name!
> *Parent:* I can understand that. I wonder why she called you a name? Could you have done something that annoyed her?
>
> *Child:* The other kids made me do it.
> *Parent:* You mean to say that you're a puppet on strings and that everybody else pulls your strings but yourself? (Schaefer, 1978, p. 100).

The goal in the reversal is not to win a verbal contest. Instead, the adult acts in a spirit of concern rather than accusation. By holding a mirror up to the student we help the youth concentrate on the contribution he or she can make to solving problems. Or, as one such youth once said, "You find the answer to everything somewhere inside yourself."

CONDUCTING GROUP MEETINGS

Peer group programs generally meet in formal group counseling sessions with an adult leader for 1 to 1½ hours daily. The typical process in a group meeting begins as students take turns reporting problems that they have had since the group last met; group members may then note any problems that a member has failed to bring to the group. (Most youth find it more desirable to share their own problems than to have peers point them out.) This procedure sets the stage for determining which individual will receive the help of the group during that meeting. Group members ordinarily concentrate their effort on one individual for most of the remaining time. A typical agenda is provided below from Vorath and Brendtro (1974, pp. 85–86). The group meetings follow a clear agenda that systematically involves all members and yet provides wide latitude for spontaneous individual expression. The meeting is not operated in a laissez-faire manner but is structured for efficient problem-solving. The meeting consists of four distinct parts, but an established group moves so smoothly through the meeting that an untrained observer perhaps would not notice the overall plan.

1. **Reporting problems.** During the first part of the meeting every member reports on the problems he has had since the last session as well as on other problems he has not yet brought to the group's attention. Each member is responsible for bringing out all problems in a clear yet brief manner, and if he omits any, other group members may call this lapse to his attention. The problem session varies in length but typically lasts 15 minutes.

2. **Awarding the meeting.** After all members have reported their problems, the group must decide who will "have the meeting." This decision is based on who needs help most that day. After the members reach a consensus they are ready to work with that one individual. Deciding who is to have the meeting generally takes about 5 minutes.

3. **Problem solving.** Here the group members concentrate on understanding and resolving one member's problems. If the group has been able to cover earlier steps efficiently, considerable time is available to work on problems. The problem-solving session typically lasts almost an hour and constitutes the major portion of the meeting.

4. **The summary.** Here the group leader engages in his most active role of the meeting. His summary of what has occurred teaches group members to become more effective in operating their meetings. The leader allows approximately 10 minutes for his summary.

Although an adult group leader is present and may intervene, the intent of the adult's intervention is to enhance the functioning of the group rather than to take away the counseling role from group members. In a well-functioning group the adult group leader plays a rather low-profile role through much of the meeting unless communication bogs down. Most interventions are phrased as questions, such as:

— "Why does the group think Maria acts so silly when group members ask about her school failure?"
— "Does Rodney think that by being angry at those who are trying to help, the group will give up on him?"
— "Why does the group think that Toby is afraid to trust group members?"

Ordinarily most of the group leader's direct comments are reserved until the end of the meeting when he or she summarizes the process, elicits suggestions as to how the group might continue to help a person in the future, and recognizes the positive contributions of members.

An attempt is made in group meetings to keep the discussion, insofar as possible, on the here and now, rather than dealing with remote, obscure issues. Furthermore, the group leader must strive to keep the task positive and productive. Although some might feel that focusing on a problem is in itself negative, the entire thrust of peer group programs must be to make problem-solving a positive process. Too often young people have learned that to show a problem is to acknowledge illness, deviance, or inadequacy. Staff in peer group programs strive to change this perception so that problem-solving comes to be seen as a positive, adaptive skill. Solving problems can be an immensely rewarding opportunity for learning and growth rather than a reason to feel inadequate or ashamed.

A positive culture is achieved only as a group is brought successfully through predictable stages of development. These stages include:

1. *Casing.* Students are guarded and lack trust in one another. They do not have a good idea of what to expect in the group and try to seek information about one another without exposing themselves. They are defensive and may scapegoat weaker members.
2. *Limit-testing.* The students experiment with techniques of participation in group meetings and thus begin revealing themselves. Tension is high and cliques are prevalent. Although students may recognize problems, they cannot yet function as a positive group.
3. *Group polarization.* As students discover alternatives to previous values or behavior, they must decide whether they are serious about changing. Although some youth desire to embrace new values, others cling to old patterns. Cliques become tenuous and anxiety or aggression may increase. The group may be divided against itself, but members are on the verge of forming a strong sense of group solidarity.
4. *A positive culture.* Students coalesce into a cohesive clique-free group marked by mutual care and concern. The group relies less on adult control and places positive expectations on members. Young people work with eagerness and sincerity to solve the problems of their peers.

Experience with group programs in many settings has produced a considerable knowledge base of practical methods for conducting effective group meetings and developing a positive peer culture. For a more extensive discussion of these procedures, the reader is referred to Vorrath and Brendtro (1974).

PEER GROUP TREATMENT WITH YOUNGER CHILDREN

One of the most frequently asked questions about peer group programs concerns their applicability to younger populations. There are some qualifications and contraindications in applying these procedures with younger age groups. The following observations were provided by JoAnne Milburn based on her experiences integrating a peer group approach with a social learning theory methodology in the treatment of pre-adolescent children.

Considerations of Development and Learning

Children in the "latency" stage (6–13) are developing a peer orientation. The process normally begins at about age 8 as the child becomes cognitively more aware of external realities and differences between himself and others. During latency, the child is evolving a personal morality. This morality changes from one based on strict rules laid down by adults to one that incorporates peer influence and involves personal decision-making and problem-solving. The process of moving from adult to peer influence is gradual, with some lapses and considerable individual differences. This process can bring the child into conflict with adults, and the reinforcing power of the adult becomes at times less than that of the peer group. The latency-age child is still aware, however, that he or she is realistically dependent on adults for survival and, therefore, still retains some orientation toward adults.

The peer group serves as one of the main sources of learning, providing models for imitation and sources of reinforcement. Peers, therefore, have the potential to influence each other for better or for worse. Adults can ensure that this potential is used in a positive way by reinforcing those who are positive models, by teaching children directly how to provide positive reinforcement to peers, and by guiding the selection of behaviors that are reinforced by peers.

Advantages of Peer Approaches with Younger Children

A number of aspects of peer group approaches are compatible with social learning theories and can be applied with latency-age children.

These aspects include:

1. The emphasis on care and concern among peers and the rela-beling of behaviors to reflect these values.
2. The emphasis on giving help rather than receiving help.
3. Emphasis on the here and now, because problems that have earlier origins will tend to repeat themselves and can be dealt with more effectively in the present.
4. Seeing problems as opportunities for change and the pinpoint-ing of problems as the first step in bringing about a solution.
5. The emphasis on high expectations, on "greatness," and on rejecting any behavior that hurts self or others.
6. Developing in the child a sense of personal accountability rather than projecting blame for his or her problems; employing the "reversal" technique whereby problems are turned back on the one who must do the changing.
7. Use of the "problem list" in which problem behaviors are clearly defined as a way of pinpointing them, provided that the positive alternatives are also specified.
8. The expectation that children exert a positive, responsible influ-ence on the behavior of their peers.
9. The emphasis on assuming responsibility through task and work activities in which the group can succeed.
10. The emphasis on developing positive self-images. Like adoles-cents, younger children develop positive self-images from a sense of mastery and from positive inputs from peers and adults.

Limitations of Peer Group Counseling with Younger Children

Peer-oriented treatment approaches have considerable usefulness for the older latency child, with some limitations. These methodologies have been developed primarily for use with adolescents and must be modified to meet the needs of the developmentally younger group. Such modifications might include:

1. *Motivation.* External reinforcers may be necessary to increase positive peer behavior. Group contingencies and contracts may be necessary to increase motivation to participate with peers in positive ways.
2. *Skills.* Peer approaches require problem-solving skills that may not be in the repertoires of latency-age children. These skills may

need to be taught directly through didactic approaches, role-playing, behavior rehearsal, and cognitive restructuring.

3. *Group sessions.* Because of limited attention spans, lengthy formal meetings are counterproductive. Adjustments should be made so the content of the meeting can be accomplished in a shorter time.

4. *Formal problem list.* Some of the behavior listed may not be age-appropriate to the younger population, as the problem statements may not be sufficiently specific for the younger and more delayed child to understand. Learning the problem list and the labeling process may become a demand that is diversionary and irrelevant with some younger children.

5. *Confrontation.* This must be monitored very closely with the younger group because of the danger of abuse. The younger child may tend to derive satisfaction from "tattling" to others, enjoying hurting rather than helping, or building up his or her own limited self-esteem by putting down others. The younger child may also lack the skills to convey caring and concern when confronting others about problems. In a latency-age group with an age span of several years, very marked differences in size, developmental level, experience, cognitive understanding, and peer group orientation may exist. Staff may need to be more active to make sure older, more sophisticated children do not dominate and bully.

With the younger group, positive relationship with staff must form the foundation of the program. Staff should be alert to times when the child has "unfinished business" from situations outside the group that would be more appropriately discussed with a staff member alone. With the younger child, the group should not be considered the only therapeutic medium necessary.

Peer group counseling is a highly verbal approach, and younger children may not have the verbal repertoires to feel successful in the group. Care must be taken that expressions of pro-social behavior are not produced only on a verbal level, but that positive behavior occurs also and that the emphasis is on what children *do* as well as what they say.

Peer group treatment makes a distinction between values and rules and stresses teaching "helping" values rather than adhering to rules. This is a desirable goal, but the younger child still needs explicit rules, although they may be presented in the context of how they are designed to foster consideration of others.

Although "demand for responsibility" for one's problems is useful and desirable, realistically many of the child's problems could be ameliorated by having responsive and positive staff, teachers, and parents. Having the child assume responsibility for his problems does not relieve the adults of their share of responsibility.

SCHOOL-BASED PEER GROUP COUNSELING

Garner (1982) reviews the development of peer group programs, particularly as applied to nonresidential settings. School-based programs have as their target not just the treatment group but the entire school culture. Typically, such programs meet during school hours and are offered for credit with educationally oriented titles such as "leadership training." Generally peer group membership is not confined to negative leaders, but is drawn from all indigenous factions of the student body including both positive and negative leaders.

Although guided group programs in school settings typically have a more relaxed structure than those originally designed for residential milieus, many of the same procedures and techniques for group development apply. Most groups initially follow a formal problem-solving approach as a mechanism for building trust and openness. Under adult guidance, youth learn to identify problems and differentiate between giving advice and truly solving problems. Once young people experience success at helping one another, they are able to shift their focus from personal problems of group members to the other members of the student body. Like their residential counterparts, youth in school-based groups are encouraged to move beyond verbal discussion of problems and demonstrate responsible, concerned behavior in their everyday relationships with peers, adults, and family members. Helping behavior is extended beyond the group by developing working relationships with school psychologists, truancy officers, guidance counselors, and administrators who provide opportunities for youth to be of service to other young people who are not formally part of the program. A typical example is to use peers to reach out to school truants in the hope of reducing the likelihood that they will become dropouts. Such groups have had a positive effect on reducing school-based delinquency, racial conflict, and student–staff tensions (Howlett & Boehm, 1975).

Summarizing his review on the application of positive peer culture to school settings, Garner concludes:

> School administrators find themselves in a classical "double bind" as they face the dilemma of disruptive behavior. Their training and their school boards lead them to strong direct action to solve the problems in their school. However, the problem of disruptive behavior in secondary schools is in part a reaction by adolescents to strong adult control. Stu-

dents are seeking a greater sense of potency and control over their own lives. It appears to be a problem with a lose–lose situation. Strong adult action engenders strong negative reactions in the adolescent peer group.

Positive peer culture does seem to offer a win–win outcome where both educators and students are able to achieve their respective goals and, in fact, discover common goals to be pursued in cooperation. The adults in school beseiged with disruptive behavior must act decisively to establish structures and programs which capture the power of the adolescent peer group for positive ends (1982, p. 23).

A CURRICULUM FOR CARING

The school bears a primary responsibility for developing what Bronfenbrenner has called "a curriculum of caring." This does not mean that children should be taught *about* caring, but rather *how* to care (Fantini, 1980). We have discussed ways in which students could be taught concern for other members of their group. However, caring for one's close peers is not the ultimate proof of humanity—even members of criminal gangs have such solidarity. Although peer group responsibility is most desirable, programs that are to make a lasting impact must generalize helping behavior beyond the in-group. If a caring community is to be effective and enduring, it must exist not only in the classroom and the school, but beyond, to involve the community (Bronfenbrenner, 1980).

A promising approach is the planful use of volunteer activity for enhancing a student's personal and educational development, which has come to be called *service-learning*. Although service-learning is of potential value to all youth, it offers unique opportunities to troubled children and adolescents. As these young people become involved in community service and person-to-person helping projects, they become a valuable resource instead of a liability. This challenges the established negative stereotype held by the citizenry, as well as the self-concepts of the youth themselves.

The use of service-learning as a major treatment intervention with troubled children and adolescents has created considerable interest in regular, alternative, and residential schools. A wide range of helping projects have been described by Brendtro and Nicolaou (1982) and Allen and Mitchell (1982). Some of these projects are of short duration, whereas others are carried on regularly over a period of many months. Among the service-learning projects have been the following:

— Serving as teacher aides at a community day care center
— Operating summer recreation programs for neighborhood children

— Assisting in Special Olympic events for the handicapped
— Working with retarded children at a special school and a state hospital
— Chopping firewood for the disabled
— Helping senior citizens by carrying groceries and shoveling snow

As Fantini (1980) has said, the range of possible service-oriented activities is virtually without limit if educators use a little thought and imagination.

Frequently troubled youth disparage values of service or giving of self to others. They may in fact take pride in their exploitive behavior as they present the image of macho and bravado (a demeanor common in problem youth of either sex). Always needing to appear strong, these young people feel vulnerable to criticism from peers if they should show their gentle or more positive side. In order to succeed, service-learning programs must overcome this reluctance and find ways of appealing to the natural interests and motivations of young people. For example, many are more receptive to approaches that reinforce their maturity ("you can be of real help to these people") than to approaches that maintain their dependence ("this will help you with your problems"). Helping others needs to be seen as an act of strength ("this will be a tough job") rather than weakness ("this will be easy").

Service projects must also be seen as spontaneous and exciting rather than routine and regimented. Perhaps highly adventuresome projects will be rare (although groups of youth have built levees to stop a flood and performed disaster work after a tornado). Yet, with creative planning, it is possible to eschew repetitive, nonchallenging projects in preference to those with interest, variety, and challenge.

Although service-learning with adolescents has received the most attention, these programs can be effective with younger children as well. The following projects were successfully completed by emotionally disturbed boys and girls between 8 and 12 years of age.

— Preparing a house and yard for a new refugee family, planting flowers, bringing toys to welcome the children.
— Buying canned goods for needy families using money accumulated by the children as a result of no breakage or vandalism in the school over an extended period.
— Visiting residents in a state center for the retarded; socializing, playing games, going bowling with a group of retarded adults and assisting with score-keeping.
— Collecting for UNICEF at Halloween and raising money for the Heart Fund by neighborhood caroling.

— Culminating a week-long summer school module on "Helping Someone Else" by putting on a rhythm band concert at a camp for the mentally retarded.

Young people need continuity and security as well as change and stimulation. Successful helping projects can be neither "one-night stands" devoid of relationships nor institutionalized rituals without meaning. Students must perceive that they are in fact meeting some genuine human need. Furthermore, since many troubled youth have been deprived of positive interpersonal relationships, projects involving people-to-people service are preferable to depersonalized, more abstract helping.

Experience with service-learning activities has given rise to a core of practice wisdom concerning the ingredients of successful projects. When groups are first beginning, it is usually best to attempt small, simple projects with limited time horizons. A highly disorganized group may also respond better to a project that is heavily motoric than to one requiring sophisticated interpersonal relationships. One such group readily accepted the challenge of painting the bridges in a city park; another group had a very positive experience chopping firewood for a large family of small children in which the father was temporarily disabled. Success in such limited projects can then lead to helping relationships of a more complex nature. Thus, a more mature group assumed responsibility for rebuilding a burned-out picnic shelter at the Camp Fire Girls' campground. This project called for a great deal of cooperative behavior over an extended period of time, and resulted in a high level of community recognition for the young people involved who became veritable heroes for their feat.

Although sound planning is important for the successful resolution of complex problems, this does not preclude the possibility that successful activities can develop around events that are spontaneous, serendipitous, and even a bit adventurous. For example, a group of youth who had been highly disorganized and incapable of complex helping projects responded enthusiastically when they were called upon to join in a search of the woods for a lost pre-school child. Staff were even able to involve the negative peer leaders in the group who, although resisting more mundane service projects, readily participated in an activity with a flair for adventure. When negative leaders find that they can obtain satisfaction also from positive leadership roles, the foundation for further service-learning has been laid. In effect, youth who previously derived satisfaction from exploiting others have become hooked on helping.

A somewhat different example of a spontaneous project was seen in a group that successfully solicited surplus flowers from a department store the day after Mother's Day so that they could be redistributed to residents of a nursing home "who didn't have anybody give them flowers on Mother's Day."

The variety of helping projects offers many opportunities for integrating service-learning with other areas of the curriculum, as evident in the following examples:

— Students who participated in a "Sitting Tall" program of horsemanship for physically handicapped children were simultaneously studying the history of the handicapped in our society as well as learning communication skills that would enable them to relate to the severely disabled.
— In constructing the picnic pavilion for the Camp Fire Girls, students worked closely with their industrial arts instructor to master the woodworking and building trade skills necessary for completing this particularly complex project.
— A group of students studied clowning in art and drama, which led to a series of clowning performances for small children in the community day care center.
— A program of visitation to the community senior citizens' home led to a study of the process of aging and death in the social science curriculum. This was particularly relevant, since upon return visits to the senior citizen center students would typically find that someone they had helped at a previous visit had subsequently died.

Conventional practice in most schools is to give the highest recognition to students for self-serving personal achievements, such as scholarships to the gifted and trophies or letters to those with athletic prowess. Although competitive activities by individuals and groups do receive their share of attention, teachers should also attempt to dramatize and reinforce the importance of successful helping projects by giving them equal billing. This includes bulletin board displays with photographs from various projects, the posting of letters of appreciation from community leaders, and, when appropriate, encouraging newspaper publicity surrounding a particularly interesting and successful community service activity.

In spite of the great diversity of projects, most service-learning activities can be seen as consisting of three stages, namely, identification of project, orientation, and implementation.

1. *Identification.* In this initial stage, staff work independently or with youth to identify potential areas of service. The projects must meet several criteria. They must not be "make-work" but reflect a genuine need that exists in a community. Care must be taken that students are not exploited through the particular voluntary work they are to under-

take. The task must be appropriate to the maturity of the young people involved. For example, the students mentioned above who worked with crippled children were quite capable of carrying out extended relationships with a group of seriously handicapped persons; not all groups would be ready to undertake such a complex project initially. Staff must determine that the project is in fact feasible and that the logistics of money, regulations, travel, etc., will be manageable and not interefere with the successful consummation of the project.

2. *Orientation.* The next stage is to orient students to the proposed project and to determine their possible interest in service. This involves exposing young people to concepts, people, or situations so that they become aware that a need for service exists. In some cases the need may be dramatically self-evident. In the case of the tornado, one had only to explain to the group that an entire community had been devastated and volunteers were sought to help clear the rubble. In another situation, the need may be introduced more obliquely to arouse interest. A psychologist from a state hospital for retarded children came to present a color slide show on mental retardation. This created initial interest, which was followed by a tour of the hospital. Only at that point, dependent on the reaction of young people during this period of orientation, was it decided that a specific proposal for involving the youth as recreation aides would be placed before the students. When students are aware of a need and motivated to be of service, then staff and youth can begin planning the third stage, participation in service activity.

3. *Implementation and evaluation.* In this phase, young people are involved to the maximum extent possible in organizing the project, executing the activity, and evaluating the service experience. As apparent from the great variety of activities, each project requires its own unique pattern of organization and implementation. Successful participation in providing a genuine service to others usually increases motivation for further service. The project can continue until the need is met, or until new challenges are desired, or both. At that point, students and staff are again ready to identify further potential areas of service. Almost all evaluations of projects have been based on informal, interpersonal feedback among staff and students. In the final analysis, the goal is to create a positive caring atmosphere in which service to others becomes a life-style; youth should not view such activity as some kind of treatment program, but as a community of humans reaching out to one another. Although qualitative evaluation is useful, there remains a need to develop creative investigative designs to assess more precisely the impact of service-learning on students and on those they serve.

As with any other educational activity, service-learning programs

are not without their problems. However, once the young people
become invested in a project, they encounter surprisingly few difficulties as there is strong peer support for succeeding. Staff make an
attempt to have the entire program seen as belonging to the young
people themselves and not imposed by adults. Perhaps the most frequent difficulty has been in dealing with isolated members of the group
who resist involvement when most of the group is motivated for a
project. The responsibility for dealing with such problems is left with
the group, as is seen in these two accounts:

— A class group was planning on a project at the state hospital for
  the mentally retarded when a particular youngster became
  rather adamant in his refusal to join in this activity. After his
  peers talked with him for some time about his feelings, it was
  finally revealed that his own mother was mentally retarded, a
  fact which he had tried to hide from his friends. His conflict
  about being ashamed of his mother while still loving her was
  brought into focus by the anticipated helping project with retarded children. After expressing these feelings, the youth was
  able, with the support of the group, to enter into a most successful service-learning activity that helped him gain a new perspective on the difficulties and challenges experienced by his
  mother.

— A 17-year-old unmarried student whose girlfriend was about to
  deliver their child was generally reluctant to participate in any
  helping projects. Rather than continue trying to convince this
  youth that he should care more about others, the group
  members adopted the strategy of initiating a car wash, with all of
  the proceeds being given for the support of his soon-to-be-
  born child. This young man was noticeably moved by this
  expression of concern from his peers and he became a fully
  contributing member of the group.

Once young people experience the satisfaction that comes from
helping others, they frequently express concern about how they might
be able to continue service. This poses a most ironic situation: youth
who previously were the greatest troublemakers now desire to help
others, but the school and community have developed few appropriate
roles for such service. Too often the student encounters reluctance and
distrust on the part of faculty who remember the past and are skeptical
about the youth's motivation. Unless personnel are exposed to the
concept of service-learning, they will have little sensitivity for using
once-troubled youth in these important roles.

If the student is returning from a treatment setting to public school,
it is crucial to communicate carefully the changes that have occurred

in the young person and give examples of positive service activities in which he or she has been involved. The idea of service-learning is not inherently difficult to communicate, and many school counselors and principals are ready to use the student in a positive role as soon as they understand the concept. Thus one youth, upon returning to a public school setting, was assigned for a portion of the day as a peer helper in a resource room for the handicapped. Another student worked part-time with the guidance department in a peer counseling program. A third youth, with the help of a counselor, found a paid role in a community recreation agency and subsequently entered a college training program in social work. These examples suggest that to fail to provide an avenue of service for motivated youth who have learned to help others is a waste of human resources just as if nurses, teachers, or lawyers were deprived of opportunities for practicing their skills.

The systematic utilization of service-learning can make a decided contribution toward transforming youth who are viewed as societal liabilities into valuable assets. However, as Saurman and Nash (1980) caution, preoccupation with the personal development of youth must not be allowed to obscure the basic purpose of service to others, lest this become yet another kind of narcissism, however self-fulfilling. Keith-Lucas (1979) has suggested that even though positive growth is an outcome of service, the overriding goal should always be the self-actualization of those being served, not of those doing the service. Otherwise, concludes Buber (1970), those who enter into helping with the expectation of satisfying their own needs are condemned to a relationship that will never be complete.

CAUTIONS AND LIMITATIONS

Considerable controversy has surrounded the effectiveness of peer group treatment programs. This is understandable, since these methods are still developing and there is no doubt that many earlier applications were principally peer-*control* programs that lacked substantial long-range impact on youth themselves. A number of authors have suggested caution about claims that the peer group methodology is superior to other approaches (Gold, 1974; Sarri & Selo, 1974). Other more recent studies have found positive benefits (Garner, 1982; Howlett & Boehm, 1975; Lybarger, 1976; Mitchell & Cockrum, 1980; Petrock, 1976; Wasmund, 1980). The positive results reported in a number of school-based programs suggest that many of the earlier criticisms of peer group treatment apply to the institutional milieu in which early programs developed, rather than to the methodology per se.

Although there has been considerable critical analysis of this methodology by external observers, there have been comparatively few data from *participants* in such programs about the potential for misuse or the critical components for program success. Brendtro and Ness (1982) surveyed staff and youth in 10 such programs, seeking to identify significant problems in the application of this methodology and to propose guidelines for practice. Based on their survey in varied kinds of schools and residential settings, ten potential areas of misuse were identified. These are presented in Table 7-3 listed in order of frequency with which they were cited. As the table shows, all but one of the staff teams expressed concern about the potentials for *abuse of confrontation*. They documented a tendency for intense hostile verbal interactions to develop unless staff carefully monitored the process. Marathon-length sessions, the use of hostile language in the guise of helping, and even physically aggressive behavior were noted as potential dangers unless clear standards are set by staff.

Programs reported concern about *mechanical, jargon-based communications* in problem-solving sessions. This was most frequently noted with respect to the compulsive use of problem labels (e.g., "fronting," "authority problem") wherein youth were facile with the vocabulary but did not seem to be engaged in genuine communication. Another abuse in verbal communication was excessive use of the reversal technique (described earlier) such that normal conversations could not be carried on, resulting in an adversarial tone to communication. Although the utility of these verbal techniques was not questioned, they clearly have the potential for being misused.

Table 7-3. Potential Misuse of Peer Group Methodology as
Reported by Staff in 10 Programs

Issue	No. of staff teams raising issue
Abuse of confrontation	9
Mechanical verbalizations	6
Family estrangement	6
Poor listening skills	5
Lack of individualization	5
Distant staff relationships	5
Staff abuse of control	3
Inadequate professional training	3
Group leader superiority	2
Purist rigidity	2

Another commonly identified issue was *family estrangement*. This concern was apparent in public school programs as well as institutional programs. Community-based programs reported a tendency for parents to become threatened by the possibility that youth would be carrying information about families into the group situation and thus fearful that the program could separate them from their offspring. The most common problem in residential settings was the existence of elaborate structures to minimize contact with parents (sometimes operating simultaneously with rhetoric suggesting that staff were family-oriented).

Staff in one-half of the programs said that *inadequate listening skills* were a key limitation to effectiveness. Although young people rather quickly learn how to confront one another and "preach," they need much more careful training in order to learn to listen and be sensitive to the nuances of nonverbal and verbal behavior.

Staff respondents in half the programs suggested that *a lack of attention to individual needs* may result from excessive emphasis on the group. For example, individual counseling has traditionally been forbidden in some peer group programs under the assumption that it would undermine the group effort. In effect, students in such a program were free to seek help from everyone except staff. When staff see the group as the answer to all problems, the potential exists for compromising a person's individual integrity and identity.

Respondents in half the programs specifically identified *distant staff–student relationships* as potentially problematic. In some cases adults used the group as a cop-out for exercising their own authority, backing off from significant involvement in the life of the group. Some staff are overly concerned with not becoming familiar. When staff are distant and unable to model positive caring relationships, the group is thereby deprived of this important staff component.

Respondents in three residential programs identified *staff abuse of control* as a significant problem. This problem seems to occur when staff subvert the focus of the program from treatment to control. Once a group culture is established, staff typically find groups to be more manageable than before. This allows staff to take advantage of the group by domineering or even provoking youth, with the security of knowing that the group will suppress any revolt. As Harry Vorrath has said, "Once the program pulls the teeth from the tiger, the most cowardly staff become courageous." Because of the potency of this intervention in a total environment, there is always the danger that staff will conscript the group into service as an enforcer, thereby mutating the treatment focus of the program.

Two programs noted concern about *inadequate professional training*. In the past some peer group programs have operated with limited professional staff under the assumption that the adult group leader primarily needs to "be a good delinquent." There appears to be growing recognition that professional training is necessary if staff are to understand fully the individual and group dynamics within the program.

Two programs also identified *group leader superiority* as an issue. This problem could be manifest both in a residential program, where the group leader overused the concept of confidentiality to enhance his status as a group therapist, and in a public school program, where the group leader alienated other school faculty through similar elitist isolation.

A final issue was that of *purist rigidity*, which was noted by staff in two settings. They noted the tendency of a particular program to become "cast in stone," thereby preventing free evaluation of assumptions or creative extension of the program. It was also noted that advocates of peer group programs have frequently been characterized by an evangelical fervor as if they possessed a panacea that would cure the world. Such unrealistic expectations alienate other professionals and oversimplify complex problems.

In interviews with youth in these 10 settings, Brendtro and Ness (1982) found that young people were generally enthusiastic, somewhat reluctant to criticize the program, and eager to describe their ability to help others and profit from the program. Nevertheless, a number of themes emerged from the interviews with youth supporting various suggestions that had been raised by staff. In particular, youth stressed the need for periods to escape from the intensity of group interaction for more unstructured time and privacy. They also objected to the tendency of staff to use group-imposed restrictions, i.e., making the entire group suffer because of the activity of one of its members. In some residential settings, youth reported that parent contacts were excessively monitored and they felt that they should have open access to their family.

After interviewing all of these staff and youth, the authors were impressed with their collective wisdom and their ability to evaluate their experience in peer group treatment. Most staff and youth felt ownership of the program, were secure in what they were doing, and were free to share examples of problems they had experienced. Virtually every conceivable misapplication of the methodology had been marked and, perhaps more importantly, had been resolved by some of the programs. Nevertheless, numerous "blind spots" were noted, since staff were unaware that certain practices would be viewed as malpractice by some of their colleagues in other programs. A number of specific guidelines are offered for operating quality peer group treatment programs.

1. *Replacing peer coercion with peer concern.* Assigning peers the responsibility for helping one another carries with it no authority to employ punitive interventions. Staff must ensure that attempts to confront youth with the reality of their behavior are carried out in a manner that minimizes the possibility of antagonism by any of the parties involved. Harassment, name-calling, screaming in someone's face, hostile profanity, and physical intimidation have no place in a quality program. Since physical restraint is a restriction of a most basic freedom, it should properly be used only in *extreme* situations where lack of intervention would lead to greater harm. Programs based on peer coercion instead of peer concern cannot be called treatment.

2. *Establishing authentic communication.* Any structured system of problem identification, labeling, and resolution is valuable only insofar as it facilitates communication. Staff must ensure that the medium does not become the message. Therapeutic communication must always be genuine, intensely human, and not mechanical. For communication to be effective, youth need skills in listening and understanding equivalent to their ability in confronting.

3. *Building positive staff relationships.* It is a misconception that staff cannot have therapeutic relationships with individual students in peer group treatment. Successful programs are marked by strong, caring bonds between adults and youth. If staff model interactions that are aloof, coercive, or hostile, the group will follow. Full staff involvement also entails a willingness to reassert adult authority if the group members are unable to handle problems in a responsible, caring manner.

4. *Providing private time and space.* Every individual needs and deserves periods during which he or she can be physically and psychologically alone. No individual should have inner feelings continually exposed to group confrontation. No group regimen should be so all-encompassing as to stifle a person's individual interests or relationships with family and friends.

5. *Involving the family.* Parents must be seen as full partners with the treatment team. Attempts to limit family contact deny parents this proper role. Likewise, parental contact cannot be used as a reinforcer for appropriate behavior any more than one would deprive a student of contact with another member of the team.

6. *Developing total professional competence.* The complexity of problems presented by youth will not yield to simplistic panaceas. Thus, the skills of every team member must be developed to the maximum extent possible. No staff member should assume that one person's contributions are more important than another team member's, and no treatment model should be assumed to have all the answers.

7. *Generalizing caring behavior.* If young people are to develop competence and self-esteem, they must experience opportunities to affect the world (White, 1971). Deprived of opportunities for productivity, shunted into consumptive roles, young people come to learn that their presence makes very little difference in the world. Unless caring behavior can be generalized beyond the immediate peer group, we shall not achieve lasting change in youth. There is no shortage of potential roles for volunteer service by young people, considering the wide range of unmet needs that exist in every community.

Peer group approaches offer strong potential for improving educational and treatment programs for children and youth. However, this methodology is still emerging, and practitioners should avoid rigid commitment to any narrow application of this model. An ancient Chinese proverb suggests that wisdom lies in being able to remain "stalwart as a pine on principles, but flexible as a willow on details." Unless commitment is tempered with open-mindedness, the most creative and dynamic principles soon become dogmatic practice.

REFERENCES

Allen, A. & Mitchell, M. Helping the community: An untapped resource for troubled children. *Pointer*, 1982, *26*,(3), 29–33.

Brendtro, L., & Ness, A. Perspectives on peer group treatment: The use and abuse of guided group interaction/positive peer culture. *Children and Youth Services Review*, 1982, *4*(4), 307–324.

Brendtro, L., & Nicolaou, A. Hooked on helping. *Synergist*, 1982, *10* (Winter), 38–41.

Bronfenbrenner, U. Foreword. In E. Wynne, *Looking at schools: Good, bad, and indifferent*. Lexington, MA: Lexington Books, 1980.

Brophy, J., & Rohrkemper, M. The influence of problem ownership on teachers' perceptions of and strategies for coping with problem students. Research monograph, East Lansing: Institute for Research on Teaching, College of Education, Michigan State University, August 1980.

Buber, M. *I and thou*. New York: Charles Scribner and Sons, 1970.

Empey, L., & Lubeck, S. *The Silverlake experiment*. Chicago: Aldine, 1972.

Fantini, M. Disciplined caring. *Phi Delta Kappan*, 1980, *62*, 182–184.

Garner, H. Positive peer culture programs in schools. In D. Safer (Ed.), *School program for disruptive adolescents*. Baltimore: University Park Press, 1982.

Gold, M. A time for skepticism. *Crime and Delinquency*, 1974, *20* (January), 20–24.

Gordon, W. In an exchange of letters with LaMar T. Empey and Jerome Rabow, *American Sociological Review*, 1962, 27(2), 256–258.

Hamachek, D. *The self in growth, teaching and learning*. Englewood Cliffs, NJ: Prentice-Hall, 1965.

Hobbs, N. Helping disturbed children and their families: Project Re-ed 20 years later. Paper published by the Center for the Study of Families and Children, Institute for Public Policy Studies, Vanderbilt University, Nashville, TN, 1979.

Howlett, F., & Boehm, R. *School-based delinquency prevention: The Rock Island experience.* Austin, TX: Justice Systems, 1975.

Keith-Lucas, A. Foundations of caring. *Residential Group Care,* 1979, *4,* 1–5.

Keller, O., & Alper, B. *Half-way houses: Community centered correction and treatment.* Lexington, MA: D. C. Heath, 1970.

Lerner, M. *Values in education: Notes toward a values philosophy.* Bloomington, IN: Phi Delta Kappa Educational Foundation, 1976.

Lybarger, W. The effect of positive peer culture on the self-concept and rate of exhibition of inappropriate behavior of the emotionally disturbed adolescent male. *Dissertation Abstracts International,* 1976, *37* (September–October).

McCorkle, L., Elias, A., & Bixby, F. *The Highfields story.* New York: Henry Holt, 1958.

Mitchell, J., & Cockrum, D. Positive peer culture and a level system: A comparison in an adolescent treatment facility. *Criminal Justice and Behavior,* 1980, *7*(4), 399–405.

Petrock, F. Guided group interaction in public schools: Managing student behavior through peer group advocacy. Doctoral dissertation, University of Michigan, Ann Arbor, 1976.

Phillips, E., Phillips, E., Fixsen, D., & Wolf, M. *The teaching-family handbook: Group living environments administered by professional teaching parents for youth in trouble.* Lawrence, KS: University Printing Service, 1972 (rev. 1974).

Pilnick, S. Guided group interaction. In R. Morris (Ed.), *Encyclopedia of social work* (Vol. 1). Washington, DC: National Association of Social Workers, 1971.

Sarri, R., & Selo, E. Evaluation process and outcome in juvenile corrections: A grim tale. In P. O. Davidson, F. W. Clark, & L. A. Hamerlynch (Eds.), *Evaluation of community programs.* Champaign, IL: Research Press, 1974.

Saurman, K., & Nash, R. An antidote to narcissism. *Synergist,* 1980, *9*(1), 15–18.

Schaefer, C. *How to influence children.* New York: Van Nostrand, 1978.

Vinter, R., Kish, R., & Newcomb T. (Eds.). *Time out: A study of juvenile correction programs.* Ann Arbor, MI: University of Michigan, National Assessment of Juvenile Corrections, 1976.

Vorrath, H. *Positive peer culture: Contents, structure, process.* Minneapolis: Minneapolis Center for Group Studies, 1972.

Vorrath, H., & Brendtro, L. *Positive peer culture.* Chicago: Aldine, 1974.

Wasmund, W. A research evaluation of the Woodland Hills Residential Treatment Program. Duluth, MN: Woodland Hills, 1980.

Weeks, A. The Highfields project. In R. Gillombardo (Ed.), *Juvenile delinquency: A book of readings.* New York: Wiley, 1976.

White, R. The urge towards competence. *American Journal of Occupational Therapy,* 1971, *25*(6), 271–274.

Whittaker, J. *Caring for troubled children.* San Francisco: Jossey-Bass, 1979.

Re-education Through Recreation   8

CHARLES L. MAND

> The bow cannot always stand bent,
> nor can human frailty subsist
> without some lawful recreation.
> —Cervantes in *Don Quixote*

Many troubled youngsters have been deprived of social success, skill acquisition, and a sense of identity in their lives. Rather, they have experienced too much failure, frustration, and anxiety, leading in many cases to social isolation, inactivity due to fear of failure, self-abuse, and aggressive behavior. A sound recreation program can help to redress some of these maladaptive behaviors in conjunction with more traditional forms of intervention. Recreation for therapeutic purposes seeks to (1) promote social experiences for participants, (2) assist students to regain a sense of confidence through the acquisition of recreational skills, and (3) prescribe recreational activities for individuals with special needs.

In this chapter we shall discuss briefly the purposes and development of recreation as a re-educational tool. Typical activities will be noted, with emphasis on the potential significance of the activities to those being served. Leadership and administrative organization will also be examined so as to place the activity program in perspective.

THE SIGNIFICANCE OF PLAY

Play, as a significant phenomenon both in the fabric of an individual's life and collectively as a measure of society, has provided the foundation for the development of general recreation and subsequently therapeutic recreation over the last hundred years. This focus on play dates from the end of the nineteenth century, when various intellectuals began a systematic examination of play and its significance in people's lives.

One of the first prominent theories of play is attributed to the German philosopher Schiller and aptly called "surplus energy" (Meyer & Brightbill, 1964). According to this view, individuals play to maintain the body's homeostasis, and vigorous play enables people, particularly children who do not work, to rid themselves of excess energy. Although this is a nineteenth-century theory, it has a familiar ring: "Build a recreation center and keep the kids off the streets."

At about the same time that Schiller proposed the surplus energy theory, which was basically a biological description of play, the alternative theory of "re'creation," a mentalistic concept, was developed and attributed to Spencer (Meyer & Brightbill, 1964). This concept explains play as an exercise to relieve the boredom and repetitiveness of life in the work world of the late nineteenth century. Where were spontaneity, joy, risk, adventure, thrill, and fun to be found but in the world of play? Those who participated in play were renewed, stimulated, refreshed, and once again able to resume the daily chores of life with a light step and clear mind. Perhaps the clearest support for this re'creation theory can be found during exam week on a college campus, as students between exams and serious bouts of study flock to the campus recreation facilities to swim, shoot baskets, lift weights, roller skate, or engage in almost any activity to provide release and refreshment from the academic tensions.

Other theories of play advanced during this period are equally intriguing, yet, as with most theories, they are incomplete and unsatisfactory as full explanations of this complex phenomenon. Gross proposed the "instinct-practice" theory on the basis of a lifetime observing the animal world (Meyer & Brightbill, 1964). A kitten crouches, stalks, and pounces upon a ball of yarn as practice for capturing mice or rabbits as an adult. Kittenhood is a time to prepare for life as a cat, and play represents the medium of progression. Similarly, children and adolescents practice skills necessary for adults in our world, but the practice period is much longer since our adult life is very much more complex than that of animals.

C. Stanley Hall, an eminent educational psychologist of his time who was influenced by the work of a contemporary, Charles Darwin, developed the "recapitulation" theory of play (Meyer & Brightbill, 1964). Hall noted that children in each part of the world, in industrial as well as pre-industrial cultures, assume similar play forms. Furthermore, these play forms repeat the historical stages of human development — of man as hunter, gatherer, and agriculturalist — through chasing and fleeing games, collecting activities, or hiding and finding pastimes. A particular result of this theory was the inclusion in playgrounds of swings, which represent an arboreal period in the history of the race. Is there a reader who, given the opportunity, wouldn't swing on a rope over water and land with a great splash, or who does not thrill to the Tarzan movies and wish that such convenient vines were available in his or her playscape?

As suggested, these early theories were incomplete, even romantic rather than truly scientific, but the theories and the very prominent individuals who sponsored them had a significant effect: play became a serious matter and worthy of study. Perhaps even more important was the notion derived from such early work that play was a developmental phenomenon, and not merely frivolous. In fact, in 1906 a number of prominent Americans established the Playground Association of America. The membership included G. Stanley Hall, John Dewey (educator), Gifford Pinchot (of the U.S. Forest Service), Clark Heatherington (physical educator), Jane Addams (social worker), Joseph Lee (philanthropist), and Luther Gulick (of the Camp Fire Girls), and the honorary chairperson was Theodore Roosevelt. The membership, much more extensive than that listed above, represented a variety of academic backgrounds and lent great authority to the notion that play was an important element in the life of an individual and collectively in the quality of society. The Playground Association of America eventually became the National Recreation Association, which in turn realigned its functions and is now named the National Recreation and Park Association. It is through this organization that therapeutic recreation derives its support and organizational energy.

However, the story of play theory and its relationship to recreation and eventually to therapeutic recreation is still incomplete. In the twentieth century, the examination of play continues, and three theories are particularly relevant.

1. In *Man, Play and Games,* Callois (1961) provides a continuum for the play experience from *ludus* to *paedia*, from the simple and spontaneous to the complex and highly organized. Play can take forms that are as different as frisbee is from varsity football or as solitaire is from contract bridge. Callois assists us in understanding the commonality of play among different age groups although the forms of play vary widely.

2. The cultural theory of play described in *Homo Ludens* (Huizinga, 1962) maintains that culture in any society is a product of the play forms in the culture. In certain pre-industrial regions of the world, truth is determined by which of two adversaries is judged a superior dancer by members of the tribe. This, of course, is not very different from a court of law in a country such as the United States. Prosecutor and defense attorney act as adversaries to present evidence that a jury evaluates to determine innocence or guilt. The courtroom is a very

competitive environment and, in Huizinga's view, probably to the consternation of academic jurists, it evolved as a play form rather than as a logical extension of thought. Marriage, church, and family, as well as law, are traced by Huizinga to cultural origins in play.

3. The most significant contribution of play theory to the eventual development of therapeutic recreation is found, however, in the work of analytic psychiatrists such as Anna Freud (1965) and Erik Erikson (1963). The psychodynamic theory of play includes four factors: (1) mastery, (2) impulse outlet, (3) relief from anxiety, and (4) pleasurable moment.

Mastery, in a strict psychological frame of reference, refers to recognition by an individual of the limits of reality through the illusionary world of play. Imagine, for example, a 10-year-old girl who has suffered the death of her favorite grandmother. When she plays with dolls, she has a doll for her sister, brother, mother, father, and favorite grandmother. This play practice may persist for months after the grandmother's death. One day the child plays the scene with only four dolls: mother, father, sister, and brother. There is no doll for grandmother and, in effect, the youngster has mastered her death.

A secondary thread related to mastery is the notion that the acquisition of skill in the play world, be it an athletic, intellectual, or aesthetic skill, leads to mastery of the real world of daily living.

Impulse outlet refers to the many games that foster aggressive behavior. However, the aggressive behavior is modified by the rules of the game, and penalties occur if the rules are broken. Thus, although games can be quite violent, even when they do not include written rules or when third parties such as referees are not present, security against play that is too aggressive is an unwritten but obvious element of most activities. Observe an elementary group playing in the corner of the football field at a high school game. Whoever clutches a hat is fair game to be tossed to the ground and mauled until the hat is released. As soon as the hat is released, aggressive behavior stops. Furthermore, it is possible to play and never hold the hat and therefore to escape any mauling. A true safety net seems to be available in many play forms: a chance to be violent but not dangerous because of the rules of the activity. One is in a sense protected against oneself.

Relief from anxiety is probably best exemplified by the fact that most of our pastimes include costumes. A helmet, shoulder pads, cleated shoes, a numbered and colored shirt typify a football player. A 13-year-old boy, seeking manhood and anxious about being masculine, certainly achieves a temporary measure of relief from such anxiety when appearing in costume with the other boys. Even the adults accept the role and costume, thus reinforcing the mechanism.

Pleasurable moment refers to the gratification of an animal's need for big muscle activity, which is called for in many sports and games. Domestic animals stretch luxuriously after confinement; girls and boys race about the school yard upon release from the classroom. Individuals play partly to achieve the satisfaction of physical release in strenuous pursuits.

As with other theories, the analytical model provides some insight into the world of play, but like other theories, it overstates or ignores certain play behaviors among specific groups. What the model does provide for the analytically trained is a ready vehicle for observing and analyzing behavior of a nonverbal nature.

The summation of these theories leads to the notion that play can be expressive, nonconsequential, very intense at times, absorbing, highly organized, exhausting, and exhilarating. Yet it also can be passive, casual, spontaneous, and relaxing. It can take a variety of forms, be a social or a solitary experience, childlike yet important in the adult world, and almost limitless in application. A most cogent and complete but simple definition may be that of B. F. Skinner, who defines play as "serious activity for non-serious purposes."

The most important contribution of play theory is that it has led to the institutionalization of play and the acceptance of play as an essential human need. It is only a short step to recognize that exceptional people, although perhaps placed in a rehabilitative center, retain their human needs. Thus the institutional forms of play, games, sports, drama, music, camping, and organized recreation appear not only in schools, churches, and parks, but also in hospitals and residential centers for special populations.

DEVELOPMENT OF THERAPEUTIC RECREATION

Recreation for special populations in America originated in playgrounds and settlement houses at the turn of the twentieth century (Rowthorn, 1978). One of the most influential early pioneers was Boston lawyer–philanthropist Joseph Lee, who organized a model playground for boys whom he had seen arrested for playing in the streets. Another early force leading to the development of therapeutic recreation was the American Red Cross, which assumed responsibility for providing recreational services to hospitalized veterans of World War I. It was during and after World War II, however, that recreation for troubled persons received its greatest impetus for growth. One class of veterans was traumatized by the horrors and degradation of war and required extensive treatment for emotional and mental illness rather than for the traditional physical injuries of such conflicts. A large number of psychiatric hospitals were opened by the Veterans Administration and they included sophisticated recreational facilities. This represented a large step forward for recreation services in therapeutic environments. Within a short time, general hospitals serving long-term patients began to include recreation for patients. Other treatment facilities have followed this pattern, and there is growing emphasis on recreation for clients with behavioral problems or emotional disability as well as for those with special physical needs.

Actually, a paradox has grown from these events, and to some extent it plagues the continued development of therapeutic recreation within the medical model. Very little group treatment exists in hospitals that provide interventions on a one-to-one basis — doctor-to-patient or therapist-to-patient. The evolution of the professional child care worker or *educateur* promises to alter this state of affairs drastically by emphasizing the importance of leisure time and of recreational activities.

LEISURE COUNSELING

The growth of leisure counseling has led to a significant advance in professionalism for recreation programs. Leisure counseling does for recreation what tests of reading or mathematical skills do for educational programs. These sorts of diagnostic tools help provide information about the leisure ability, interest, skills, experiences, assets, and liabilities of an individual. They provide a base for building a coherent program of activities.

Think for a moment about what sort of information is available about a youngster who is enrolled in a re-educational program. It has been common to accumulate data about special educational needs, family background, psychological functioning, medical status, and social agency contacts. However, typically almost nothing has been known about how the youngster uses spare time. That sort of information has not seemed important even though many more hours in the day and in the week are spent in non-school activities and beyond the presence of psychologists, social workers, or other counselors. Does the youngster enjoy athletic activities? Is the student skilled? Does he or she collect, paint, play an instrument? Does the person enjoy organizing events, helping others, traveling? Are there deficiencies in the student's leisure pursuits? Is the youth asocial, afraid of peers, resistant to certain types of authority figures, threatened by large groups or by being alone? Does the youngster need special encouragement to try something new?

The first step in leisure counseling is to seek some answers to these questions and others like them. Robert Overs (1970) provides a model for the process of leisure counseling, which is shown in Table 8-1. It should be noted that although materials such as Overs' model are useful as a guide, this model as well as other illustrative materials must be modified and adjusted to the needs of specific programs serving a particular population. For example, in Overs' model, the client has complete choice of activities, although only after discussion and counseling with a therapist. In re-education, the treatment team is more likely to modify choices and prescribe activities as part of the therapeutic process.

There are several ways to elicit information about the recreational practices of students before enrollment in special programs and periodically thereafter. A simple but highly revealing data collection technique is a self-report form completed at periodic intervals by students. The youth are asked to fill in a schedule of their activities on an hour-by-hour basis for a typical 24-hour day. A variety of other instruments can be used to determine interests and skills as well as limitations in the recreational background of a student.

A most complete scheme to determine recreational interests is the Miranda Leisure Interest Finder (Miranda, 1973), developed in Milwaukee for community adult recreation. This approach uses a questionnaire to assess interest in a large number of possible recreational activities. The principal feature of this system is the production of a profile sheet for an individual that displays high- and low-interest areas in categories such as these: games, sports, nature, collection, homemaking/home craft, art/music, educational/entertainment/cultural, and volunteer organizations.

Finally, the data gathered must be compiled, synthesized, and maintained in a record-keeping system that is available and administratively practical. In sum, leisure counseling seeks to provide a measure of the individual's interest patterns and life activities during unstructured personal time so that this information can be used in activity planning.

ACTIVITY PROGRAMMING

Certainly, the fundamental question for the participant is, "What can I do in this place?" Staff may have their own agendas of proposed programs, but the principal concern for the student is the activity, the skill, and the social milieu. A typical program includes a wide variety of

Table 8-1. Leisure Counseling Scheme

Action initiated	Client choice	Methods or instruments
Identification of interests and aptitudes of client		Measured by: expressed interests interest inventories psychological tests analysis of the life history data observation of demonstrated interests in occupational therapy and work evaluation
Identification of physical, mental, and emotional limitations		Medical evaluation
Systematic exploration and identification of suitable avocational activities	Client selects one or more fields of activity to explore	Avocational Activities Inventory (AAI)
	Client narrows down choices to one or more activities for which outlets are potentially available	

Systematic exploration of the Avocational Activities File to locate activity opportunities appropriate for the activity choices made

Activity testing. A client tries out one or more activities. Referral by counselor or recreation worker to activity agency if appropriate. Detailed check of client's eligibility for activity if appropriate. Arrangement for transportation, writing for information, purchase of equipment, etc.

Tentative choice of one or more apparently available suitable activities

Final Choice: Client initiates activity. Client makes final choice of activity which is demonstrated to be fully available to him

Avocational Activities File

Referral network

241

pursuits, probably from A to Z, but certainly from archery to yoga. For our purposes, it is helpful to classify this great variety of activities in order to examine their potential contributions (Table 8-2). Classification schemes vary from source to source in the descriptive labels used, but they generally include a similar range of pursuits.

Sports and Athletics

This category includes a number of alternative forms of physical activity. Team sports such as volleyball or basketball can be either recreational or very competitive. The use of competitive athletics with emotionally disturbed populations poses important questions (Phillips, 1981). Many troubled youngsters are not eager to participate in team games of a highly competitive nature because of fear of failure or ridicule, which are very possible in such situations. Furthermore, team games require role-playing by the participants. Not everyone can be a

Table 8-2. Typical Activities Program[a]

Sports and athletics	Social activities	Creative arts
Volleyball	Parties	Modern dance
Soccer	Tournaments	Painting
Basketball	Movies	Sculpture
Softball	Skating	Choral music
Tennis	Trips	Instrumental music
Track and field		Theater
Golf	Special events	Crafts
Archery	Learning caravan	Photography
Fencing	Creative supper	
Gymnastics	Olympics	Outdoor pursuits
Body building	Help Another Day	Camping
Conditioning	Founder's Day	Bird watching
Weight lifting	Holiday programs	Earth watch
Judo	Aquatics	Backpacking
Yoga	Swimming	Rappelling
New games	Life saving	Kayaking
	Canoeing	Outward Bound
Hobbies	Sailing	
Gardening	Fishing	Work–service
Model building	Water skiing	Maintenance
Stamp collecting		Incentive work
Current events		Environmental improvement
Language groups		Human service
Folk dance		
Collectibles		

[a] Partial listings.

high scorer in basketball or be the pitcher in baseball and, in a sense, serve as a center of attraction. Rather, individuals must submerge personal feelings for the group welfare and in some cases for the benefit of another individual. Although a notable purpose of such activities is to develop these qualities, they are beyond the capability of many troubled youth. Thus, the usual competitive elements of traditional team sports may have to be modified, and competitive activities that include physical contact such as football or wrestling may have to be avoided. For these reasons there has been increased interest in developing noncompetitive but physically vigorous *cooperative* activities with troubled youth such as those advocated by the New Games Foundation (Fluegelman, 1976).

Individual sports such as archery, golf, or track permit physical exertion but provide almost a self-pacing element of competition. For example, one can lose a race in track or a pole vaulting competition and yet have matched or exceeded a personal record. The competition in these activities may be with self and environment, and not necessarily with other people. In addition, many individual or dual sports also have a strong recreational connotation in the culture rather than a strictly competitive emphasis. For every Jack Nicklaus or Tom Watson, there are thousands of weekend golfers seeking to break 100. It is all right not to be the best!

A very popular form of physical activity for adolescents is in the area of conditioning and body-building. Young people at this age seek a "body beautiful." At least, large numbers of young people participate regularly in these activities and take pride in the results of an improved figure for girls, and, for boys, bigger muscles, more strength, and a macho image. Some of this enthusiasm probably stems from serious anxiety about body image, but at the very best, participation in these sports produces a positive response to the concern.

The martial arts such as yoga, judo, karate, and T'ai Chi are unique. Oriental in origin, these sports require an absolute discipline on the part of the participant, combine mind and body, and seem to be totally absorbing. It is ironic that many young people who participate are in rebellion against authority, disdain tradition, and abhor structure. Yet, these very people engage in these sports, which are typified by a rigid structure, are rote in practice, and are completely authoritarian. They are growing in popularity and obviously satisfy personal needs.

A proper sport and athletic phase of a therapeutic recreation program requires a balance among offerings and a generous amount of sensitivity regarding the modification of activities. A projection of traditional athletic programs to populations of troubled students may be an invitation to failure. The heterogeneous nature of the anxieties of disturbed youngsters requires a variety of choices and an opportunity to participate on grounds of self-satisfaction rather than community-desired outcomes.

Aquatics

The aquatic environment seems particularly relevant for therapeutic activity. Such activities as swimming, diving, canoeing, and scuba diving can be developed as instructional, recreational, or competitive events. The age range for participation is almost unrestricted, and certain activities beyond swimming are quite easy to master to the point of self-satisfaction. Water skiing is an excellent example of a popular activity for adolescents. It is an "in" sport. It is important and has prestige among other young people. It has a costume and a vernacular—"cut," "rooster tail." Yet, given reasonable swimming skills for safety in the water, a motor with sufficient horsepower, and a patient instructor, just about anyone can ski a simple course on two skis. It is a great morale booster. Obviously, to become an expert skier involves a different set of conditions.

Other aquatic activities have aesthetic overtones, promote tranquility, and yet can create a rare sense of risk and adventure, such as in white water canoeing.

A word of caution, however, is in order regarding water-related activities. The consequence of poor safety can be very sudden, abrupt, and complete — drowning. Most accidents around water result from poor judgment. The poor judgment could be caused by limited knowledge, or by irresponsible behavior that is drug-related or impulsive. This rich program area requires strong leadership and effective contingency controls to establish safety in a group situation.

Creative Arts

Many troubled youngsters seek an avenue of expression, social experiences, and skill acquisition in creative arts rather than athletic or physical games. Although this is not an either – or proposition, a relatively large number of youngsters, many of whom seem less aggressive and acting-out, seek satisfaction almost exclusively in music, art, theater, and similar creative activities. Unfortunately, too often therapeutic recreation personnel have traditionally been hired on the basis of an athletic reputation. These people, in turn, have not seemed to appreciate creative arts nearly as much as athletic or more vigorous pastimes. This is a serious error and is prejudicial to a large segment of the treatment population.

A desirable feature of these activities is the potential for integrating various art forms. A stage production combines the talents of musicians for accompaniment, actors, artists for set design, writers, photographers, and craftsman for costumes and props. A theater production company becomes a close-knit unit working toward common goals; its members are dependent on each other to meet deadlines for opening night. A thorough discussion of the rich contributions of the creative arts follows in Chapter 9.

Hobbies

Some years ago, while the author was working with troubled adolescents in northern New England, a small group of youngsters asked to accompany a staff member to an antique auction. This seemed a reasonable off-campus trip. Upon return, the youngsters decided that antique collecting and refinishing furniture seemed an interesting pastime. So at the next weekly auction, several youngsters, using some of their own money, bought pine dressers, chests, or similar pieces of furniture. (It should be added that unrefinished pine chests brought less than $10 to the seller. The antique dealers had not reached northern New England at that time.) The students then refinished the furniture and in many cases sold it at a profit to neighbors in the surrounding community. The group grew, and interest increased in the entire range of collectibles available in the area. Before long, a club was established for collectibles. Students purchased, refinished, and sold antiques; in fact, they created a modest mail-order business in the area. Members of the photography club produced a brochure illustrating finished pieces, and a process for delivery, payment, and distribution was established at the center. A simple activity engaged a number of students in a very educational and stimulating enterprise. This is just one example of the value of hobbies in fulfilling the mission of a recreation program.

Social Activities

A wide range of large group activities is necessary to balance the program offerings. Some of the social activities are participatory;

others involve spectator events. Weekly or scheduled movie programs, large parties, large-screen viewing of television spectaculars such as the inauguration of the President or a space launch are welcome additions to any recreation program although they are basically spectator activities. In addition, small group off-station trips, tournaments, and special event holiday carnivals, which are more participatory in nature, also contribute to breaking the routine and promoting interest and enthusiasm.

The trick in recreation programming is to establish a balance among small and large group activities, viewing versus participating pursuits, routine versus innovative programming.

A principal criticism of the recreational diet of many youth is a program consisting of passive, consumptive activity like watching television or listening to rock music. These pastimes may have merit but only in the perspective of a total program that includes a variety of participatory and spectator activities, some of which have primarily social purposes, but others of which foster skill, challenge, adventure, creativity, and mutual interests.

Outdoor Pursuits

Outdoor activities have been used for therapeutic purposes with troubled children and adolescents for many decades. McNeil (1957) provided one of the early reviews of the background and rationale of therapeutic camping. More recently Loughmiller (1979) advocated the use of adventure camping as a re-educational tool. Probably the most dramatic example of the widespread interest in outdoor pursuits is found in programs like Outward Bound. Actually, Outward Bound is a nonprofit corporation that promotes outdoor activity for the purposes of increased self-awareness and improved group relationships. The activities employed to achieve these purposes include rock climbing, rappelling, backpacking, canoeing, mountain climbing, kayaking, and similar outdoor environmentally oriented pursuits. The activities are exotic, but the technique of conducting the program is what creates the extraordinary impact of the experience. Outward Bound and many similar outdoor adventure programs provide highly stressful experiences.

Outdoor adventure learning challenges participants to high levels of risk. The risks are real and involve serious consequences for failure. Stepping off a cliff on a rappel rope; canoeing in white water; climbing almost vertical rock faces; being alone for several days in the wilderness with little or no prepared food; being responsible for weaker members of the group or being dependent on stronger members; being hungry, cold, wet, scared of failure, yet miserable about continuing and physically tired—tired almost beyond hurt or caring—are typical descriptions by participants in these experiences. The challenges are physical, mental, and emotional; the risks are very personal; and the consequences of failure, quite high. The popularity of these programs has stimulated discussion about the psychology and basic principles underlying "risk recreation" (Allen, 1979). Whatever the motivation, the fact remains that many troubled youth who avoid traditional recreation programs are highly captivated by such adventurous pursuits.

Others enjoy less stressful outdoor activities than those proposed by Outward Bound. Some programs incorporate backpacking, canoeing, and climbing with ecological imperatives, and the emphasis is on understanding the environment rather than examining self and group relationships.

This area of outdoor pursuits is now well established in recreation settings, yet it seems to hold great promise as a medium for re-education.

Special Events

Even the most dynamic youth program can settle into a routine of boredom and lethargy. A good recreation program including an ample measure of special event activities can aid in overcoming some of the listlessness that frequently occurs at certain times in the school year.

> Six weeks into a summer program for troubled adolescents, a "creative supper" was held for the population of 120 people. Students and staff volunteered to prepare their favorite meal, frequently ethnic in derivation, and together prepare dinner for the entire group. Each person who participated as a cook provided enough of his or her specialty for approximately 8–12 people. A large round of beef was barbecued over a pit fire to ensure something for everyone. Probably one-third to one-half of the school population participated as chefs. The regular kitchen staff were honored guests and also served as judges for the meal. The awards were semi-comic—"most burned fingers," "most pots and pans dirtied,"—as well as for good foods. Everyone pitched in to clean and prepare the kitchen for the next morning's breakfast—everyone, that is, but the regular kitchen staff who received an evening free from dirty dishes.

This event engaged many people, placed students and staff in different roles, changed the routine, and was quite intense for a short period of time with very minimal consequences for failure.

Special events can be spontaneous or elaborately planned. They can be one-time happenings or part of on-going traditions such as holidays.

Maier (1979) highlights the importance of such social rituals in establishing a sense of shared participation and belonging. These special occasions not only break the routine but also contribute to a long-term sense of rhythm in the community life.

An example of an elaborate special event is described by Mand and Green:

> The most popular school feature of the summer was the learning caravan. A minibus which held eight students, two staff and camping gear for one week was used to sponsor trips in science, history, and the arts. A typical one week trip in American history would emphasize the theme of Benedict Arnold's expedition to Quebec during the Revolutionary War. During the week prior to the trip, students would plan the menu, develop individual projects, establish the itinerary including camping sites and learn to use the cooking and tenting gear. Research materials were secured from local libraries and historical societies. Typical projects included the significance of Quebec City in 18th century North America, a biography of Benedict Arnold prior to his defection, a comparison of Arnold's defection with Vietnam draft evasion, biography of Colonel Enos and similar subjects. During the trip, students paddled up the Kennebec River as did Arnold, slogged through part of the Carry Pond portages, wandered in French Quebec Province and eventually spent two days in Quebec City. The trip included an excellent dinner at a fine French restaurant.
>
> Upon return the students spent the next week writing and presenting their reports. If satisfactory, a quarter credit in American History was added to their high school transcript.
>
> This technique of learning while traveling seems to hold great fascination for this group of young people. Many have a history of failure in traditional school programs, but the somewhat exotic nature of the caravan seemed to reawaken their motivation. It was very exciting to see certain youngsters who had been ejected from a variety of public and private schools, and were almost totally defeatist about any formal learning possibilities, working on papers related to these trips. Some even took pride in their efforts (1973, p. 7).

The great importance of special events in re-educational programs is the vitality created by manipulating the usual standards of time, staff, and environment.

Work–Service

Service and work activities are related in the nature of the activity performed but quite different in the minds of adolescents and adults in this society. There is little question that everyone should contribute to the common welfare of the school, residence, or community. Everyone has responsibility for helping others and sharing to make life more pleasant. Certainly, assignments and contingencies should be established to promote this notion.

Work, on the other hand, differs from service in that it is a mark of adult society and is rewarded tangibly for its worth. All the messages young people receive underscore the ideas that work has value and to work means that you have worth in and to the society. Youth provided only with recreation pastimes or academic pursuits that prepare them for work miss the ritual of work itself. Life based solely on the pleasure principle soon leads to anxiety and dissatisfaction. The adolescent as well as the adult and the senior citizen seeks work to reaffirm his or her worth to the society and thus to self.

In addition to service-learning activities described in the previous chapter, students can benefit from formal work experiences in which they are paid for their labors, just as in the real world. Opportunities abound to promote work. The grounds require road repair, mowing, tree planting, pruning, snow removal, and other such activities. The food service provides many job opportunities also. Other such maintenance activities are predictable and can provide the basis for prescriptive assignments.

One technique for organizing a job program is to develop a job service bureau of staff and student members. All jobs are listed in the bureau, wage rates are established by the bureau, and efforts are made to match students with the work opportunities.

A more sophisticated approach to work is found in the following example. A group of students with industrial arts skills and their teacher purchased a mold to fabricate Fiberglas kayaks. The students produced boats from the mold (it is possible to build one per weekend) and sold the boats via advertisements. The cost of materials was deducted from the selling price and the remaining money divided as wages for the laborers.

An important consideration in providing work opportunities is to respond to the needs of those who wish to work but not with hammer and saw. So-called nonconstructive jobs such as typing, mimeographing, and child care are important.

The principles of work activities are simple: provide a reward for labor and create opportunities within the environment that are significant to the operation of the agency.

FOUNDATIONS OF SUCCESSFUL ACTIVITIES

The classification of activities presented above provides a wide range of possible experiences related to the treatment process. The conduct of these activities in a therapeutic environment should embody the following principles.

1. Build upon the successful characteristics and behaviors of the student.
2. Define success and progress within reasonable limits of the student's capacity.
3. Promote a wide variety of activities, with opportunity for progressive skill development.
4. Draw public attention to student achievement.
5. Promote social relationships and skill development that lead to self-direction.
6. Control potentially adverse competitive elements in activities.
7. Assist students to complete tasks.
8. Celebrate participation.

Leadership

Activities are part of the story. Good personnel adds to the likelihood of success. In fact, without competent and mature staff, the program is doomed. Competence refers simply to what the recreation leader is supposed to do. This includes leisure counseling, organizing events, training volunteers, teaching students, and a host of other duties expected of a recreation professional. Students expect high performance levels of staff and quickly ignore, avoid, or scorn incompetence. It is as if the inability to perform is a mirror of self-felt inadequacies. Maturity is a compendium of characteristics. The mature staff member communicates to fellow staff and students that they are individuals worth caring for. He or she demonstrates loyalty, sensitivity, and humor.

The role of the recreation leader must be understood in terms of multiple functions. Everybody usually understands the counseling role or direct service such as teaching an activity. However, an equally important role is that of organizer of experiences. It is almost impossible to execute a program such as described here without staff support from the community and from personnel in other departments of the treatment center. The recreation leader may recruit these people, assist them to understand their responsibilities, and at times train the volunteers to the specifics of the situation. This effort calls for a salesman's energy and the patience of a minister. In addition to exercising authority, the leader must delegate authority to fellow staff, adjunct leaders, and students.

Resources

"Have equipment, will travel" is a parody of that old television series, "Have Gun, Will Travel," so popular in the 1950's. It is not a bad thought — spending money on equipment and traveling to various facilities for activities. The vast array of interests among students almost prohibits any single campus site as sufficient to satisfy program needs. It is foolish to presume that a successful program can be achieved without a fair commitment of facilities and equipment to complement leadership resources.

However, there never will be enough financial assistance to satisfy all program requests. Some should be denied just on that basis: too expensive for value gained. The best strategy is to stretch whatever dollars are available by self-help techniques.

1. Make your own equipment. Small sailboats, kayaks, gymnastic equipment, primitive shelters for camps, docks, and a multitude of other types of equipment can often be constructed on station using existing industrial arts or crafts equipment. It is doubly valuable to use students to help construct their own environment because producing the equipment or developing a facility represents an activity in itself.

2. Budget. Regardless of how much or little money is available, an income – expenditure budget tied to long-term and operating costs will help the leader and students understand and use their program more effectively.

3. Use community resources. The use of resources, particularly unique facilities beyond the agency, is a necessary step in extending program horizons. This technique does entail a willingness to spend some money on transportation.

Organization

The general treatment model will determine the organization of the recreation program. Recreation programs in an alternative school or self-contained group home are different from those in a large state institution. Some agencies call upon their teachers or child care staff to serve as recreation leaders. Other models employ a separate recreation staff distinct from education or resident staff functions.

Two important factors to consider in any model are the degree of student participation and the degree of self-selection of activities. Student participation may be promoted by a student – staff recreation council. This council should be representative of the various population groups served by the program. This is a policy and planning body, and the shared nature of the committee demonstrates the cooperative community spirit of the recreation program. The second factor that needs clarification is the relationship between general and prescribed activities. As stated previously, a therapeutic recreation program implies specific grouping of students for purposes of engaging in prescribed activities. It also includes a general level of programming to satisfy the ordinary needs of students for activity. The allotments of time given to these enterprises need publicly established guidelines. One scheme is to allow staff to plan a portion of recreation time for prescriptive use, students to plan a portion of their recreation time, and students and staff together to plan a shared portion of recreation time at the center. Thus, some student time will involve mandatory participation and other time will be the result of self-choice. Age level, presenting problems, and other such factors will influence such an equation.

PROBLEMS AND PROSPECTS

Many of the claims made for the values of a recreation program are of a subjective nature. Since the general intent of the program is benign, few are opposed to promoting healthful, pleasant, fun-filled, socially-oriented recreation experiences. The field of recreation has hitched a ride on this fact for most of its existence. However, subjective evaluation is inadequate to provide the necessary data for realistic improvement of program or to evaluate the progress or lack of progress of a particular student. Furthermore, almost everyone else on a treatment team attempts to make judgments as a result of some type of data base. Recreation has the same responsibility and requirements for participation in the re-educational process.

Program evaluation should be multifaceted. These facets may include such factors as facility use, staffing needs, cost effectiveness, and balance between prescriptive and self-selected activities.

An analysis of the effects of the program on individual students is also essential. For example, one of the benefits claimed for recreation is the opportunity for social interaction. This is a measurable item, and a professional person attempts to gather data to determine if this goal is being realized or just hypothesized.

The *educateur* or recreation worker has a professional responsibility to gather data for purposes of evaluation. Furthermore, greater acceptance of this fledgling professional field will occur only with the collection of data to document results. There is still a need to impress others in the treatment process of the significance of an activity program.

A crystal ball projection of future trends is merely educated guesswork. This is a relatively new professional field emerging in the treatment process at a time of great concern and enthusiasm for people with special needs in society. Certainly this combination of circumstances indicates that changes will occur in the next decade with respect to training and practice. Among the changes that appear most probable are:

1. Data-based analysis and evaluation will become a more significant portion of training and practice in recreation.
2. Certification in child care and therapeutic recreation will become a legal requirement.
3. Training programs will become interdisciplinary in nature, and the fields of special education and recreation will become more closely integrated to prepare recreational specialists for re-education.

REFERENCES

Allen, S. Some basic principles of risk recreation. Paper presented at the Annual Conference of American Alliance for Health, Physical Education, Recreation and Dance, New Orleans, LA, March 16, 1979.

Callois, R. *Man, play, and games.* New York: The Free Press of Glencoe, 1961.

Cohen, W. J. *Developing controls from without.* Paoli: Devereaux Foundation Press, 1964.

Erikson, E. *Childhood and society* (2nd ed.). New York: W. W. Norton, 1963.

Fluegelman, A. (Ed.). *The new games book.* San Francisco: New Games Foundation, 1976.

Freud, A. *Normality and pathology in childhood: Assessments of development.* New York: International Universities Press, 1965.

Huizinga, J. *Homo ludens: A study of the play element in culture.* Boston: Beacon Press, 1962.

Kraus, R. *Therapeutic recreation service.* Philadelphia: W. B. Saunders, 1973.

Loughmiller, C. *Kids in trouble: An adventure in education.* Tyler, TX: Wildwood Books, 1979.

McNeil, E. The background of therapeutic camping. *Journal of Social Issues,* 1957, *13*(1), 3–14.

Maier, H. The core of care: Essential ingredients for the development of children at home and away from home. *Child Care Quarterly,* 1979, *8*(3), 161–173.

Mand, C., & Green, L. An outdoor community for troubled adolescents. *Journal of School Health,* 1973, *43* (January), 8–17.

Meyer, H. D., & Brightbill, C. K. *Community recreation* (3rd ed.). Englewood Cliffs, NJ: Prentice Hall, 1964.

Miranda, J. Miranda-Leisure Interest Finder. Joseph J. Miranda, Milwaukee Recreation Department, Milwaukee, WI. 1973.

Overs, R. A Model for avocational counseling. *Journal of Health, Physical Education and Recreation*, 1970, *41* (October), 36–38.

Phillips, K. Aggression and productiveness in emotionally disturbed children in competitive and noncompetitive recreation. *Child Care Quarterly*, 1981, *10* (Summer), 148–156.

Rowthorn, A. *A history of the evolution and development of therapeutic recreation services for special populations in the United States from 1918–1977.* Ann Arbor, MI: University of Michigan, 1978.

Re-education Through the Creative Arts

9

KRISTEN D. JUUL AND NOBEL L. SCHULER

> Creativity is an instinct
> which all people possess, an
> instinct which we primarily
> use to solve and express
> life's problems.
> — Viktor Lowenfeld (1957)

Throughout history, art in its various forms has served an important function in enriching the lives of individuals and nations. The healing and therapeutic power of art has also been known for a long time. It was no coincidence that the ancient Greeks made the noble Apollo both the god of music, dance, and poetry and the healer of physical and moral illness.

During the past several decades, much evidence has accumulated both from informal observations and from systematic studies regarding the positive impact of the arts in education and therapy. There is already a very substantial body of literature on the use of drama, creative movement, music, visual arts, and other art forms with children and youth with special needs.

There are some schools and other psychoeducational programs in which the arts constitute an important part of the curriculum. However, compared with the actual need, relatively little is being done. This is particularly the case in public school special education programs. As a whole, art has a low priority in our nation's schools. Eisner (1981) reports, that, on the average, elementary school teachers devote 4% of school time each week to instruction in the fine arts. In programs for the handicapped the situation is even more discouraging. According to an estimate by the National Committee on Arts for the Handicapped, only 12% of children in special education receive any art instruction at all.

255

The main purpose of this chapter is to call attention to the rich and valuable resources that are provided by the arts in fostering normal development and overcoming behavioral problems in emotionally disturbed and socially maladjusted youth.

THE ARTS AND THE HANDICAPPED IN HISTORY

Ancient Times

The curative force of the aesthetic impulse was known long before the beginning of recorded time. In pre-literate and early societies ritual dance, drama, music, and song were used to drive out evil spirits and to cure the afflicted. The Old Testament describes how King Saul called upon the harp player David to dispell his evil moods.

At the dawn of civilization the relationship between medicine and the arts was already firmly established. When the Egyptian physician Imhotep (ca. 2900 B.C.) was posthumously given divine status and elevated to the god of medicine, a temple in his honor was erected in Memphis. This temple served both as a medical school and as a sort of psychiatric hospital in which the patients were encouraged to participate in music, dance, painting, and recreational activities.

The early Greeks believed in the close relationships among art, beauty, and health. The natural condition of man was considered one of complete harmony with the divine order of the universe, whereas illness was thought to be a disruption of this balance. Harmony was restored in part by steering thoughts and feelings in the direction of the beautiful and the good, and by participating in and enjoying the arts. The center for healing in Greece was the city of Epidauros, which was dedicated to Aesculapius, the god of medicine. This city was also a center for culture, with temples, theaters, schools of learning, a library, and a sports arena. Some of its buildings represented the most exquisite architecture in Greece. In the theaters, the patients watched or participated in performances of the plays of the great dramatists or joined in the reading or chanting of epic poems. The Greeks were well aware of the inner cleansing or catharsis wrought by a dramatic enactment. Theories regarding music therapy were brought to a high level of refinement. Selected musical instruments or songs were recommended for specific problems, such as sleep disturbances in children; according to Aristotle, flute music was an effective antidote for revelers who could not snap out of the excitement they had worked themselves into during Dionysian orgies.

The Middle Ages and the Renaissance

Throughout the Middle Ages and the Renaissance the close relationship between physical and spiritual health was generally accepted, and physicians were perceived as healers of both the body and the soul. Among the arts, music in particular was regularly used in the treatment of both physical and mental disorders, and musicians had a high status as an ancillary medical profession (Ruud, 1980).

There are numerous reports about the use and the effectiveness of music in what one today would call the promotion of mental health and adjustment. One of the best known is the story about the famous Italian singer Carlo Farinelli (1705-1782). He was called upon by the Spanish court to help cure King Philip the Fifth who had sunk into a state of deep depression and despondency. His music so affected the king that he recovered and returned to his duties. For 10 years the singer remained at the court and he sang daily before the king. It is also reported that the 18th-century composer Vivaldi created a major part of his music to be performed by orphaned, illegitimate, and handicapped girls in the institutions of Venice. The value of the music in their rehabilitation was well recognized.

Starting in the 14th century, a strange epidemic disorder was widespread in Central Europe. It was called tarantism because it was believed that it was caused by bites from the spider tarantula. The victims would wake up in the morning with acute chest pains, headaches, and an intense thirst. They ran into the streets or to the market place where they jumped about in great excitement, covered themselves with flowers and leaves, and often acted indecently. The only effective treatment was to dance the tarantella, a rapid Italian folk dance. The dancing went on for several days until the patients collapsed from exhaustion and were cured. Groups of musicians traveled around and were available to provide the therapy. The connection between the spells and the spider bites was eventually disproved, but the epidemics continued. Contemporary medical historians believe that the "disease" was a remnant of the Greek Dionysus cult, which was suppressed with the coming of Christianity (Sigerist, 1962).

The Age of Science

Gradually new modes of thinking emerged emphasizing rationalism and empiricism, and by the 19th century positivistic philosophy had become dominant, supported by the many discoveries and inventions in science and technology. Scientific advances in the conquest of disease led medicine to abandon its ties with the transcendental and the arts. There were some notable exceptions, however. In France, three great physicians, Esquirol (1772–1840), Itard (1775–1838), and Seguin (1812–1880) were inspired by the ideals of both science and humanitarianism in devising educational programs for the severely mentally retarded. All three experimented with music, and Seguin also pioneered in the use of visual arts and movements in his teaching.

Much of the 19th and the beginning of the 20th century was dominated by an optimistic faith in progress and by the rather naive belief that science and technology would eventually solve most human problems. The rise of totalitarian dictatorships and the devastations of the Second World War changed all this. Science was used to produce weapons of destruction that almost defied imagination, and technology was employed to construct extermination camps. Unspeakable and senseless atrocities were committed on a large scale by people who had reaped the benefit of our so-called advanced civilization. The war made many people question the ability of the physical sciences to provide answers to the human dilemma and to human suffering, and they turned to psychology and psychiatry for solutions.

It was widely believed that the cause of war and destruction could be found in the psychopathology of individuals and nations. Thus a better world could be built only on the foundation of improved personal and collective mental health. The motto of the United National Educational and Scientific Organization reflects this vision: "Since wars begin in the minds of men, it is in the minds of men that the defenses of peace must be constructed."

MODERN THEORIES ABOUT THE ARTS

In their practice, art therapists have generally relied strongly on some distinct theoretical system for support. In tracing these diverse and changing conceptual paradigms over the last 40 years, one is struck by how similar they are to the remediation models for behavior-disordered children discussed in Chapter 1. One big difference is the significant role that the humanistic model has assumed in the arts, in contrast to special education, where it has had decidedly less impact. In the pedagogical realm, the humanistic impulse has been incorporated largely in the countercultural strategies. Another difference is the continuing importance of the psychodynamic model in the arts, whereas behavior modification is finding limited application for such fields. The opposite is the case in special education. This section consists of brief presentations of seven major theoretical models that are currently drawn upon when the arts are applied in the re-educational process.

Psychodynamic Models

When the mental health movement gained momentum in the mid- and late 1940's, the psychodynamic or psychoanalytical theories of Sigmund Freud and his followers were in their ascendancy. These theories were widely accepted by psychiatry and the other healing professions. When mental health programs were gradually established in schools, child guidance clinics, and psychiatric hospitals, Freudian methods — usually under the supervision of a psychiatrist — were the accepted treatment modalities. Artists who entered the mental health field also subscribed to these theories.

In the visual arts, Naumberg (1950, 1953, 1975) is perhaps the most eloquent representative of this school. She asserted that a major purpose of the arts was to gain access to the patient's unconscious conflicts, in the interest of both diagnosis and therapy. Her studies of the free art expressions of children and adolescents, first published in 1950, reflect this approach.

Kramer (1958, 1971, 1975, 1979) also bases her approach on psychoanalytic theory. In contrast to Naumberg, she finds the art activity itself a healing experience. She spent several years as an art therapist in the famous Wiltwyck School for delinquent boys in New York (Kramer, 1958). She found herself cast in the roles of artist, therapist, and teacher, and she discovered the potentially civilizing force of art as it served to reconcile and sublimate basic conflicts. Her record of her experience in the children's community is a rich source of inspiration and ideas for those working with troubled youth.

A similar orientation was practiced by Berkowitz and Rothman (1951, 1960) in their teaching in Bellevue Psychiatric Hospital and the Livingston School for Girls in New York City, respectively.

The psychoanalytic model is in current use at the Henry Street School for delinquent adolescents in Manhattan, where art therapy is the primary clinical treatment modality (Wolf, 1975). An underlying theoretical assumption in this program is that delinquents have experienced a premature withdrawal of maternal love. The antisocial and destructive behavior is an attempt by the child to provoke the environment to respond in such a way that the child may re-experience this lost relationship (Wolf, 1979). In this accepting and facilitating therapeutic setting the youth are encouraged to express and live through their early traumas and disillusionments which have blocked their capacity for emotional and social growth and adjustment. Several art media are integrated in the therapy (Wolf, 1978), including the novel Polaroid technique (Wolf, 1976).

Another psychodynamic approach to art therapy has evolved from the theories of Carl Jung, a Swiss psychiatrist and an early collaborator with Freud. Jung believed that man has inherited from his racial past certain unconscious personality themes that are in opposition to each other. The lack of reconciliation of these themes becomes the basis for emotional disturbances. In creative activities, particlarly in a support- ive group setting, these conflicts can be made conscious and can be accepted and incorporated in the personality. In Jungian therapy, the mandala or the circle is important as a symbol and expression of the integration of the personality. The St. George Homes in California use Jung's ideas as the foundation for their treatment of severely disturbed adolescents. In these homes the mandala is present in art work, decora- tions, furniture, games, and religious rituals. Jung's principles have been applied in a number of other therapeutic settings (Dougherty, 1974).

Several art therapists have specifically used drawing or filling in mandalas as an instrument in psychological evaluations and treatment (Kellogg et al., 1977). Edgar (1978) bases his poetry therapy on Jungian concepts, and he has found that the personality emerges through a cycle of stages similar to what Jung had observed in dreams.

With an Adlerian framework, Dreikurs (1965) has used music ther- apy successfully in child guidance clinics. In conformity with Adler's personality theories, the general goals of the therapy were to deal with the child's undue demands for attention, struggle for power, desire to hurt, and flaunting of actual or assumed deficiencies. The sessions involved instrumental music, singing, rhythms, and dance, as well as the finely tuned interaction between therapist and child.

Humanistic Models

From a foundation in psychodynamic thinking another movement with diverse strands has developed which is often labeled humanistic psychology. It has a more optimistic view of human nature than Freud's instinct-oriented determinism. Maslow is a prominent expo- nent of the humanistic viewpoint. He theorizes that innate in human nature is a striving for self-actualization. This can be achieved only if a hierarchy of other needs has been met. They consist of physiological needs, safety needs, needs for affection and belonging, esteem needs, cognitive needs, and aesthetic needs. The humanists stress the impor- tance of a person's self-image and self-esteem.

The arts have a central position in the humanistic approach to creative development and to therapy. Garai (1979) has cogently presented the humanistic contributions in the expressive arts.

Another crucial dimension of the humanistic view is its conception of the child as a whole. The Gestalt theories of Perls fit well within this paradigm. Pioneering work in Gestalt art therapy has been done by Rhyne (1973) and Kronsky (1979).

Bonny uses music as an entrance into different and deeper states of consciousness and to peak experiences that bring about positive personality changes (Bonny & Savary, 1973). Nordoff and Robbins (1971, 1977) also place themselves within a humanistic framework in their work with handicapped children. They combine artistic talent and skills with a profound insight into the needs and nature of children, in moving them through music toward better adaptation and adjustment.

Transcendental Models

With the evolution of a scientific world view and the growth of rational thought there has been a corresponding loss of transcendental beliefs and of a feeling for the mystical in existence. The historian Theodore Roszak belongs to an increasing number of thinkers who lament this situation and advocate a return to the visionary sources of our culture. This position, which has much in common with humanism, has also found its place among the therapeutic movements. The St. George Homes have many of these features with their use of Jungian symbolism, Senoi dreamwork, and the immersion in the rituals and mysticism of the American Indians.

The transcendental view has found its most eloquent expression in therapeutic homes and schools conducted according to the philosophical and educational principles of Rudolf Steiner (1861–1925). Steiner became dissatisfied with the materialism and secularism of his time and founded a reform movement called anthroposophy, which means the wisdom of man.

Its spiritual foundations are Christian, but it contains elements of oriental mysticism. Thus reincarnation and karma are incorporated in the anthroposophic view of human destiny, as are the poetic visions of Goethe, Emerson, and Thoreau.

In addition to many provocative theories on such topics as politics, economics, agriculture, and medicine, Steiner also formulated some new principles of child development and education. His pedagogical system is called the Waldorf Method. In the Waldorf or Steiner Schools, balanced attention is given to the intellectual, emotional and social, aesthetic, and practical dimensions of the curriculum. This approach was originally intended for normal children, but it soon proved to have equal relevance with handicapped children as well.

According to the anthroposophic view, the child's inner personality remains intact regardless of the nature and the severity of a handicap. The child can be helped in overcoming his disabilities in a carefully designed educational and therapeutic setting in which all his diverse developmental needs are met. These needs are addressed through family-style living with close human relationships, multi-faceted education, community participation, work, and worship. Proper nutrition is of central importance, and most of the food is derived from biodynamic farming.

The Waldorf method as applied to the handicapped is called "curative" or "healing education." Descriptions of this education can be found in several books (Grahl, 1970; Pietzner, 1966; Weihs, 1971), and in more recent articles by Ogletree (1974) and Juul (1978). A volume that consists mainly of pictures portrays well the role of the arts in the curriculum (Healing Education Based on the Anthroposophic Image of Man, 1974).

A special branch of anthroposophy is the Camphill movement. In several countries it has established schools and villages where handicapped villagers and normal co-workers live together on the basis of spiritual equality.

Beauty and the arts suffuse these villages. The carefully selected picturesque setting, the landscaping, the architecture, the decor, and the prominent display of art works combine to pervade the visitor with an unparalleled sense of well-being. The anthroposophists have created novel styles of architecture and have invented new therapeutic art forms and musical instruments. Representative of the anthroposophic conceptions in architecture is the school building in Führenbühl, a children's community in West Germany. The structure itself looks like it came out of a fairy tale, with its irregular form and rounded walls. In the center of the building is the theater, which is in daily use with plays, dance performances, and musical events. The hallway spirals gently upward inviting the young to start their arduous journey toward learning. The first grade room is at the bottom. It is round in shape. For the following grades the classroom becomes a polygon with fewer and fewer sides, as if gradually releasing the child from an embrace. The order of the classrooms is a daily reminder to the pupils of how far they have come and how far there is to go.

Eurythmy is one of the therapeutic art forms invented by Steiner. It may be described as visible speech or visible song, as the movements of the arms and the body express the vowels and consonants of speech and the tones and intervals of musical melody (Ogletree, 1976). Eurythmy can be performed individually or in groups. At Führenbühl, the week starts Monday morning with a gathering of all the chldren and teachers in the school theater for half an hour of enjoying beloved poetry and music being translated into movement of great beauty and power.

Another innovation is a form of combined color, light, and movement therapy. A teacher stands behind a white screen and is illuminated by strong, multicolored lights. As he dances to slow, soft lyre music, he is perceived in the audience as an indistinct moving form enveloped by waves of color. Attending such a performance is remarkably calming and has been especially effective with agitated and hyperactive children.

In the schools one finds several unique musical instruments, such as the Choroi flutes and a special lyre. At an adolescent center in Jarna, Sweden, the music teacher has designed a kind of violin to be played by two. The teacher and the student sit facing each other while they play. It is a good way of capitalizing on attention, relationship, and imitation, which are so important in teaching and learning music.

The arts are pervasive in the curriculum, and they are often woven into the academic subjects. Drama brings historical events to life, and drawings make the abstract concepts of science and mathematics more concrete. The teachers utilize their own artistic talents in different ways. At House Christophorous in the Netherlands, the teacher had illustrated an episode in Norse mythology with an elaborate drawing in color chalk on the blackboard showing the god Thor thundering through the clouds in pursuit of the Jotuns. Similarly, a science lesson on the arctic regions in a class in Scotland was made more interesting through a chalk drawing of icebergs floating on the frigid seas. In the same school, the Murtle Estate, puppetry was used in the Bible class to tell the story of Daniel in the lion's den. Perhaps the most lasting memory of a visitor to these gentle counterculture communes was an outdoor performance of "A Midsummer Night's Dream" at the Ochil Tower School for emotionally and socially troubled youth near Edinburgh. It was a lovely day in late June, and the lawn outside the stately old manor house was hedged in by rhododendron bushes laden with pink and red flowers. There was music and there was dance, and the young actors did their parts with such joy and high spirits that the Bard himself must have smiled at them from his privileged place among the stars.

Developmental Models

In recent years there has been a change of emphasis in the arts from therapy to growth and a shift of allegiance from psychiatry to education. There has been an increasing realization that helping a troubled child does not necessarily consist of a direct confrontation with his pathology but may occur by supporting the child's normal emotional and developmental needs. Bettelheim, who is a forceful and eloquent exponent of psychoanalytic therapy, also embraces this point of view: "The absence of self-respect is a central issue in all functional disturbances. The most important task of therapy is not to have the patient gain insight into his unconscious, but to restore him to a high degree of justified self-esteem (1975, p. 21). And he adds that his experience has convinced him that "everything that increases the feeling of being a good, worthwhile person is curative (p. 23).

Lowenfeld (1957) is perhaps the most influential theorist with regard to the therapeutic potential of art education. His chapter "Therapeutic Aspects of Art Education" in his monumental volume *Creative and Mental Growth* states his position forcefully. He believes that creative activities in themselves serve as a means for emotional release and adjustment. They promote independence and social interaction, and they lead to improvements in thinking and communication. The role of the art educator in therapy is not to make speculative inferences and interpretations of symbols but to free the child from the barriers to his environment imposed by the handicap.

Lowenfeld places great emphasis on the art educator's rapport with the child and his ability to empathize with him and put himself in his place. In a published case study of a young girl's liberation from neurotic inhibition through art, Lowenfeld (1941) gives a good example of his principles in action. Another of his contributions is a richly illustrated schema of the stages in artistic development. This graphic chronology is useful both for understanding and fostering normal growth and as a reference point for indications of atypical art productions.

A succinct description of the application of the developmental model in therapeutic art education has been provided by Williams and Wood (1977). Their book is based on their experiences at the Rutland Center for Emotionally Disturbed Children at the University of Georgia. Others have related the model to all the major handicaps, including behavior disorders (Anderson, 1978, Rubin, 1978).

In her book *Art for All Children*, Anderson (1978) asserts that art, above all, has an intrinsic value in meeting the child's basic drive to create. But it also enhances communication and cooperation skills, builds a positive self-concept, and aids in reinforcing academic skills. She envisions eventually an art-centered curriculum, and she offers numerous illustrations of how art experiences can be integrated with mathematics, science, and social studies. With a vocabulary speckled with such terms as behavior objectives, task analysis, and accountability, she has clearly assumed much of the identity of the modern teacher in special education.

In music education and therapy, Gaston has served a leadership role similar to that of Lowenfeld in the visual arts. He maintains that exceptional children must be undestood in the light of normative growth and development. They have the same emotional needs as other children. To Gaston (1958, 1968) it is essential that the music therapist have a strong and adequate relationship with the client and a belief that when children perform in the best manner possible for them, they get their recompense in personal satisfaction, status, security, and acceptance.

The developmental point of view has a special relevance in the psychoeducational programming for delinquent youth. As mentioned earlier, psychoanalytic theorists assume that many delinquents are blocked in their emotional growth because of early traumas. There is evidence that similar arrests tend to occur in the sensory–motor, perceptual, and cognitive dimensions and in the awareness of physical and social causality. In the re-education process instituted by Guindon (1973) and implemented in such places as the Boscoville School in Montreal (Seeder, 1973) there is a heavy reliance on the epigenetic principles of Erikson and Piaget and much use of the formative arts, expressive movement or "gestes," and psychomotricity. The treatment program goes through four states, of which the first is in some ways equivalent to Piaget's sensory–motor period. At this stage, art activities generally intended for younger children would be appropriate.

The merger in the concepts of therapy and education has led to a broadening of the traditional roles of educators and therapists in the arts, an overlapping of functions, and occasional conflicts. Some call the situation an "identity crisis," and the respective professional organizations have taken steps to bring about a solution. Packard and Anderson (1976) have made a comprehensive outline of the disparate and overlapping areas of art education and art therapy and have made suggestions for a mutually more beneficial relationship.

In the meantime the teacher is emerging as a potentially significant contributor to the arts curriculum. The growing evidence of the usefulness of the arts in both social and emotional adjustment and in academic learning has placed the responsibility on the teachers to have skills in the arts that can be implemented with the students in their care. Except for the teachers in the Steiner Schools who receive intensive training in the arts, most special educators have little background in this field. A National Committee, Arts for the Handicapped, has recently sponsored in-service workshops in the arts for teachers in special education. Some teacher training institutions already include arts courses as requirements or electives in the special education curriculum. What makes the involvement of the teacher so crucial is the simple fact that art therapists are practically nonexistent in the public schools, and the art educators have such an enormous number of regular students to serve that there is little time left for those with special needs.

The Learning Disabilities Model

In the late 1960's, a new category of handicap called "learning disabilities" was established. Some children were found to have inherent problems of motor, perceptual, and cognitive functioning that interfered with their learning. Often they also had difficulties of an emotional or social nature that were either primary or secondary reactions to their frustrations in living. It has also been found that many juvenile offenders are learning-disabled, and efforts have been made to institute intervention services consisting of remedial education programs, group therapy, and family and individual counseling.

A superb example of the utilization of the arts in the education of learning-disabled students is The Lab School of the Kingsbury Center in Washington, D.C. (Smith, 1979). In this school, half the day is devoted to the arts, which include woodwork, all the arts and crafts, the graphic arts, sculpture, music, dance, drama, puppetry, and filmmaking. The students also belong to clubs that study the historical ages from the cave man to the present. In the clubs, the students immerse themselves into the atmosphere of the period, and the arts are integrated in the teaching of history, geography, civics, and literature.

The artists and art educators make important contributions in detecting underlying causes of learning difficulties, in confirming previous diagnoses, or in finding new relationships between behavior and learning. For example, a dance teacher discovered that several children who could not subtract or use the past tense in their language, were also unable to move backward. Opportunities to work in several art forms also give students a chance to find where their strengths and abilities lie. In several instances, artistic talents have been unearthed that have motivated the young people to a career in an art field.

A significant experiment on the effect of art therapy on learning-disabled children has been conducted by Carter (1979). He took issue with theorists who base their remediation on direct visual perceptual training in favor of an approach taking into consideration the whole child and his or her personality. He relied specifically on previous research by Krippner (1964), who had found a relationship between mental health scores and the capacity to benefit from a remedial reading program. In the investigation by Carter, the control group had a formal program in perceptual motor development while the experimental group had arts experiences. The latter class gained significantly higher scores in visual alertness, motor coordination, work recognition, linguistic ability, spatial relations, and perceptual age. These students also did better on a child behavior rating scale. Other innovative approaches in using the arts to reach students with behavioral and learning problems have been developed by Gair (1975, 1977, 1981).

Behavioral Models

In the mid-1960's, behavior modification appeared as a major force in rehabilitation and special education. In the arts, the approach found immediate acceptance among music therapists. In a 1968 issue of the *Journal of Music Therapy*, Madsen, Cotter, and Madsen presented their rationale for this procedure in music therapy. Madsen and Madsen (1968) also reported on the successful use of lessons on a guitar and recorded music as contingencies to eliminate the inappropriate behavior of a 15-year-old delinquent boy who had physically abused his mother and threatened others with a gun.

Another case of using guitar lessons as a contingency has been described by Michel (1976). In this instance the lessons were also used with a 15-year-old delinquent boy whose problem was truancy. He earned the guitar lessons and later the guitar itself by reporting weekly on regular school attendance and by showing evidence of completed school work. Similarly, Eisenstein (1974) found that using guitar lessons as a contingency led to marked improvement in reading.

Listening to music as a reinforcement has been used by Jorgenson (1974), who found it effective in eliminating behaviors that interfered with learning. Miller, Dorow, and Greer (1974) used both music and art as reinforements to improve arithmetic scores in a class of emotionally disturbed children. The classroom had an activity center with drawing and coloring supplies, and a tape recorder with rock music. Children who met the criterion for reinforcement were given free time in the activity corners.

Some music therapists take exception to the ways in which the behaviorists use music and maintain that such procedures should not be properly called music therapy. Others staunchly defend these techniques. One supporter is Steele (1977), the head of the music therapy program at the Cleveland Music School Settlement. She uses behavior analysis structures, targeting of objectives, and contingency management to modify inappropriate behavior patterns and ineffective learning in children referred to the program. She has found the procedure successful. The objective goals and evaluations employed have also been useful in documenting the effectiveness of the program before the community agencies that support it financially.

The Biophysical Model

In recent years support for the arts has come from neurobiological theory and research. For a long time it had been assumed that the right side of the brain was just an unimportant spare for the left. It now appears that both hemispheres perform different but complementary functions with regard to learning and the utilization of experience. The left hemisphere seems to be specialized for analytical thinking, logic, and language, whereas the right counterpart appears to have more holistic, sensory, and creative functions.

Brooks and Obrzut (1981) have made an outline of the contrasting functions of the two hemispheric processes, part of which is reproduced in the following tabulation:

Left	Right
analytic	synthetic
verbal	visual-spatial
linear	holistic
rational	intuitive
deductive	inductive
causal	coincidential
realistic	idealistic
mathematical	artistic

It is also known that the two sections of the brain are closely interconnected through a complex network of nerve fibers and that they share much of the information relayed via the sensory channels.

This hemispheric theory gives a rationale for the observation that abstract learning is facilitated by concrete and sensory experiences. It also helps to explain the positive correlations between art activities and academic improvement found in some studies.

Basing her research on the hemispheric model, Silver (1978) questioned whether art procedures can bypass language disorders and lead a child to the fundamental mathematical or logical ideas that are usually learned through language. In a series of ingenious experiments with hearing and language-disabled students she gathered considerable support for this idea.

The new research on the brain has profound implications for both regular and special education. Galin (1976) maintains that our culture has overemphasized analytic left-hemispheric skills. To develop all of a child's capabilities, curricula and materials must be designed for both sides of the brain and the two kinds of consciousness and experiencing of the world that they represent. The arts should have a respected place in this new kind of education.

MODEL PROGRAMS

The *Educateur* and the Arts

One promising development in the incorporation of the arts in the re-education of troubled youth is the evolution of the *educateur* profession in the United States. This profession had its origin in France where it was developed after the Second World War in response to the mental health needs of a large number of emotionally disturbed and socially maladjusted children and youth who were victims of the war's ravages. The *educateurs specialisès*, as they are called in France, met a genuine demand, and there are currently over 40 training colleges in the country.

The curriculum for the degree of *educateur specialisès* has a substantial segment devoted to the arts and crafts. An official governmental bulletin, published in 1973, has a list of recommend topics that includes the following: creative drama; theater; costumes; puppetry; creative movement; vocal and instrumental music; choral singing; story-telling; painting; drawing; pottery; work with plaster, mosaic, enamel, felt, glass, and wire; wood carving; basket weaving; weaving; tapestry making; and paper cutting. Obviously, no single college can offer training in all these subjects. However, the senior author found on visits to two of the training centers that they both had several options. The Institut de Formation d'Educateurs Specialisès at the University of Dijon had strong drama and photography departments. One of the graduates worked at the Centre Educatif in Velarssur-Ouche, a residential school for deliquent boys. It was impressive to watch the *educateur* direct the production of a film about the problems of incarcerated youth and to observe a suspenseful film he and his students had previously made about the resistance movement during the Nazi occupation.

The professional equivalent in Canada, the *psychoeducateur*, also uses the arts as an important educational and therapeutic resource. The training program at the University of Montreal places emphasis on

creative movement and offers two elective minors, one in psychomotricity and one in *gestes,* which might best be translated as mime or
expressive movement. Pierre Girouard has had an important role in
developing the latter program. As a *psychoeducateur* he has experimented with *gestes* and other art forms at the Centre d'Orientation, a
residential school for bright but severely disturbed boys.

One of Girouard's innovations is the teaching of history as a therapeutic medium. In the course of the school year his classes cover seven
major epochs: Prehistory, Ancient Greece, Rome, the Middle Ages, the
Classical Period, the Modern Period, and the Contemporary Period. In
the art workshop the students relive in a personal way the developmental stages and the changes in the arts. They study the arts of each period
and also create art themselves with the media appropriate for the age.
Drama and mime are used extensively to recreate historical events, and
a collection of clay figures made by the students shows that they have
been able to capture the essence of historical epochs with genuine
insight and artistic force. At the end of the year, the students review
their experiences in the course. They are helped to see their own lives
in historical perspective, and they begin to formulate their own des-
tinies as carriers of a cultural heritage from the past, through the
present, and into the future.

The Integrated Arts: Starr Commonwealth

One program that incorporates many if not all of the theoretical
models and art modalities in the re-education of troubled youth is The
Starr Commonwealth Schools in Michigan and Ohio.

The creative arts program offers students a variety of opportunities
for exposure and involvement in activities designed to aid their intellectual, physical, social, and emotional development. More specifically, the program is organized to accomplish the following objectives:

1. To program easily attainable and successive levels of learning
which will increase individual feelings of self-esteem, recognition, and
belonging.

2. To redirect undesirable behavior patterns and reinforce desirable behaviors such as the ability to work with people, accept responsibility, follow directions, and exercise leadership.

3. To lengthen the individual's attention span through the use of
selected activities and to increase the student's problem-solving abilities and general thought processes.

4. To develop gross and fine motor coordination, improve sensory
awareness, and heighten the student's body image and concept.

5. To program creative experiences specific to each person's strength and special needs in order to develop successful participation in the fine arts and pre-vocational activities.

6. To develop a repertoire of art skills and an appreciation of beauty which provide avenues for release of tension and constructive use of leisure time.

7. To provide observations and feedback to staff for use in evaluation and treatment.

The implementation of this program involves the participation of *educateurs*, classroom teachers, and several art specialists. These specialists, with expertise in the areas of industrial and fine arts education, music therapy, and the creative use of drama, work directly with youth as well as provide training workshops and supplementary art information to other staff.

Music. Music classes foster active participation in diverse activities that stimulate creative thinking, feeling, and self-expression. These activities include writing, singing, listening, discussion, progressive relaxation, creative movement, dancing, and the making and playing of instruments.

Another emphasis of the music program is to encourage the growth and development of the creativity and talent in individual students. Many students take part in weekly half-hour lessons in vocal or instrumental music. The lessons are structured to foster successful learning of musical skills, which can improve self-esteem and provide an avenue toward appropriate use of leisure time. An opportunity for the acquisition of vocal skills is also available through participation in an all-school choir.

For those students who do not actively participate in the music program, another facet of music is offered. Listening is the focus for concerts held throughout the year, which present many varied styles of music. Students have attended the performances of rock 'n roll bands, bluegrass, folk groups, symphony orchestras, jazz ensembles, classical pianists, and choirs. Without judging any one style of music, the program staff hopes that this exposure encourages open-mindedness and a widened perspective.

Creative Drama. In creative drama classes the activity of play is utilized as a therapeutic vehicle. Emphasis is placed on experiential activities that develop the personal resources of concentration, senses, imagination, physical self, speech, emotion, and intellect.

One of the most important of these activities is sociodrama. Through spontaneous role-playing and characterization, students explore creative problem-solving by playing out imagined situations. Pantomime is then introduced with story-telling through movement and body gestures. Simple charades progress to more advanced mime techniques as students work together developing interactive and communication skills. Students attend community and high school productions, and, on occasion, Broadway touring shows. A creative arts troupe meets weekly to explore many facets of drama, such as mime, puppetry, dance, formal acting, and the creative use of makeup and costume. This group performs regularly for a variety of organizations and campus events.

Visual Arts. Visual arts and crafts are offered through four components of the educational program: cottage activities, industrial art classes, fine art classes, and museum activities. Many of the creative arts experienced in the cottages have a seasonal or holiday focus, whereas others correspond to academic lessons being taught in the schools. These activities have included candlemaking, macramé, woodburning, mural painting, batik, découpage, basketry, mosaics, mobiles, plaster and sandcore sculpture, drawing, screen-printing, ceramics, photography, and even filmmaking. Although the art specialists may provide introductory information or assistance, most cottage-based art projects are implemented by the *educateurs*.

Industrial arts and crafts focus on teaching pre-vocational and practical home skills such as carpentry, drafting, and welding. However, within these classes are activities closely aligned with the creative behaviors nurtured through the fine arts program. Activities such as stained glass, woodcraft, wire sculpture, and photography are directed toward the development of self-awareness, personal expression, and communication.

Service-Learning and the Arts. Values of helping and caring are expressed through the arts. Senior citizens, unable to leave their living quarters, or children from day care centers are often entertained with laughter and song and even special art lessons. The creative arts troupe has had a major service commitment to a local nursing home. This project consists of short performances, usually skits presented in pantomime and visitations to individual rooms.

A very special event held each spring is a school-wide fine arts festival. This one-day celebration is the culmination of a year's involvement with creative arts activities. It provides a unique opportunity for students, staff and their families to meet together in an atmosphere of fun and creativity.

PROBLEMS AND PROSPECTS

This chapter has been devoted to the mainly unrecognized potenti- alities of the arts as instruments for growth, healing, and learning. However, it is also important to suggest cautions in the application of the arts.

The usefulness and effectiveness of the arts can be no greater than the skills of the practitioners and their ability to adapt their medium to the needs of individual children. Obviously, a teacher without exten- sive formal training cannot compete with the consumate expertise of those with a lifetime experience in the arts. However, even the longest journey starts with the first step, and a teacher with no formal back- ground in the arts but with a realization of their value may do many positive things to enhance learning and adjustment through artistic creativity.

It has been common practice both in education and in mental health to respond to an innovation with initial bursts of enthusiasm some- times bordering on fanaticism. Converts tend to push a new approach with the fervor of a crusade and with unrealistic claims and sensational publicity. Lauer (1978) has provided some sobering observations of such abuses among the proponents of poetry therapy.

Research on the therapeutic and educational impact of the arts is still in its infancy, and studies dealing with behaviorally disordered populations are rare. Kalenius (1978), summarizing 138 studies of the arts for the handicapped, found strong support that handicapped chil- dren increased their feelings of self-worth and improved their aca- demic skills as a result of arts activities.

It should be recognized that although individual children have made remarkable improvements in adjustment or learning through the arts, these instances are atypical. With troubled youth, no single approach is likely to bring about dramatic or lasting changes. The problems of these children are often rooted in their biology, in their life histories, in the social fabric, in almost insurmountable domestic stress, and even in adverse and destructive conditions in the very schools and therapeu- tic institutions that are supposed to help them. Nevertheless, in the face of these challenges, the arts show promise in making a distinctive contribution toward the creation of a quality holistic educational experience.

REFERENCES

Anderson, F. *Art for all children. A creative sourcebook for the impaired child.* Springfield, IL: Charles C. Thomas, 1978.

Berkowitz, P., & Rothman, E. Art work for the emotionally disturbed pupil. *The Clearing House*, 1951, *26*, 232–234.

Berkowitz, P., & Rothman, E. *The disturbed child. Recognition and psychoeducational therapy in the classroom.* New York: New York University Press, 1960.

Bettelheim, B. *A home for the heart.* New York: Bantam Books, 1975.

Bonny, H., & Savary, L. M. *Music and your mind. Listening with a new consciousness.* London: Harper & Row, 1973.

Brooks, R., & Obrzut, J. E. Brain lateralization: Implications for infant stimulation and development. *Young Children*, 1981, *36*(3), 9–16.

Carter, J. L. Art therapy and learning disabled children. *Journal of Art Psychotherapy*, 1979, *6*, 51–56.

Dougherty, C. A. Group art therapy: A Jungian approach. *American Journal of Art Therapy*, 1974, *13*, 229–236.

Dreikurs, R. Music therapy. In N. J. Long, W. C. Morse, & R. G. Newman (Eds.), *Conflict in the classroom.* Belmont, CA: Wadsworth, 1965.

Edgar, K. The epiphany of the self via poetry therapy. In A. Lerner (Ed.), *Poetry in the therapeutic experience.* New York: Pergamon Press, 1978.

Eisenstein, S. R. Effect of contingent guitar lessons on reading behavior. *Journal of Music Therapy*, 1974, *11*, 138–146.

Eisner, E. W. The role of the arts in cognition and curriculum. *Phi Delta Kappan*, 1981, *63*, 48–52.

Gair, S. B. An art-based remediation program for children with learning disabilities. *Studies in Art Education*, 1975, *17*, 55–67.

Gair, S. B. Form and function: Teaching problem learners through art. *Teaching Exceptional Children*, 1977, *9*, 30–32.

Gair, S. B. Teaching problem learners through the arts. *Directive Teacher*, 1981, *3*, 16–17.

Galin, D. Educating both sides of the brain. *Childhood Education*, 1976, *53*, 17–20.

Garai, J. E. New horizons of the humanistic approach to expressive therapies and creativity development. *American Journal of Art Therapy*, 1979, *6*, 177–183.

Gaston, E. T. Functional music. In N. B. Henry (Ed.), *Basic concepts in music education.* Chicago: University of Illinois Press, 1958.

Gaston, E. T. *Music in therapy.* New York: Macmillan, 1968.

Grahl, V. *The exceptional child.* Spring Valley, NY: The Anthroposophic Press, 1970.

Guindon, J. The reeducation process. *International Journal of Mental Health*, 1973, *2*, 15–26.

Healing education based on the anthroposophic image of man. New York: Anthroposophic Press, 1974.

Jorgenson, H. The use of contingent music activity to modify behaviors which interfere with learning. *Journal of Music Therapy*, 1974, *11*, 41–46.

Juul, K. D. European approaches and innovations in serving the handicapped. *Exceptional Children*, 1978, *44*, 322–330.

Kalenius, W. G. The state of the research. In *The arts and handicapped people: Defining the national direction.* Washington, D.C.: The National Committee, Arts for the Handicapped, 1978.

Kellogg, J., MacRae, M., Bonny, H. L., & DiLeo, F. The use of the mandala in psychological evaluation and treatment. *American Journal of Art Therapy*, 1977, *16*, 123–134.

Kramer, D. *Art therapy in a children's community.* Springfield, IL: C. C. Thomas, 1958.

Kramer, D. *Art as therapy with children.* New York: Schocken, 1971.

Kramer, E. Art and craft. In E. Ulman & P. Dachinger (Eds.), *Art therapy.* New York: Schocken, 1975.

Kramer, E. *Childhood and art therapy.* New York: Schocken, 1979.

Krippner, S. Relationship between reading improvement and ten selected variables. *Perceptual and Motor Skills*, 1964, *19*, 15-20.

Kronsky, B. J. Freeing the creative process: The relevance of Gestalt. *American Journal of Art Psychotherapy*, 1979, *6*, 233-240.

Lauer, R. Abuses of poetry therapy. In A. Lerner (Ed.), *Poetry in the therapeutic experience*. New York: Pergamon Press, 1978.

Lowenfeld, V. Self-adjustment through creative activity. *American Journal of Mental Deficiency*, 1941, *45*, 366-373.

Lowenfeld, V. *Creative and mental growth*. New York: Macmillan, 1957.

Madsen, C. H., Cotter, V., & Madsen, C. K. A behavioral approach to music therapy. *Journal of Music Therapy*, 1968, *5*, 69-71.

Madsen, C. K., & Madsen, C. H. Music as a behavior modification technique with a juvenile delinquent. *Journal of Music Therapy*, 1968, *5*, 72-76.

Michel, D. E. *Music therapy: An introduction to therapy and special education through music*. Springfield, IL: Charles C. Thomas, 1976.

Miller, D. M., Dorow, L., & Greer, R. D. The contingent use of music and art for improving arithmetic scores. *Journal of Music Therapy*, 1974, *11*, 57-64.

Naumberg, M. *An introduction to art therapy*. New York: Teachers College Press, 1950.

Naumberg, M. *Psychoneurotic art: Its function in psychotherapy*. New York: Grune & Stratton, 1953.

Naumberg, M. Spontaneous art in education and psychotherapy. In E. Ulman & P. Dachinger (Eds.), *Art therapy in theory and practice*. New York: Schocken, 1975.

Nordoff, P., & Robbins, C. *Therapy in music for handicapped children*. New York: St. Martin's Press, 1971.

Nordoff, P., & Robbins, S. C. *Creative music therapy*. New York: John Day, 1977.

Ogletree, E. J. Curative education and Rudolf Steiner. *Journal for Special Educators of the Mentally Retarded*, 1974, *10*, 146-159; *11*, 3-9.

Ogletree, E. J. Eurythmy: A therapeutic art of movement. *Journal of Special Education*, 1976, *10*, 305-319.

Packard, S. P., & Anderson, F. E. Shared identity crisis: Art education and art therapy. *American Journal of Art Therapy*, 1976, *16*, 21-28.

Pietzner, C. *Aspects of curative education*. New York: The Anthroposophic Press, 1966.

Rhyne, J. The Gestalt approach to experience, art and art therapy. *American Journal of Art Therapy*, 1973, *12*, 237-248.

Rubin, J. A. *Child art therapy. Understanding and helping children grow through art*. New York: Van Nostrand Reinhold, 1978.

Ruud, E. *Hva er musikkterapi?* Oslo: Gyldendal Norsk Forlag, 1980.

Seeder, M. The Boscoville School. The educateur model in operation. *International Journal of Mental Health*, 1973, *2*, 33-42.

Sigerist, H. D. *Civilization and disease*. Chicago: The University of Chicago Press, 1962.

Silver, R. A. *Developing cognitive and creative skills through the arts*. Baltimore: University Park Press, 1978.

Smith, S. L. *No easy answers. Teaching the learning disabled child*. Cambridge, MA: Winthrop, 1979.

Steele, A. L. The application of behavioral research technique to community music therapy. *Journal of Music Therapy*, 1977, *14*, 102-115.

Weihs, T. J. *Children in need of special care*. London: Souvenir Press, 1971.

Williams, G. H., & Wood, M. M. *Developmental art therapy*. Baltimore: University Park Press, 1977.

Wolf, R. Art psychotherapy with acting out adolescents: An innovative approach for special education. *Journal of Art Psychotherapy*, 1975, *2*(3/4), 255-266.

Wolf, R. The Polaroid technique: Spontaneous dialogue from the unconscious. *Journal of Art Psychotherapy*, 1976, *3*, 197-214.

Wolf, R. Creative expressive therapy: An integrative case study. *Journal of Art Psychotherapy*, 1978, *5*, 81–91.

Wolf, R. Re-experiencing Winnicott's environmental mother: Implications for art psychotherapy of anti-social youth in special education. *Journal of Art Psychotherapy*, 1979, *6*, 95–102.

Conclusion

In this book we have outlined a psychoeducational approach which blends practice wisdom with theory in order to create effective strategies for re-education. We have identified the foundations for powerful interpersonal environments and have discussed selected formats for teaching and treatment. It has been our thesis that the most effective programs for troubled youth entail a holistic synergy which results from skillfully harmonizing many important variables.

Regardless of the methodology employed in education, treatment, and child care, the outcome hinges, in the large measure, on the nature of the underlying human interactions. Thus we view the critical foundations of re-education to be the quality of individual, group, and organizational relationships.

The most successful teachers and youth workers are invariably those able to build strong human bonds with children who may not readily identify with adults. This relationship process has been defined as the enhancement of communication, social reinforcement, and modeling. Specific procedures for establishing and maintaining effective relationships have been outlined, and the common pitfalls in work with adult-resistant youngsters have been discussed.

The best efforts of concerned adults are often rendered impotent by the power of the peer group. Behavior managers have regularly been frustrated by their inability to compete with the reinforcers dispensed by a negative youth subculture. A major thrust in this book has been to identify procedures for the creation of a responsible group process, and for generalizing this helping behavior beyond the classroom or treatment group.

Perhaps the most neglected set of relationships in child and youth service organizations are those that are organizational in nature. Re-education is a complex process that requires teamwork, both among professionals and with parents and significant others in the child's life. Without such close cooperation, the various players in a child's ecology find themselves working at cross purposes. We have reviewed at some length the factors that produce a dysfunctional organization and have proposed a model for achieving total teamwork.

In several chapters of this book we have discussed a range of intervention strategies that can be built upon the foundations of solid individual, group, and organizational relationships. Because behavior is a result of unique personal and situational factors, we believe that the needs of children are best served by a holistic approach to re-education. Thus we have sought to show how approaches that have sometimes been seen as incompatible or contradictory can be brought together in synergy to create powerful re-educational interventions.

We propose a model of differential diagnosis and intervention based upon an assessment at both the behavioral and affective-emotional levels. Strategies for managing behavior, intervening in times of crisis, and affective re-education are considered. We have included discussions of the principles, procedures, and pitfalls of individual communication strategies (such as the life-space interview) and of group guidance techniques (such as positive peer culture). Two further areas which have often been neglected in this field are recreational activities and the creative arts. Therefore, we have drawn on colleagues with special expertise to relate these areas to the process of re-education.

Various chapters have stressed the need for evaluation in order to understand troubled youngsters and measure the effectiveness of our efforts. But in the current state-of-the-art, our assessment is most precise when measuring narrow, specific, isolated behaviors. Unfortunately, the questions which can be readily quantified are often those of least importance, and as our measurement becomes more precise, our purposes become more unclear (Nash, 1978; Boyer, 1980).

Perhaps the greatest challenge confronting those who embrace a holistic, psychoeducational strategy is to create evaluation systems which match the breadth of their model. As Whittaker (1977) suggests, we need to learn more about what works and what does not in children's programs. Our approaches cannot be esoteric but instead must be practical, problem-focused, and action-oriented. This will require the use of a range of evaluation methods. Among the components of this evaluation strategy might be:

1. Individual measures of behavioral, academic, and affective change.
2. Measures of the quality of the individual, group, and organizational interactions.

3. Consumer evaluation by students and their parents.
4. Follow-up studies of outcome that go beyond narrow definitions of success.

If evaluation is to achieve its proper role in child and youth service organizations, then researchers and evaluators must be brought into closer contact with the real issues and concerns of those who work on the front lines with troubled youngsters. As Tukey (1963) suggests, it may be better to seek the approximate answer to the right question rather than a precise answer to the wrong question. Equally important, practitioners must overcome their reluctance to submit their programs and procedures to careful scrutiny. In the words of Carl Rogers (1964), "Even if evaluation or research does not support fully what we are doing, this cannot be seen as a threat, for knowledge can only help us improve."

REFERENCES

Boyer, E. L. Quality and the campus: the high school-college connection. *AAHE Bulletin,* May 1980, *32*(9), 5–6.

Nash, R. J. & DuCharme, E. D. Preparing new educational professionals for non-public school settings. *Journal of Teacher Education,* July-August, 1978, *29*(4), 36–41.

Rogers, C. This is me. In G. Bennis, Edgar H. Schein, David E. Barlew, and Fred I. Steels (Eds.), *Interpersonal dynamics.* Homewood, IL: Dorsey Press, 1964.

Tukey, J. The future of data analysis. *Annals of Mathematical Statistics,* 1963, *33,* 13–14.

Whittaker, J. The changing character of residential child care: an ecological perspective. *Social Science Review,* March 1978, *52*(1), 21–36.

Index

Absenteeism, 99; *see also*, Organization, dysfunctional
Acceptance, 72, 73; *see also*, specific areas
Accountability, 96, 112
 in residential groups, 112
 in social institutions, 96
Achievement Place, 5, 36; *see also*, Teaching family Model
Achilles, 34
Activity programming, role in re-education, 239–249
Addams, Jane, 4
Adler, Alfred, 8
Adolescence, 70, 73
 power relationships, 73
 reference group, 70
Adult attractiveness, in residential treatment, 50
Adult role, abdicating, 60; *see also*, Overidentification
Adventure, need for, 5; *see also*, Behavioral problems
Affective re-education, in crisis management, 157–163
Aichorn, August, 8, 40, 52, 128
Alcohol or drug problem, 211; *see also*, Problem-solving
American Association of School Administrators, 55
American Red Cross, 237
Anger, *see* Problems
Anthroposophy, 261; *see also*, Steiner, Rudolf; Transcendental Models
Antiseptic bouncing, in behavior management, 141, 142
Anxiety, relief from through play, 236
Aquatics, use in re-education, 244
Aristotle, 256

Art
 history of, 256–258
 model programs, 269–272
 role in therapy, 258–270
 theories, 258–270
Art for All Children, 264
Art of Loving, The, 63
Assessment, 17–19, 129, 130, 164, 278
 of behavioral problems, 129, 130
 is ecological, 17–19
 of social skills, 164
Australia, programs in, 118
Authoritarian interference, in behavior, 144
Authoritarian/nonauthoritarian managers, 105; *see also*, Leadership
Authority
 administrative, 106, 111, 113
 delegation of, 106
 in relating to youth, 58
Authority problem, in problem-solving, 210
Autonomy, enhancing, as a goal, 160
Aversiveness, minimization of, 52
AWARE Project, 169

Bedlam, organizational, 101; *see also*, Communication
Behavior
 emotional levels, diagnosis of, 129–134
 generalization of, 168
 holistic, 17, 20, 21
 management, 131–148
 modification of, 6, 8, 21, 145, 148–151; *see also*, Social skills training
 objectives, 166